D0706629

# THE NATURE OF EXISTENCE

# THE NATURE OF EXISTENCE

BY

## JOHN McTAGGART ELLIS McTAGGART,

LITT.D. CAMBRIDGE, LL.D. ST ANDREWS,
FELLOW AND LECTURER OF TRINITY COLLEGE IN CAMBRIDGE,
FELLOW OF THE BRITISH ACADEMY

### VOLUME I

EDITED BY

## C. D. BROAD, LITT.D.

FELLOW OF TRINITY COLLEGE

CAMBRIDGE
AT THE UNIVERSITY PRESS
1921
REPRINTED
1968

Published by the Syndics of the Cambridge University Press
Bentley House, 200 Euston Road, London, N.W. 1
American Branch: 32 East 57th Street, New York, N.Y. 10022

PUBLISHER'S NOTE

Cambridge University Press Library Editions are re-issues of out-of-print standard works from the Cambridge catalogue. The texts are unrevised and, apart from minor corrections, reproduce the latest published edition.

Standard Book Number: 521 07425 8
Library of Congress Catalogue Card Number: 21–13018

First published 1921
Reprinted 1968

First printed in Great Britain at the University Press, Cambridge
Reprinted in Great Britain by John Dickens & Co. Ltd, Northampton

TO

MY WIFE

FOR ALL HER HELP

# PREFACE

I AM deeply indebted to Dr G. E. Moore for his kindness in reading the whole of this volume, and in giving me very great and valuable assistance. I am also much indebted to Dr A. N. Whitehead and to Dr C. D. Broad for their most valuable criticisms on several chapters which they allowed me to submit to them.

J. M<sup>c</sup>T. E. M<sup>c</sup>T.

TRINITY COLLEGE,
CAMBRIDGE.
*July*, 1920.

# TABLE OF CONTENTS

## BOOK I.   INTRODUCTORY

### CHAPTER I.  INTRODUCTORY

### CHAPTER II.  REALITY AND EXISTENCE

## CHAPTER III. METHOD

# BOOK II.   SUBSTANCE

## CHAPTER IV.   EXISTENCE

## CHAPTER V.   QUALITY

## CHAPTER VI. SUBSTANCE

## CHAPTER VII. DIFFERENTIATION

## CHAPTER VIII. RELATIONS

## CHAPTER IX. DERIVATIVE CHARACTERISTICS

## CHAPTER X. DISSIMILARITY OF SUBSTANCES

## CHAPTER XI. SUFFICIENT DESCRIPTION

## CHAPTER XII. DETERMINATION

## CHAPTER XIII  MANIFESTATION

# BOOK III.  GROUPS

## CHAPTER XIV. SIMILARITY OF SUBSTANCES

## CHAPTER XV. GROUPS

## CHAPTER XVI. COMPOUND SUBSTANCES

## CHAPTER XVII. EXCLUSIVE COMMON QUALITIES IN GROUPS

## CHAPTER XVIII. THE UNIVERSE

## CHAPTER XIX. UNIVERSAL DETERMINATION

## CHAPTER XX. ORGANIC UNITY

## CHAPTER XXI. SUMMARY OF RESULTS

## CHAPTER XXII. INFINITE DIVISIBILITY OF SUBSTANCE

# CHAPTER XXV. DETERMINING CORRESPONDENCE
## AS CAUSAL

## CHAPTER XXVI.   DETERMINING CORRESPONDENCE
### (*continued*)

## CHAPTER XXVII.   EXCLUSIVE COMMON QUALITIES
### (*continued*)

# CHAPTER XXX. THE DIFFERENTIATION OF PRIMARY PARTS

# CHAPTER XXXI. THE UNITY OF THE UNIVERSE

# BOOK I

## INTRODUCTORY

# CHAPTER I

## INTRODUCTORY

**1.** In this work I propose to consider what can be determined as to the characteristics which belong to all that exists, or, again, which belong to Existence as a whole. I shall also consider what consequences of theoretical or practical interest can be drawn from these general characteristics with respect to various parts of the existent which are known to us empirically[1].

The Existent is, I conceive, *primâ facie* a species of the Real. All that exists must, it is universally admitted, be real, while the position has been maintained that there is reality which does not exist. The first question, then, for us to consider is what is meant by reality, or Being—the two words, as generally used, are equivalents.

**2.** Reality is indefinable. The proposition "whatever is, is real," although true, does not help us to define reality, or to determine it in any other way, because in "whatever is" the "is" involves being, and being is the same as reality. But the proposition, though tautologous, is not, I think, useless, since it brings before us the wide denotation of reality.

Reality, then, is an indefinable characteristic, of which it can be said that whatever is, is real. It may thus be said to be universal in its denotation, but this does not mean that all predication of unreality is contradictory. The predication of unreality, indeed, is often correct. The fourth angle of any triangle, and the Duke of London in 1919, are both unreal[2].

---

[1] The first of these enquiries occupies Books II, III and IV, which are contained in this volume. The second enquiry will be pursued in Books V, VI and VII, which will appear subsequently.

[2] It has been objected to this that, *e.g.*, the fourth angle of a triangle must be real, if we can predicate anything of it with truth. And thus any predication of unreality would contradict itself. But this seems to me to be mistaken. In order to make any predication about anything, I must have an idea of that thing, and the idea—the psychical event in my mind—must be real. But a real idea of such an angle does not involve the reality of the angle. This subject will be discussed in Book VI.

**3**. It has been held that reality is an ambiguous term, *i.e.*, that to say that anything is real is to say nothing definite, unless we say something more. Before we can say whether Mrs Gamp is real or not, we must determine of what world the question is asked. She may not be real in the world of our ordinary life, and yet she may be real in the world of Dickens' novel, and perhaps in my dream world.

Now of course any one may, if he chooses, use the word reality in such a sense that, in that sense, something could be unreal in the world of waking life, and real in the world of fiction or of dreams. Between this use of the word, and the one which I have adopted, there is no question of truth and falsity, but only of convenience and inconvenience. But it seems clear to me that there is such a quality as that which I have called reality, and that it is this quality to which the name is usually applied, so that this use of it is the more convenient. And, in this sense, a thing is either real or not real, independent of qualifications. My dream of Mrs Gamp is, of course, real—not only in a particular "world," but absolutely. But Mrs Gamp herself is not real in a dream, since one person cannot be a part of another person's dream. Nor is she real, as I suppose her to be during my dream, in a non-dream world, since my supposition during the dream was wrong. (Of course, it might turn out that what I now think to be waking life was the dream, while the supposed dream was waking life. Then Mrs Gamp would be real, and the man I thought I saw five minutes ago would be unreal.)

**4**. Reality, in the sense in which we have taken it, is not a quality which admits of degrees. A thing cannot be more or less real than another which is also real. It has been said that reality does admit of degrees. But this can, I think, be traced to one of two confusions, and, when these are removed, it seems clear that there are no degrees of reality.

Sometimes reality has been confused with power, and a thing has been said to be more real in proportion as it exerted more power on other things. But power and reality are quite different, and a thing which exerts more power is not more real than one which exerts less.

Sometimes, again, it would seem that the possibility of

degrees of reality has been based on the possibility of degrees of truth. Even if $A$ is not $X$, we may misrepresent its real nature less by calling it $X$ than we should by calling it $Y$. And in that case it is usual, and not, I think, improper to say that "$A$ is $X$" is more true than "$A$ is $Y$," though neither of them is perfectly true. And then, because we may say that "$A$ is $X$" is more true than "$A$ is $Y$," it is supposed that we may say that $AX$ is more real than $AY$. If, for example, it should be truer to say that the universe was an organism than that it was an aggregate, then it is supposed that we may say that an organic universe is more real than an aggregate-universe. But this is a mistake. "$A$ is $X$" may misrepresent the nature of $A$ less than "$A$ is $Y$," but, unless it is quite true that $A$ is $X$, then $A$ is not $X$, and $AX$ is not real at all. Unless it is quite true that the universe is an organism there is no organic universe which has any reality.

**5.** We have now, I think, succeeded in identifying the indefinable conception of reality. But what about existence? Can we define existence in terms of reality, or is existence, as well as reality, indefinable? I think that it must be pronounced indefinable. We are, indeed, able to say in what cases reality involves existence. If a substance or an event is real, it is existent. A man, a table, a battle, or a sneeze can only be real by existing. And it seems to me that we should also say that the qualities and relations of existent substances and events exist, and also the qualities and relations of those existent qualities and relations and so on. Not only does Socrates exist, if he is real, but so does his quality of wisdom, and his relation of moral superiority to Nero, and, again, the quantitative relation in which his wisdom stands to the wisdom of Aristotle. But, on the other hand, the quality of wisdom, and the relation of superiority, taken in themselves, and not as belonging to, or connecting, particular existents, do not exist, even if they are real. And, again, the proposition "Socrates is wise" (as distinguished on the one hand from the man Socrates who is wise, and, on the other hand, from the psychical event of my knowledge that Socrates is wise) does not exist, even if it is real.

It might perhaps be doubted whether the characteristics of the existent should themselves be classed as existent. But if

Socrates exists and is wise, it surely would be unreasonable to deny that his wisdom exists. And his wisdom is nothing but his quality of being wise. In the same way, does not the moral superiority of Socrates to Nero exist? And this is nothing but a relation in which Socrates stands to Nero.

To this it may be objected that in this case real wisdom would both exist and not exist. It would exist as a quality of Socrates, but not as a quality in general. But, as we shall see in the next chapter, it is not certain that any qualities or relations are real apart from their existence. And even if it should be the case that qualities and relations were both existent, as qualities and relations of existent things, and non-existent, in their general aspects, I do not think that this would be an objection to our view. Qualities and relations are very different from substances, and the fact that a substance cannot be both existent and non-existent does not prove that qualities and relations—which are universal, and not particular as substances are—could not be existent in one aspect, and non-existent in another.

Thus we know in what cases reality involves existence, but this will not give us a definition of existence. For when we come to define substance, we shall find that it is necessary to introduce the conception of existence as part of the definition. And events will be found to be a class of substances, so that the conception of an event will likewise require the conception of existence as part of its definition. The conception of the qualities and relations of the existent, and the conception of their qualities and relations, again, can clearly not be defined without introducing the conception of substance. Thus an attempt to define existence by means of substances and events, and their qualities and relations, would involve a vicious circle.

But the statement of the cases in which reality involves existence, though it would be vicious as a definition, is valuable as an explanation. The conceptions of a substance, of an event, of a characteristic[1], and of a proposition, are conceptions of

---

[1] I use the term Characteristics as a common name for qualities and relations. It is convenient to have a common name for both, and no other seems available. It is true that a relation cannot be correctly called a characteristic

which it is easy to give examples, and which are much more familiar to us than the more abstract conception of existence. And so the nature of existence becomes clearer to us when we realise that existence belongs to real substances, real events, and their characteristics, but not to characteristics in general, nor to propositions, should characteristics in general and propositions be real.

**6.** But *is* there anything real which is not existent, or are the only things which are real of such a sort that their reality implies their existence? If this should be the case the spheres of reality and existence would coincide. This point will be discussed in the next chapter, and I shall endeavour to maintain that there is no reason to hold that there is anything real which is not existent, and that, even if there is any such non-existent reality, its relation to existence is such that, in studying existence, we study the whole of reality.

But even if this should not be so—if there is reality which is non-existent, and it should be of such a sort that we should not be studying all reality in studying existence—yet the nature of existence would have special interest for us. For, from the point of view of our practical interests, nothing is of any moment to us except the existent. In that which exists we have all of us practical interests of one sort or another. But it seems very difficult to suppose that any person could feel any practical interest in non-existent reality, for its own sake, and independent of any effect it may have on the existent[1].

With purely theoretical interest the case is different. Many

---

*of* anything, as a quality can. But, as we shall see later, every relation generates, for each of its terms, a Relational Quality which is a characteristic of that term. The relation may thus be said to characterise each of its terms, though it is not a characteristic *of* either of them, and this may justify us in calling it a characteristic.

[1] It may be said that we have a practical interest, not only in the existent, but in the possibilities of existence. It is true that I have a practical interest in the possibility that it may rain to-morrow, but that only means that I am interested in to-morrow's weather, and do not yet know all its characteristics. Now to-morrow's weather is existent, for existence is as much a predicate of the future and past as of the present. On the other hand, the possibility that it might have been raining now, when in point of fact it is not raining, has no *practical* interest for me. The difference between these two kinds of possibility will be discussed in the next chapter (Section 35).

people have a strong interest in knowing the truth as such, and this theoretical interest could be excited about non-existent reality as much as about existent reality. And this gives them an interest in non-existent reality, if there is any such reality, though an interest of a different kind from that which is taken in the existent. For with the non-existent all that we should desire would be to know what the nature of the real is. We should have no desire that it should have one nature rather than another, except in so far as it might affect the existent. In so far as it does affect the existent, of course, we might desire that it should have one nature rather than another. Any desire, for example, that its nature should not be such as to render our knowledge of it limited or untrustworthy, would come under this head, since knowledge, if real, is existent.

We can, then, have interest in the real, even though it should not be existent. But it is only that interest which we have in knowledge for its own sake. All our other interests—in happiness, for example, in virtue, or in love—-deal exclusively with the existent, the study of which would thus in any case have a special importance for us.

# CHAPTER II

## REALITY AND EXISTENCE

**7.** We have now to discuss the question whether there is anything real which is not existent, or whether, on the other hand, the only things which are real are of such a sort that their reality implies their existence, so that the spheres of existence and reality would coincide. I shall endeavour to maintain that there is no reason to hold that there is anything real which is not existent, and that, even if there is any such non-existent reality, its relation to existence is such that, in studying existence, we study the whole of reality.

We must consider separately the various classes of things which have been asserted to be real without existing. In the first place, it has been asserted that Propositions are real without existing. By a Proposition is meant such a reality as "Socrates is wise," or "the multiplication table is green," as distinguished on the one hand from anyone's belief that Socrates is wise or that the multiplication table is green (which belief would, of course, be existent), and on the other hand from any existent thing about which the proposition may be made—such as, in the case of our first example, the existent Socrates. Secondly it has been said that characteristics can be real without being existent. And finally it is said that possibilities are real but not existent.

**8.** Let us begin with propositions. The argument for their reality is that there are mental states which are true or false, and that their truth or falsity can only be determined by their correspondence to a true proposition or a false proposition respectively.

It is beyond doubt that there are mental states which are such that each of them must be true or false. There are certainly beliefs, and every belief must be true or false. And besides beliefs, there are Assumptions[1]. If I assert "Smith is bald," that is a belief. But if I do not assert that Smith is bald, but only consider whether he *is* bald, or if I assert "if Smith is bald, he must wear a wig," then I have not a belief about Smith's baldness, but an assumption—the assumption "that Smith is bald." And this assumption is true or false, according as Smith is or is not bald, though, since it is not an assertion, it is not knowledge if it is true, nor error if it is false.

But does the reality of true and false beliefs and assumptions involve the reality of true and false propositions? Since whatever considerations are applicable to belief in this connection are also applicable to assumptions, I shall, for the sake of brevity, speak only of beliefs.

**9.** What is it that makes a belief true? It has sometimes been maintained that the truth of a belief lay in its coherence with other beliefs, or in its completeness, or in the possession of a systematic nature. It seems quite clear to me that all such views are false. Such characteristics, or some of them, may possibly be criteria of truth, but they cannot make the belief true. If I say "the table is square," the only thing which can make my assertion true is the fact that the table *is* square— that is, the possession by the table of the quality of squareness. The only belief which can be made true by the coherence, or completeness, or systematic nature, of any belief $M$, is the belief that the belief $M$ is coherent, or complete, or systematic.

And in the same way we must reject the theory that what makes every belief true is a relation to the knowing subject. It is said that my beliefs are true because they work for me, or because they give me satisfaction, or because they are self-evident to me. It may be that these characteristics, or some of them, are criteria of truth, but they cannot be what makes a belief true. The only beliefs which are made true by any relation to the knowing subject are beliefs about that subject. And the only belief which could be made true by the working for me of a belief $M$, or by its satisfying my nature or being self-evident to

[1] I use Assumption, as will be seen, as the equivalent of Dr Meinong's Annahme.

me, would be a belief that the belief *M* did work for me, or satisfy my nature, or was self-evident to me[1].

**10**.  It seems to me that truth, as a characteristic of beliefs, may be defined as a relation in which the belief stands, and which is a relation of correspondence to a Fact.  I should define a Fact as being either the possession by anything of a quality, or the connection of anything with anything by a relation.  (In this definition I use "anything" to include both substances and characteristics.)  A fact exists when the thing about which it is a fact is existent.  Thus the squareness of the table is a fact, in distinction from the belief about it, which is an event in my mind[2], and the proposition about it which the view which we are opposing asserts to be also real.

The other elements in our definition of truth do not admit of further definition.  We shall see in the next Book that we cannot define the characteristic of being a relation.  The characteristic of correspondence is also, I think, indefinable.  And when we ask what sort of correspondence it is which constitutes truth—for not all sorts of correspondence would do so—we find that we cannot define the particular sort of correspondence. And, it may further be noted, we cannot even give other examples of it.  It is just that sort of correspondence which is the relation of truth.

**11**.  Are we right in taking truth as a relation in which things stand, and not as a quality which they possess?  In favour of the latter view it might be said that truth is affirmed of beliefs simply.  We say that a belief is true, without any mention of a term other than a belief.  Surely then truth cannot be a relation between a belief and some other term.

There is, no doubt, a quality of being a true belief, which is

---

[1] Thus the only case in which a belief could be made true by its own coherence, or by its own satisfaction of my nature, would be the case in which it was a belief that it itself was coherent, or satisfied my nature.  Most beliefs are not about themselves, but some are.  The belief "all my beliefs satisfy my nature" is a belief about itself and others.  And the belief "the last belief I shall ever hold satisfies my nature" is a belief about itself and about nothing else, if it happens that this belief is the last I shall ever hold.

[2] My belief "the table is square" is, of course, itself a fact.  It is a relation to this fact which gives truth to the further belief "I have a belief that this table is square," should circumstances lead me to make this further assertion.

possessed by true beliefs. But a belief only has that quality because it stands to some fact in that relation of correspondence of which we have been speaking. It is only a matter of convenience whether we give the name of truth to the relation in which the belief stands, or to the quality which arises from the relation. It seems better to give it to the relation, because the relation is logically prior to the quality. The belief does not stand in the relation because it has the quality. It has the quality because it stands in the relation—indeed, its quality is just the quality of being a term in the relation. It is the relation which is fundamentally important, and it is therefore more convenient that it should bear the name of truth, especially as there is no other name for this particular sort of correspondence.

In the case of any belief whose nature is known, it is sufficient to say that it is a term which stands in this relation to something. It is not necessary to specify the other term, because there is only one term to which any particular belief can have that relation, and we know what that term is, when we know what the belief is about. If the belief "the table is square" is true at all, it can only be by correspondence to one thing—the squareness of the table. It would be superfluous to say that the belief that the table was square was true of the squareness of the table. And thus the fact that truth is a relation tends to fall into the background, since, in any particular case, it is superfluous to mention one term of the relation. But this does not make the relation any less real.

**12**. Our theory that truth consists in a certain correspondence with a fact, which correspondence is not further definable, must not be confused with the theory that truth consists in resemblance to a fact—a view which has been sometimes called the "copy theory" of truth. Resemblance is a correspondence, but all correspondence is not resemblance, and the particular correspondence which constitutes truth is not resemblance. Nor does it involve resemblance. Of course all true beliefs must to some extent resemble the facts believed in, because everything resembles everything else to some extent. But there is no special resemblance between the belief and the fact. If I truly believe A to be a man, my belief has no greater resemblance to the quality of being a man than it has to the qualities of being a woman or a child. And my belief that *A* is a man has no greater resemblance to *A* than a belief that *A* was a woman would have, although the first belief is true, and the second would be false.

At the same time we must recognize that the copy theory of truth has several important features in common with the theory which we have adopted, and that, if our theory is true, the copy theory is considerably nearer the truth than various others are. For the copy theory makes the truth of a belief depend upon its relation to a fact, and it holds that relation to be a relation of correspondence. And in these points it is right, though it is wrong in holding that the particular relation of correspondence in question is resemblance.

**13**. There seem to be two reasons why it should have been supposed that the correspondence in this case was resemblance. In the first place, many thinkers are very unwilling to admit any fresh ultimate and indefinable conception—an unwillingness which is often very salutary, but can easily be carried too far. And, as the reality of the relation of resemblance cannot be denied, it would diminish the number of indefinable conceptions if the relation of truth-correspondence could be taken to be resemblance. And, in the second place, a true belief gives us information about the object of a belief, and from the nature of one resembling thing we can gain knowledge of the thing which resembles it. It was not unnatural, though it was illogical, to conclude that the relation was the same in both cases.

I suspect, however, that some thinkers who have been accused of holding the copy theory of truth have in reality only held that the truth of a belief depends on its correspondence with a fact, and that it has been their critics who have been in error in supposing that the correspondence asserted could only be the correspondence of resemblance.

It may be noted that the theory of truth which we have adopted, though it cannot be identified with the copy theory, might be called with some appropriateness the picture theory of truth. For while a picture gives information about the object pictured, it does not do so by being an exact copy of that object. A picture may contain, on a surface of two dimensions, two

figures of very different sizes. But from it we may learn that
the objects represented are two three-dimensioned human bodies,
approximately equal in size, standing at some distance from
each other in a particular direction.

I do not say that our theory would be in any way explained
by calling it a picture theory. For in order to explain the
relation which a faithful picture bears to its object, we must
say that it represents it. And this, I think, involves that the
picture gives us knowledge of the object. Thus the conception
of knowledge, and therefore the conception of truth, would be
required to explain the explanation of truth. But the relation of
a picture to its object, while not an explanation of the relation of
truth, seems as appropriate a metaphor for it as can be found.

**14.** Now if we accept this theory of what is meant by the
truth of beliefs, there is, I maintain, no reason to hold that the
truth of beliefs involves their correspondence with true propositions. We shall agree with the advocates of propositions that
the truth of a belief involves its correspondence with something.
But we shall say that in every case the truth of a belief involves
its correspondence with a fact, and that there is no need for
any further correspondence with a proposition.

The supporters of the reality of propositions would not deny
that every true belief did correspond to a fact. Every belief
asserts that something (in the widest sense of "something")
possesses a quality, or is connected with something by a relation.
If the belief is true, then that thing does possess the quality, or
is connected with something by the relation. The possession of
such a quality, or the connection by such a relation, is a fact,
according to our definition. And if the belief is true, it will
correspond to the fact. It may also correspond to a true proposition, but then it will have two correspondences—to the true
proposition and the fact. What reason is there, then, to believe
in the reality of the proposition at all? The only ground given
for the reality of the proposition was that there must be something, correspondence to which constituted the truth of the
belief. Our theory admits this, and relies on the admitted
correspondence to the fact. What reason can be given why a
further correspondence to a proposition should be necessary?

**15**. Two reasons have been given for the necessity of this further correspondence, neither of which seems to me to be satisfactory. The first of them is that many things are true which are never thought of. The second depends upon the assertion that all truth is timeless.

It is said that many things are true which, in all probability, are never known or assumed. Take, for example, the number of mosquitoes born on this planet between the death of Caesar and the death of Queen Anne. What are the chances that any person has ever entertained any belief or assumption at all on this subject? And if there had been any such belief or assumption, what chance is there that it would have been true? And yet, it is asked, can we deny that there must be some number such that it is true that it is the number of those mosquitoes? Now, if there are no propositions, nothing could be true about this number except beliefs and assumptions. And, consequently, the fact that there is a truth, where there is neither belief nor assumption, proves the reality of propositions.

In reply to this, some thinkers have admitted that, if propositions are not real, every fact must be present to some mind, but have endeavoured to avoid the reality of propositions by relying on the existence of an omniscient being, who entertains true beliefs about every fact[1]. But even if the existence of such an omniscient being should be proved, and should render it certain that nothing could be true without being known, the

---

[1] It does not seem very satisfactory that the possibility of truth should be dependent on the existence of a being who was occupied in knowing, not only the truth that red is not green, but the truth that it is true that red is not green, the truth that it is true that it is true that red is not green, and so on through an infinite series. Such beliefs grow less significant and important as the series progresses, and consequently it would follow that the proportion of the beliefs of such a being which fell below any standard, however low, of significance and importance, would be infinitely greater than the proportion which fell above it.

It is not necessary that an omniscient being, if there were one, should be occupied in this way. For, if all reality were existent, a being whose knowledge was intuitive and not discursive might be fairly said to be omniscient if he had an intuitive knowledge (somewhat analogous to our perception) of all that exists, although he did not believe all truths—or, indeed, any truths. But the existence of an omniscient being whose knowledge was of this sort would not meet the difficulty discussed in the text.

believers in the reality of propositions would not be silenced. For their objection could be put in a more fundamental form, which could not be met in this way. Even if every truth should be known, is it not certain, they may ask, that its truth does not depend upon its being known? "$X$ is $Y$" is not true because I have a true belief in it. My belief in it is true because it is true that $X$ is $Y$. And thus, it is said, the truth is independent of the belief, even if the existence of an omniscient being ensures that every truth is believed. But, if so, there is something true besides beliefs. Truth is objective, and a thing cannot be made true by believing it to be true.

**16**. It follows, no doubt, from the theory which we have adopted that nothing is true but mental states. But I do not think that any of the untenable consequences, which have been asserted to follow from this, do really follow from it. For, although on this theory there is no truth independent of the beliefs, there is something else which is independent of the beliefs—the facts to which the beliefs correspond. Now these facts hold the same position as independent of the beliefs, and as determining their truth, as the propositions were asserted to hold by those who believed in them. Take the case of a man who was selfish without his selfishness being suspected or contemplated, either by himself or by any other person. Then there would not be a real truth, "$X$ is selfish," but there would be the real fact of $X$'s selfishness. And supposing that his selfishness was known—either by an omniscient being or by anyone else—the truth of the belief in his selfishness need not depend on any proposition, since it would depend on the fact that he *was* selfish.

And thus it seems to me that the alleged difficulties disappear. The element in them which was valid was the fact that it is essential to a true belief that it depends for its truth on its correspondence to something. But that is satisfied by its correspondence to the fact. There is no necessity that it should depend for its truth on anything *true* other than itself, and it is the assumption that there was such a necessity which makes the objection of our opponents invalid.

Nothing, it has been said as an objection to our theory, can be made true by believing or assuming it to be true. And it has been argued that if nothing is true except beliefs and assumptions, then "$X$ is $Y$" would be made true by believing or assuming it to be true. But there is an ambiguity here. Does "made true by believing it to be true" mean only that the belief is essential for the truth, or does it mean that it is all that is essential for the truth? It is only if the phrase is taken in the second sense that it must be admitted that a thing cannot be made true by believing it to be true. And it is only if the phrase is taken in the first sense that our theory involves that a thing is made true by believing it to be true.

The mere fact that an assertion is believed is certainly not all that is required to make it true. But then our theory does not say that this is all that is required. It says, on the contrary, that it is essential, in order that a belief should be true, that it should correspond to a fact. Otherwise it will be false. And so our theory does not assert that the belief in anything is sufficient to make it true. It does assert that nothing is true unless it is believed, but there is nothing untenable in this when it is realized that, besides being believed, it must correspond to a fact.

**17.** In the second place, it has been said that whatever is true at all is timelessly true, and that this fact renders propositions indispensable, since in them, and in them alone, can this timelessness be found. It cannot be found in the belief in the fact, since all beliefs are unquestionably in time. Nor can it, in many cases, be found in the fact which is believed, since that is often in time. It is timelessly true, it is said, that the date of the battle of Waterloo is 1815. Nothing timeless can be found, either in the battle itself, or in anyone's belief about it, as they are both in time. But if propositions are real at all, they are certainly timeless, since they would be non-existent, and nothing but the existent can be temporal. Here, and here only, is the necessary timelessness found, and therefore propositions must be real.

The supporters of this view would not deny that a belief, which corresponded with a true proposition, would be properly called true, although it was in time. But they would say that the truth of such a belief was only derivative, and depended on its correspondence with the proposition. It is the truth of the proposition which is the ultimate truth, and so the time-lessness of truth would be saved by the timelessness of the proposition.

But is it certain that what is asserted in *every* true belief is timelessly true? It is clear that nothing would be timelessly true which is true at one time, and not at another. And there are beliefs which *primâ facie* assert something which is true at one time and not at another. The belief "I am now hungry"— if those words are really the complete and unambiguous ex-pression of my belief—is sometimes true and sometimes false, and therefore, when it is true, cannot be asserting anything which is timelessly true. But there is an explanation of what is meant by "I am now hungry" which would avoid that result. With that explanation I cannot agree, but the point cannot well be discussed here[1].

**18.** Nor is it necessary to do so, for it does not affect the force of the present argument. It may or may not be the case that what is asserted in some beliefs is sometimes true and some-times false. But it is certain that what is asserted in the majority of beliefs is not sometimes true and sometimes false. If any beliefs assert what is sometimes one and sometimes the other, it is only those which contain some reference to past, present, or future. All other beliefs assert something which is true or false without reference to the time at which it is asserted. "The date of the battle of Waterloo is 1815" was a belief which was true during the battle, will be true a million years hence, if anyone happens to remember it, and would have been true a million years ago, if anyone had happened to prophesy it.

We must not say, however, that such beliefs as these are always true, since this would imply that the same belief can

---

[1] It will be discussed in Book V. The solution of this and similar problems, which will be put forward there, will involve the theory that time is unreal, and that, in consequence, nothing changes. But such a result will not support the argument for timeless propositions which is discussed in the text. For that argument demanded propositions as a refuge for the timelessness which was not to be found in beliefs. It will therefore be invalid if it should finally appear that beliefs, together with everything else, are timeless.

exist at different and separated times, which is not the case. A belief is a psychical fact in a man's mind, and my belief now cannot be the same as your belief now, or as mine next year. We must rather say that such beliefs are true or false without reference to the time when they are made. From this it follows that, if any such belief in $X$ is true or false, all such beliefs in $X$ will be true or false respectively, whenever they are made[1].

But this does not justify us in concluding that such beliefs correspond to timeless true propositions. Of course, if there were timeless true propositions, then all beliefs in any such propositions would be true whenever they were made. But the converse does not hold. It does not follow that, if there are beliefs which would be true whenever they are made, they must correspond to timeless propositions, or to anything timeless. If a belief which makes an assertion $X$ corresponds to a fact in such a way as to be true, then all beliefs which make the same assertion will be true, whenever they are made, unless the assertion contains a reference to past, present, or future. It does not require anything timeless to secure that beliefs that the date of Waterloo is 1815 shall be true whenever they are made. That is secured by all the beliefs referring to the same fact, and not referring to it as past, present, or future.

**19**. It is possible, then, to account for the truth of true beliefs without basing it on their correspondence to true propositions, and so far we have found no reason to believe in the reality of propositions. But how about false beliefs? Such beliefs do unquestionably exist, and it may be maintained that they can only be false by corresponding to false propositions.

What is it that makes a belief false? We saw that the truth of a belief does not lie in its coherence, or completeness, or systematic nature, or in the fact that it works for me, or satisfies me, or is self-evident to me. And in the same way it seems clear that the falsity of a belief does not lie in its want of any of

---

[1] It may be asked what is meant by two different beliefs being beliefs in the same thing. In the case of true beliefs, which we are at present considering, the answer is simple. Two true beliefs are beliefs in the same thing when their truth consists in correspondence to the same fact. What is meant by it when the beliefs are false will be considered in Section 21.

these characteristics. The absence of one of them may be a criterion of falsity, but it does not constitute falsity.

It seems to me that a false belief owes its falsity, as a true belief does its truth, to a relation to fact. It cannot, of course, be a relation of correspondence to a fact, since then the belief would be true. I think that the relation in question is a relation of non-correspondence to all facts. If $A$ has not the relation of correspondence to $B$, it has the relation of non-correspondence to it. And I submit that what makes a belief false is just that there is no fact anywhere to which it corresponds. If I say "my table is of gold," this is false because it is not a fact that there is anything which possesses the characteristics of being my table and of being golden. If I say "my table is not of wood" this is false because it is not a fact that there is anything which possesses the characteristics of being my table and of not being wooden. If I say "no Cambridge college in 1919 has a chapel" this is false because it is not a fact that there is anything which has the characteristics of being a group of all Cambridge colleges in 1919, and of being a group all of whose members are devoid of chapels. If I say "whatever is a Cambridge college must be an elephant," this is false because it is not a fact that there is anything which is the characteristic of being a Cambridge college and which itself possesses the further characteristic that whatever has it must be an elephant.

**20.**   Against this view it has been argued that every belief must refer to some object. But this seems to me to be due to a confusion between two truths. One of these is that every belief professes to refer to some fact, and, more specifically, to correspond to it in the way which we have already discussed. But this only means that every belief professes to be true, or, in other words, that to believe anything means to believe it to be true. All beliefs profess to refer to some object, but only those which are true really do so. The other truth is that every belief really has a relation to some fact or facts on which its truth or falsehood depends. And this is admitted by our theory. The mistake arises from confusing the relation, which every belief really has, with the reference, which every belief professes to have, but which false beliefs have not.

**21**. It may be asked whether our theory can give any meaning to the statement that two persons, or the same person at different times, had false beliefs in the same thing. If Smith and Brown both believe that the earth is flat, it would very commonly be said that they had the same false belief. This is incorrect, for two people cannot have the same belief, since a belief is a psychical fact which cannot be in two minds. But it is impossible to deny that in some sense they have false beliefs in the same thing. Now if there were false propositions, we could say that they had beliefs in the same proposition. If their beliefs were true, we could say that they corresponded to the same fact. But with false beliefs, if our theory is true, there is no correspondence of the two beliefs to the same reality. They both, indeed, have the relation of non-correspondence to all facts, but they share that relation with Robinson's belief that Bacon wrote *Hamlet*, which would not be called a belief in the same thing.

But our theory gives us a perfectly satisfactory meaning for the phrase "in the same thing" as applied to two false beliefs. Two false beliefs are beliefs in the same thing when they both *profess* to be beliefs correspondent to the same fact. In the case of false beliefs there is no such fact, and therefore no such relation of correspondence. But the assertion of such a correspondence would be a quality of such beliefs. And, although a belief can only be true or false by means of a relation to a fact, there is no reason why two beliefs should not be beliefs in the same thing in respect of a common quality.

Again, if two beliefs profess to be correspondent to the same fact, it is the absence of that fact which makes them false. And therefore we can also say that two false beliefs are beliefs in the same thing when it is the absence of the same fact which makes both of them false. Smith's belief is made false by the absence from reality of anything which is both this planet and flat. And Brown's belief is made false by the same absence. This unites them together, and distinguishes both of them from Robinson's belief, which is made false by the absence of something different—namely, of anything which is both Bacon and the author of *Hamlet*.

**22**. Thus we can account for the falsity of false beliefs without basing it on their correspondence to false propositions, and we have still no reason to believe in the reality of propositions. We may remark that, even if we had come to the conclusion that true beliefs must correspond to true propositions, it would not have followed that false beliefs must correspond to false propositions. For the reality of true propositions would not have affected our conclusion that false beliefs correspond to nothing, and, if there were true propositions, the best explanation of false beliefs would be that they were the beliefs which did not correspond to true propositions. And this explanation would have the additional recommendation that there are several objections to the reality of false propositions which do not apply to the reality of true propositions[1].

**23**. We have thus seen that satisfactory explanations can be given of the truth of true beliefs, and of the falsity of false beliefs, without the necessity of introducing correspondence with propositions. And I do not know that any other reason has ever been given for belief in the reality of propositions except the asserted necessity of this correspondence—that is, if "proposition" is used in the sense in which I have taken it, as meaning a non-existent reality which is true or false independently of our beliefs. It is only when it is so used that the question of the reality of propositions has any bearing on the question whether it is necessary in philosophy to go beyond the study of the existent. If, for example, propositions are maintained to be real as constituents of beliefs, and not otherwise, then it would follow that such propositions would be existent, since it is impossible that a constituent of an existent thing should not itself exist. But, whether they were existent or not, we should study them in studying the existent, since there would be no propositions which were not constituents of existent beliefs.

**24**. The result of our discussion so far is that, while we have not positively disproved the reality of the propositions which we have been considering, we have arrived at the decision that there is no reason to assert their reality. But a further question arises. We have seen that every belief derives its

[1] Cp. Russell, *Philosophical Essays*, VII. p. 176.

truth or falsity from its relation to a fact or facts. Now if any of these facts are non-existent, we shall still have to assert that there is some non-existent reality, though it will consist of facts, and not of propositions.

It seems to me, however, that there is no reason to assert that there are any non-existent facts, and that the truth and falsity of all beliefs can be explained on the hypothesis that all facts are existent.

Beliefs may for the purpose of this enquiry be divided into two classes—those which profess to refer to an existent fact, and those which do not. Each of these classes contains, of course, both true and false beliefs.

With regard to true beliefs of the first class, it is clear that they do not require any relation to non-existent facts. If I say "my table exists," "my table is square," or "every Cambridge college in 1919 has a dining hall," what makes them true is their correspondence with the three facts to which they profess to refer—the possession by my table of the characteristic of existence, the possession by my table of the characteristic of squareness, and the possession by the group of all Cambridge colleges in 1919 of the characteristic that each of its members has the characteristic of having a dining hall. These cannot be facts unless the table and the group of colleges exist, and there-fore the facts are existent facts.

And it is equally clear that false beliefs of this class do not require any relation to non-existent facts. If I say "my table is golden," or "every Cambridge college in 1919 has a swimming bath," these assertions could only be true if they corresponded with existent facts. If either of them does not correspond to any existent fact, it will be false, and so its falsity is no ground for asserting the reality of non-existent facts.

**25**. We now come to the second class—to the beliefs which do not profess to refer to an existent fact. And these present a more difficult and complicated problem. "Perfection is a quality," "two sides of a triangle are always longer than the third," are beliefs of this class. But so also are all beliefs in general laws, as distinct from summaries of what takes place in each of a group of cases. "All Cambridge colleges in 1919 have dining halls" falls, as we saw, in the first class, because, in the natural sense of the statement, in which we took it, it is not an assertion of any general law, but only a summing up of seventeen facts about the seventeen colleges respectively. But take the belief "all lions are mortal." In any sense in which any person is justified in asserting this, it is not a summing up of particular facts about particular lions, since no one has observed the death of all lions, past, present, and future. It is a belief in a general law which we should still hold to be true even if no lions existed. We could not, indeed, in that case, establish it by an induction based on the observed deaths of lions, but if we established inductively the law that all animals are mortal, it would follow from this, together with the definition of a lion, that all lions would be mortal, and the conclusion would still be held to be true if we were certain that no lions ever did or would exist. Such a law as this, then, does not profess to refer to an existent fact. Does it, in reality, always derive its truth or falsity from its relation to existent facts?

**26**. All beliefs which do not profess to refer to an existent fact have one characteristic in common—they all assert that the presence of one characteristic implies the presence of another[1].

In order to make this clear, let us first note that the only beliefs which do not assert a *concomitance* of characteristics are such beliefs as "I am happy," "this is red," where the subject of the assertion is immediately perceived by the person who makes the assertion. And such beliefs are obviously among those which profess to refer to existent facts. With these exceptions, every belief asserts a concomitance of characteristics with one another. This is clearly the case when the subject of which anything is asserted is a characteristic, for what is asserted of it can be nothing but its possession of another characteristic. But when the subject is not a characteristic, it must, if

---

[1] It may be said that to include all beliefs we should have to say that presence or absence of one characteristic implies the presence or absence of another. But the absence of a characteristic may be taken as the presence of a negative characteristic, and thus the expression in the text is not incorrect.

The nature of implication will be discussed in Chapter XII. At present it will perhaps be sufficient to say that I use the word in the ordinary sense.

it is not perceived, be defined or described by characteristics, and so the assertion is that the characteristics of the definition or description are found along with the characteristic asserted. "All men are mortal" means that the characteristics which define a man are never to be found without the characteristic mortality. "Smith is wiser than Jones" means that the characteristics which enable us to identify Smith are found in a substance which has the characteristic of being wiser than Jones.

**27.** Characteristics, however, can be concomitant without one implying the other. And, in fact, many of our beliefs do assert concomitance without implication. I know, for example, that every Cambridge college in 1919 had a dining hall, not because the characteristic of being such a college in that year implies the characteristic of having a dining hall, but because I know that in that year each of the seventeen colleges had, as a matter of fact, the latter characteristic.

But beliefs which assert concomitance without implication always profess to refer to existent facts, and when we pass to beliefs which do not profess to make this reference, we find that it is always concomitance with implication which is asserted. I can assert that, if an eighteenth college had been founded in Cambridge, this college would not be an elephant, because the characteristic of being a college implies the characteristic of not being an elephant. But I cannot assert that it would resemble the existing colleges in having less than seventy fellowships, or in having a dining hall, because these characteristics are not implied by the characteristic of being a Cambridge college existing in 1919. And again, of the class of triangles, as studied in geometry, I can only assert such things as are implied by the characteristic of triangularity[1].

All beliefs, then, which do not profess to refer to existent facts, assert that the presence of one characteristic implies the presence of another. Let us first consider true beliefs of this

[1] The implication may be of such a kind that it is only known to us empirically. I can assert that if there should be a lion in Westminster Hall to-morrow it would not be green, because I have good, though empirical, evidence for the belief that the characteristic of being a lion implies the characteristic of not being green.

class, and enquire whether it is necessary that the facts to which they refer should in any case be non-existent.

**28**. Take, to begin with, such a general law as "all lions are mortal." This, as we have seen, does not profess to refer to existent facts. It asserts a connection between two characteristics which would be true if no existent being had ever been a lion or been mortal. But it seems clear to me that its truth depends on its correspondence with facts which do exist. The characteristics of being a lion, and of being mortal, do exist, since there are existent substances which possess them. The belief in the law owes its truth to its correspondence with the fact that the characteristic of being a lion has the characteristic of implying the characteristic of being mortal, and with the equivalent fact that the characteristic of being mortal has the characteristic of being implied by the characteristic of being a lion. And these facts, being each of them the possession of a characteristic by an existent characteristic, are existent facts.

**29**. This simple solution, however, is only possible because in this case the characteristics happen to be those of existent substances, which is not, as we have seen, essential to the validity of the law. And there are many beliefs which cannot be dealt with in this way—for example, "a man is more valuable than a phoenix," or "a man cannot be a phoenix." Here the characteristic of being a man is existent, but we have every reason to suppose that the characteristic of being a phoenix is not. Of course, there *may* be a phoenix. But the certainty of my belief that a man could not be a phoenix does not depend on this possibility. And in the case of such a belief as "a perfectly virtuous man would be more admirable than a conqueror of the whole world," it might well be the case that no existent substance possessed either characteristic, and so that neither characteristic existed.

There are, no doubt, various ways in which the nature of a non-existent characteristic might be determined by the nature of an existent characteristic. In the first place, the existent characteristic might be a part of the non-existent characteristic. To be a phoenix is probably not an existent characteristic, but to be a bird is. This cannot of course determine the whole nature of the non-existent characteristic, but will determine part of it. And this may be sufficient to justify the belief. Since a man cannot be a bird, he cannot be a phoenix. And thus the truth of the belief is justified by the nature of the existent characteristic "to be a bird."

In the second place, a non-existent characteristic might be determined by its relation to an existent characteristic. For example, if the nature of the characteristic of partial virtue is given, it determines, in part at least, the nature of the characteristic of perfect virtue. Thus it may be the case that if the characteristic of partial virtue is what it is, it will follow that a perfectly virtuous man is more admirable than Alexander. In that case the truth of the belief would be determined by the nature of an existent characteristic. And the same principle might apply when both the characteristics which found a place in the belief were non-existent—if, for example, the belief were that a perfectly virtuous man would be more admirable than a conqueror of the whole world.

Or, once more, the non-existent characteristic may be determined by a relation of another kind to the existent characteristic. The non-existent characteristic might be one which men have a tendency to believe to exist when they perceive anything as having a certain existent characteristic. Or it may be one whose existence would be inferred from that of the existent characteristic if some definite mistake were made in a chain of argument, of which all the other steps were logically correct.

For example, if Berkeley is right, neither space nor straight lines exist. Yet it would remain true that two straight lines cannot enclose a space. But things certainly exist which have the characteristic of being spatial sense-data. And men have a tendency to believe in the existence of space and straight lines when they perceive spatial sense-data. And, again, the existence of space and straight lines can be inferred from the existence of spatial sense-data, if a definite mistake is introduced in an argument otherwise correct. Thus the characteristics of being a space and of being a straight line are so connected with the characteristic of being a spatial sense-datum, that since the latter has the nature which it has, the nature of the two former must be such that to be a space implies the impossibility of being contained by two straight lines. Once more then, the truth of the belief is determined by its relation to the nature of an existent characteristic.

**30.** These relations between characteristics are real and important. But they will not serve our purpose. In the first place, though it would be difficult to prove that there were any characteristics as to which we hold true beliefs, which were not related to existent characteristics in one of these ways, yet it would not be easy, I think, to prove that there were *not* any which were not so related.

And, in the second place, these relations are not relations of correspondence. My belief that a man cannot be a phoenix is, no doubt, determined to be true by the existent fact that the characteristic of being a bird implies the absence of the characteristic of humanity. But it does not correspond to that fact with the peculiar sort of correspondence which constitutes truth. It does not assert anything about the characteristic of being a bird, but about the characteristic of being a phoenix. In order that it should be true, it would have to correspond to something about the characteristic of being a phoenix. And, if that characteristic is not existent, we shall not have avoided the correspondence of some beliefs with non-existent facts. The position will be the same about beliefs which make assertions about perfectly virtuous men, or (if Berkeley should be right) about space and straight lines.

**31.** But, if we go further, we shall find a way in which every characteristic is either a characteristic of the existent, or else is an element in a characteristic of the existent. For, with any characteristic whatever, it is true of everything, and therefore of everything existent, that either it has that characteristic or it does not have it. And not to have a characteristic is equivalent to having the correspondent negative characteristic. If a man cannot be a phoenix, then every man will have the negative characteristic of not-phoenix. This characteristic will be existent, and since "phoenix" is an element of "not-phoenix," it will also be existent. For it seems clear that the parts of what exist must themselves exist. And thus all characteristics will exist, whether they are or are not characteristics of existent things.

Since this is so, every assertion about a characteristic which nothing existent possesses, will be an assertion about something which nevertheless does exist, as an element in an existent characteristic. It will be remembered that every assertion which does not profess to refer to an existent fact is an assertion that a characteristic implies another characteristic. The truth of such an assertion consists in its correspondence to a relation between these two characteristics. And this relation is a characteristic of both of the characteristics. The characteristic of being a griffin, for example, has the characteristic that anything which has it cannot have the characteristic of being a phoenix. The same incompatibility is also a characteristic of the characteristic of being a phoenix. And both the characteristics of being a griffin and of being a phoenix are to be found as elements in the nature of whatever exists—they are both to be found, for example, in the nature of any particular table, since it will have the characteristics of not being a griffin and of not being a phoenix. The belief, therefore, corresponds to what is found in the nature of the table—and of everything else existent— that is to say, it corresponds to an existent fact.

It may be objected that it is paradoxical and wilful to treat it as part of the nature of a table that it is not a phoenix, or, again, not a prime number, and to place such characteristics on a level with its characteristic of being a table, or even with its negative characteristic of not being a chair. And it is true, no doubt, that from any practical point of view it is much more important to believe about any substance, which is, in fact, a table, that it possesses the characteristics of being a table, or of not being a chair, than that it possesses the characteristics of not being a phoenix, or a prime number. And even apart from all practical considerations, we shall gain more knowledge of the nature of the substance by realizing that it possesses the first two characteristics than we shall by realizing that it possesses the other two. But it remains the fact, nevertheless, that the two last characteristics are as truly and objectively characteristics of the substance as the two first are.

For it cannot be denied that any person who should assert that the table was not a prime number would be asserting something that was true. The assertion may be unimportant, foolish, a waste of time. But it is not false, and it must be true. And it cannot be true unless it is made true by the nature of that thing about which the assertion is made. If it is not a characteristic of the table not to be a prime number—if that is not part of the nature of the table, independently of whether the assertion is made or not—then, if the assertion is made, it cannot be true. And so not to be a phoenix must be a characteristic of the table.

**32.** We have thus arrived at the conclusion that the truth of true beliefs which do not profess to refer to existing facts does not imply the reality of non-existent facts. For all such beliefs assert the implication of one characteristic by another, and all characteristics exist, either in their own right or as elements in others, and therefore all facts about them are existent facts.

Everything, in the widest sense of the word, has as many characteristics as there are positive characteristics, since it will have in each case either the positive characteristic or its negative. If it should be asked what determines the number of positive characteristics, the answer must be that it is an ultimate fact, just as on the theory of real propositions the number of those propositions would be an ultimate fact. The criterion of the reality of a characteristic is that any person should be aware of it, for though there may be any number of characteristics of which no one is aware, it is impossible to be aware of a characteristic which is not real.

**33.** We now pass to the case of false beliefs which do not profess to refer to existent facts. These beliefs, like other false beliefs, owe their falsity to being in a relation of non-correspondence to all facts. Take, for example, the false belief that every man must be a philosopher. This, as we have seen, means that the characteristic of being a man has itself the characteristic that whatever possesses it possesses the further quality of being a philosopher. Now there is no fact which is the possession by the characteristic of being a man of this characteristic. And as this is the only fact to which the belief could correspond, the belief is in a relation of non-correspondence to all facts, and is therefore false.

This does not involve the reality of any non-existent fact. So long as there is no fact which does correspond to this belief, the belief will be false, whether all facts are existent or some are non-existent. But we may go further and point out that it must be the nature of the existent which makes the belief false. For what it falsely asserts is that a characteristic possesses another characteristic. Now we have seen that all characteristics exist, and this possession of a characteristic by a characteristic would, if it were real, be an existent fact. Thus the nature of the existent, by not including this fact, is sufficient to make the belief false.

We may notice in passing a difference between those false beliefs which profess to refer to existent facts and those which do not profess to refer to them. As we have seen, all those which do not profess to make this reference assert the implication of a characteristic by another characteristic. And, as we have seen, every characteristic does exist, either positively, or as an element in a negative characteristic. A false belief about a substance may be false in one of two ways. It may be false because the substance does not exist at all, as, for example, "the present High Treasurer of England is a Mahometan," or because the substance has not the characteristic asserted of it, as, for example, "the present Pope is a Mahometan." But we cannot believe a characteristic to have a certain nature without being aware of that characteristic, and every characteristic of which we are aware is real, and so exists, either positively or as an element in a negative characteristic. It follows that a belief about characteristics cannot be false in the first of the two ways in which a belief about a substance can be false.

We have now gone through all sorts of beliefs—those which do and those which do not profess to refer to existent facts, and, in each class, those which are true and those which are false. And we have found that none of them require that any of the facts, their relation to which makes them true or false, should be non-existent facts.

**34**. We saw at the beginning of the chapter that, in addition to propositions, characteristics were sometimes asserted to be real without existing. But the discussion of facts, into which we were led by our discussion of propositions, has enabled us to see that all characteristics are existent. Such characteristics as being a phoenix, or being a prime number, are not existent in respect of being themselves characteristics of anything that exists, but they are existent as elements of negative characteristics which belong to existent things. Indeed, if we knew all about the nature of any one existent thing, we should know all about every characteristic, since each existent thing has, as part of its nature, the fact of having or not having each characteristic.

**35**. It has sometimes been said that, besides propositions and characteristics, possibilities can be real without existing. Possibility is an ambiguous word, but, in whatever sense it is taken, it does not, I think, involve anything which is real but not existent.

Possibility may mean nothing but a limitation of our knowledge. Thus, if I say that it is possible that it may rain to-morrow, the most obvious sense of the words is that I do not know whether it will rain or not. In this case, clearly, it is a statement, not about any non-existent reality, but about my existent knowledge.

Possibility, however, is often asserted in cases where we know that the reality is different from what is asserted to be possible. Thus I may say that it was possible that I should not have sneezed yesterday, although I did sneeze. This may mean one of two things. It may only mean that I can see no reason why I did sneeze yesterday. In this case it is clearly once more an assertion about my existent knowledge. But, again, I may make the assertion, though I do know why I sneezed yesterday. I may say that it was possible that I should not have sneezed yesterday, but that the fact that I took snuff prevented that possibility from becoming actual. In this case the possibility means, I think, that there is nothing within some particular field of circumstances to ensure my sneezing. For example, it might have meant that the fact that I was alive on that day did not ensure my sneezing on it, as it did my breathing on it.

The particular field of circumstances, in reference to which the possibility is taken, can usually only be discovered from the context when, as in this case, the possibility is asserted about a single thing. In this case, for example, the possibility might have meant that snuff sometimes makes me sneeze, and sometimes does not. But when the possibility is asserted, not of a single thing, but of a class of things marked out by a definition, the particular field of circumstances usually consists of those circumstances which are included in the definition. If it said "it is possible that a triangle should be equilateral," this would naturally mean that the characteristic of being a triangle does not imply, either that the figure which possesses it is equilateral, or that it is not equilateral[1].

Thus, when possibility is taken in this sense, it is an assertion about the implication of one characteristic by another. And we have seen that the implication of one characteristic by another is always an existent fact. It is therefore no more necessary to accept the reality of anything non-existent when possibility is taken in this sense than when it is taken in the other.

36. It would seem, then, that there is nothing which compels us to believe in non-existent reality. There is nothing which makes it necessary for us to accept the reality of propositions, or of non-existent characteristics, facts, or possibilities. And these are, as far as I know, the only things which have been asserted to be real without existing.

But are we entitled to go further, and conclude that there are reasons for positively rejecting non-existent reality? With regard to characteristics and possibilities, the course of our argument has justified us in asserting positively that they

---

[1] In the mouth, however, of a person who was ignorant of geometry, the statement might refer to the limits of his own knowledge, and might signify that he did not know whether a triangle must be, could be, or could not be equilateral. He would be in the same ignorance about the relations of the two characteristics as we all are about to-morrow's weather.

cannot be real without existing. For we saw, to begin with, that all characteristics were existent. And all statements of possibilities have been reduced either to statements about existent knowledge or to statements about the implications of characteristics, and are therefore statements about the existent.

**37.** But how about propositions? There the matter is rather different. If a proposition, in the sense in which we have been using the word, is real at all, it must be non-existent. Thus the question before us is—are we able to assert positively that no propositions are real, or must we content ourselves with our previous conclusion that there is nothing which makes it necessary for us to assert the reality of propositions?

We can say at any rate that our theory of reality will be simpler, if the reality of propositions is rejected. It might perhaps be objected that such a belief as "a phoenix cannot be a griffin" cannot be explained as simply by our theory as by means of propositions. In the latter case the belief would be true because it corresponded to a true proposition. But if there are no propositions the truth of the belief could only be explained by falling back on the characteristics of not being a phoenix, and not being a griffin, which belong to all substances.

But this objection would be unjustified. On our theory the explanation of the truth of the belief is very simple. We say that the belief is true because it asserts that the characteristic of being a phoenix implies another characteristic, which, in fact, it does imply. And, whether there are propositions or not, every belief which does not profess to refer to existent facts is, as we saw, an assertion about the implication of one characteristic by another, and is true or false according to the nature of those characteristics.

Whatever complexity there is in our theory is not to be found in the explanation of the truth of the belief, but in the explanation of the existence of the characteristics. And this complexity is not peculiar to our theory, though the use made of it is, for even a believer in propositions must admit that, if no phoenix exists, everything existent must have the characteristic of not being a phoenix.

In this respect then, our theory is not less simple than the other. And in another respect it is more simple. For it requires only one sort of correspondence in which a true belief must stand—the correspondence between the belief and the fact. But the theory of propositions requires two such correspondences. The belief must, it is said, correspond to a true proposition. And it cannot be denied that it does also correspond to a fact. If it is true that my table is square, there must be a squareness of the table, and the belief corresponds to it.

Thus two correspondences are required, and each of them seems to be independent of the other. The truth of the proposition is, if I understand the theory rightly, taken as ultimate, and so cannot depend on the occurrence of the fact. And the fact cannot depend on the truth of the proposition. It could not be maintained that the squareness of the table depended on the truth of the proposition that the table is square.

But it is not always the case that the simplest solution of a problem is the true one. And it does not follow that there are no propositions because all the data known to us could be as well accounted for without propositions. But when we look further, we find, I think, a more positive ground for rejecting propositions—that there is no place left for them.

**38**. If I have a true belief that my table is square, there is, on the one side, this belief itself. It is true, and it is subjective, in the sense that it depends on the existence of a knowing subject, who holds the belief. On the other side there is, as the advocates of propositions would admit, the actual squareness of the table—the fact. This is objective, in the sense that it does not depend on the existence of a knowing subject. And it is not true. Between these two, propositions must come, if they come at all. On the one hand the proposition is, like the fact and unlike the belief, objective. On the other hand it is, like the belief and unlike the fact, true. Now it seems to me that if the proposition is distinguished clearly from the belief, it is impossible to keep it distinguished from the fact. When the subjective element in the belief is eliminated, it seems to me that the truth goes with it, and that we find ourselves left, not with a timeless, non-existent, and true proposition, but with nothing but the fact, which is not true (though it determines the truth of beliefs), which may or may not be timeless, and which, as we have seen above, is always, in one way or another, existent.

If this is right, the reality of true propositions would not only be superfluous but untenable. And no one, I think, would maintain the reality of false propositions, if true propositions were abandoned. The only ground, as far as I know, for maintaining the reality of false propositions was the view that the truth or falsity of every belief must be determined by its correspondence with a proposition. If this was abandoned about true propositions, there could be no ground for maintaining it of false propositions, especially as there are several objections to the reality of false propositions which do not apply to propositions which are true.

If there are no propositions, there will be nothing left to be non-existent. Substances, characteristics, and facts have all been seen to be existent. And thus we shall be entitled to conclude that there is no reality which does not exist.

**39**. But even if there should be propositions, we should still be entitled to assert that, in constructing our philosophy, we could safely confine ourselves to the consideration of that reality which is existent. For, as we have seen, every assertion either professes to refer to an existent fact, or else asserts the implication of one characteristic by another. And thus whatever was asserted in any proposition would deal with the existent.

This result depends, of course, on the view which we have taken that the characteristics of the existent, and the elements of those characteristics, themselves exist. But if this view should be rejected, the result would not be substantially different. For it would make little difference if we said, as in that case we must say, that we shall study all reality when we study what exists, together with the characteristics of what exists, and the characteristics of those characteristics.

**40**. It follows from what we have said as to the relation of reality and existence, that it is not the case, as is sometimes supposed, that what is actually existent is surrounded by a sort of framework of possibilities of existence, which limit what does exist, and do not depend on it. We saw that "it is possible that $X$ should be $Y$," if it was not a statement about the limitations of our knowledge, meant that the characteristic $X$ does not imply the absence of the characteristic $Y$. It is thus a statement about the implication of characteristics, and is not, of course, a statement about their possible implication, but about their actual implication. It is possible that a triangle should have an angle greater than a right angle, because being a triangle does not imply the absence of an angle greater than a right angle. And this is not what it possibly may not imply, but what it actually does not imply.

Thus all statements of probabilities turn out to be really statements of actualities. It is true that the actualities of which they are statements are the natures of characteristics, and that they are not dependent on the existence of those characteristics as characteristics of existent substances. Whether anything existent is triangular or not, it will still be true that to be a triangle is compatible with the possession of an angle greater than a right angle. But, as we have seen, every characteristic is existent in some way or other—either as the characteristic of an existent thing, or as an element in a characteristic of an existent thing. And, therefore, since statements of possibilities are statements of the actual nature of characteristics, they will be statements about the actual nature of existence, and will not be independent of it.

Even if, however, no possibilities are independent of the nature of existence, it will still be permissible to ask whether, within the existent, we can make distinctions between what must be as it is, and what might have been different from what it is. This question, which does not concern the present enquiry, will be discussed in Chapter XIX.

# CHAPTER III

## METHOD

**41**. It will be convenient to say something in advance of the method which I propose to employ in this work. Our object, as has been already said, is, in the first place, to consider, in Books II, III, and IV, what can be determined as to the characteristics which belong to all that exists, or, again, which belong to existence as a whole. In the second place, in Books V, VI, and VII, we have to consider what consequences of theoretical and practical interest can be drawn from this general nature of the existent with respect to various parts of the existent which are empirically known to us. The method adopted for the first of these purposes will be different in some points from that adopted for the second.

**42**. With regard to our method in the earlier enquiry, it is clear, to begin with, that it cannot rest on induction. For this there are two reasons. In the first place, as will be shown later[1], the validity of induction is by no means self-evident. If it is to be accepted at all, it will have to be proved that the nature of the existent has certain characteristics. And to prove this by induction would be a vicious circle. Consequently, in starting our enquiry into the nature of the existent, we cannot use induction.

**43**. The second reason is that, even if the validity of induction were established, it would be impossible to reach any valid results in the first part of our enquiry by means of induction. We have to enquire what characteristics belong to everything that exists, and what characteristics belong to existence as a whole. The characteristics which belong to existence as a whole cannot be reached by induction, since induction starts by observing that the same characteristic is to be found in several members of the same class—for example, that this man, that man, and the other man are mortal. Now it is clear that there

[1] Chap. xxix.

cannot be a class of things, each of which is existence as a whole. There can only be one thing which is existence as a whole. And therefore the characteristics which belong to existence as a whole can never be reached by induction.

Nor would it be possible to reach in this way any conclusion about those characteristics which belong to everything which exists. For the number of such existent things is, on any theory, so great, that the number of them in which we could observe any characteristic would be a very small proportion of the whole. And we shall find reason later on to believe that the number of existent things is infinite, so that the number in which we could observe any characteristic, which would be finite, would be an infinitely small proportion of the whole.

Now, *caeteris paribus*, the probability of an inference varies directly as the proportion of the field of observation to the field of inference. If, of one hundred things which possess the characteristic $X$, I find successively that fifty also possess the characteristic $Y$, the conclusion that all of them possess the characteristic $Y$ will become more and more probable as I proceed from the knowledge that one of the hundred has it to the knowledge that fifty of the hundred have it.

It is, no doubt, true that inductions do not vary in their probability only in the proportion of the fields of observation and inference. Indeed, it may often happen that the observation of a single case may enable us to infer with considerable probability a conclusion which covers a very large field. But, wherever this happens, it is because the possible alternatives have been narrowed down by previous reasoning[1]. And therefore it cannot happen in the initial stages of a metaphysical argument directed to the determination of the general nature of the existent. In such an argument the probability of the induction would vary with the proportion of the two fields, and as, in this case, the field of observation would be infinitely

---

[1] As if, for example, I was antecedently certain that a thousand dice were all made by the same maker, and that the maker could only be $A$, whose honesty was beyond doubt, or $B$, who was known to be dishonest, and whose interest it would be that all the dice should be loaded. In this case the discovery that a single die was loaded might be the ground of a fairly certain inference that all of them were loaded.

smaller than the field of inference, the conclusion would have no validity whatever.

This would no doubt leave it possible that in some later stage of our enquiry, when various results have been reached by processes other than induction, induction should be found capable of determining between various limited alternatives. But, in point of fact, it will be found that no opportunity will offer itself in which induction can be used.

Our method, then, cannot be inductive. It will generally be *à priori*. But in two cases our conclusions will rest directly on what is observed in perception.

**44.** I use the word perception to denote that species of awareness which we have of the existent—awareness being a mental state which is not belief, though it is knowledge. It is of great importance to be clear as to what is meant by awareness and perception, as we shall have occasion to use both terms very frequently, especially in the last three Books. I am using both terms in the sense adopted by Mr Russell, and explained by him in his paper on "Knowledge by Acquaintance and Knowledge by Description[1]."

I am aware of an object or am acquainted with an object—the phrases are used as synonymous—when "I have a direct cognitive relation to that object." "In fact, I think the relation of subject and object which I call acquaintance is simply the converse of the relation of object and subject which constitutes presentation. That is, to say that $S$ has acquaintance with $O$ is essentially the same thing as to say that $O$ is presented to $S$." "When we ask what are the kinds of objects with which we are acquainted, the first and most obvious example is *sense-data*. When I see a colour or hear a noise, I have direct acquaintance with the colour or the noise." We are also acquainted, in introspection, with "objects in various cognitive and conative relations to ourselves. When I see the sun it often happens that I am aware of my seeing the sun, in addition to being aware of the sun; and when I desire food, it often happens that I am aware of my desire for food." "The awarenesses we have con-

---

[1] *Mysticism and Logic and other Essays.* The quotations in the next paragraph are from pp. 209–212.

sidered so far have all been awarenesses of particular existents, and might all in a large sense be called sense-data[1]. For, from the point of view of theory of knowledge, introspective know-ledge is exactly on a level with knowledge derived from sight or hearing. But, in addition to awareness of the above kind of objects, which may be called awareness of *particulars*, we have also...what may be called awareness of *universals*." "Not only are we aware of particular yellows, but if we have seen a sufficient number of yellows and have sufficient intelligence, we are aware of the universal *yellow*; this universal is the subject in such judgments as 'yellow differs from blue,' or 'yellow differs from blue less than green does.' And the universal yellow is the predicate in such judgments as 'this is yellow,' where 'this' is a particular sense-datum. And universal rela-tions, too, are objects of awarenesses; up and down, before and after, resemblance, desire, awareness itself, and so on, would seem to be all of them objects of which we can be aware[2]."

This, then, is what is meant by awareness. Perception is the awareness of what Mr Russell calls particulars, as distinct from the awareness of what he calls universals. In the termin-ology which I propose to adopt, it is the awareness of substances as distinct from the awareness of characteristics. The most obvious cases of perception are the awareness of the data furnished by the bodily senses, and the awareness of the con-tents of my own mind which is given me by introspection[3].

**45.** The first case in which such an appeal to perception will be necessary is in the initial stage of the whole process— the question whether anything does exist. It would be possible to consider what characteristics are involved in being existent, or in being the whole of what exists, without raising the question whether anything did actually exist. But, in addition to deter-

---

[1] I propose to use the term "perception-data" for what Mr Russell calls "sense-data in a large sense," and to reserve the term "sense-data" for the data given by sight, hearing, etc. as distinct from those given by introspection.

[2] I could not accept without reservation Mr Russell's view as to the nature of the objects of which we are aware by introspection, but this does not affect the meaning of awareness.

[3] The distinction between substances and characteristics will be discussed in Book II. The question whether we can perceive any other substances than those mentioned in the text will be discussed in Book V.

mining what characteristics are involved in existence, we want to know whether anything exists, and therefore has those characteristics. And this can only be determined by an appeal to perception. For it is never possible for me to know that anything exists, unless I perceive it, or unless its existence is implied by the existence of something else which I do perceive.

The other case in which we shall appeal to perception will be in Chapter VII. It is on an appeal to perception that we shall rest our judgment that the whole of that which exists is differentiated into parts. It would, indeed, be possible to reach this result à priori. For I shall argue later that it is certain à priori that no substance can be simple, from which it would follow that the whole of that which exists is differentiated into parts. But the view that no substance can be simple, though I believe it to be correct, is novel and controversial, and the proof of the differentiation of the existent by an appeal to perception, if not so symmetrical, seems more likely to command assent.

In these two cases, then, the basis of our certainty will be empirical and not à priori. This, however, will not make it less certain. A judgment which is directly based on a perception may be as certain as one which is evident à priori. And in the cases before us our judgments will not be based on induction from the results of various perceptions—which would be untrustworthy for the reasons given earlier in the chapter. A single perception is sufficient to prove either of them. If I perceive anything at all, and so can judge that the thing perceived exists, that is sufficient to prove the proposition[1] "something exists," which is all that is wanted in the first case. And if I have a single perception which is such that I am entitled to judge that the thing perceived is differentiated into parts, that is sufficient to prove that the whole of what exists does not form one undifferentiated whole, since two parts, at least, are to be found in it.

**46**. A belief which is directly based on a perception experienced by the person who holds the belief may be called an

---

[1] We found reason in the last chapter to reject the reality of non-existent propositions. Having done this, it will be convenient, and not contrary to usage, to speak of beliefs as propositions, when, as at present, we are considering their content, rather than their existence as psychical facts.

ultimate empirical belief. It is properly called ultimate, since, although it is based on something—the perception—it is not based on any other *belief*. There is an important difference between ultimate beliefs which are *à priori* and those which are empirical. Those which are *à priori* can be held as ultimate beliefs by more than one person. The belief, for example, in the Law of Excluded Middle as an ultimate truth, is not confined to myself. But an empirical belief can only be ultimate if it describes a perceptum perceived by the person who holds the belief. Now it is not certain that two people ever do perceive the same perceptum. And, as we shall see, in the two cases in which we shall appeal to ultimate empirical propositions, the argument will turn very largely on beliefs such that the percepta on which they are based are themselves perceptions, perceived by introspection. Now, at any rate in our present experience, no person can perceive any perceptions except his own, and, therefore, no perception can be perceived by more than one person. I may be ultimately certain that I have now a perception of a certain sort. Smith may be certain, and justifiably certain, that I have now a perception of that sort, but for him it cannot be an ultimate certainty, but must be reached by inference.

This, however, need not prevent an argument, founded on an empirical proposition of this sort, from being effective for more than one person. If, for example, I argue that something exists because my perceptions exist, the argument will not, with that premise, prove to Smith that something exists, since he is not immediately certain of my perceptions. But it will suggest to him the analogous argument that something must exist, because *his* perceptions do so. And this argument is as valid as mine, leads to the same conclusion, and leads to it from a premise of which he is immediately certain.

**47.** In the course of the next three Books, I shall endeavour to determine successively various characteristics of the existent. The order in which they will be determined will be largely a necessary order—the characteristic $Y$ will be determined after the characteristic $X$, because the only possible demonstration of the occurrence of $Y$ is one which starts from the fact of the occurrence of $X$. But the order of the demonstration will be found not to be determined completely in this way. There are various steps which could logically have been taken in a different order from that which is actually adopted. In this case the order chosen can only be decided by considerations of clearness and convenience.

Such a method will be seen at once to have a marked resemblance to Hegel's, and it will be worth while to consider in detail the resemblances and dissimilarities between them. In the first place, by the use of such a method we endeavour to base philosophy on the discovery of the characteristics which are involved in the characteristic of existence, or the characteristic of being the whole of what exists. In a similar manner Hegel's categories owe their validity to the fact that they are implied by the original category of Pure Being—by which Hegel means either existence or reality, in the sense in which we have used these words.

Then, in the second place, our determinations of the nature of existence will form, like Hegel's categories, a single chain. They will not be divisible into separate lines of argument which are independent of one another. They will form a series, in which the exact place of many of the terms will be fixed by logical necessity, while even those whose places are not exactly determined in this way will be limited by logical necessity to a few alternative positions. The chain formed by the categories, from Pure Being to the Absolute Idea, is one of the most characteristic peculiarities of Hegel's system, and resemblance to it on this point must be of great importance in determining the relation of the two methods.

**48**. But, by the side of these resemblances, there are important dissimilarities. One of the chief features of the Hegelian dialectic is its triadic division. The whole series of the categories is divided into three parts—Being, Essence, and the Notion. Each of these again is divided into three parts, and the same principle of division is carried further, though not equally far in all parts of the series. We shall not find that our process from characteristic to characteristic shows any such triadic rhythm.

Again, the triadic division in Hegel's system is closely connected with something still more fundamental, which he calls
the negative aspect of the dialectic. This depends on the fact
that, according to Hegel, the dialectic process is a movement
from error—that is, partial error—to truth. When we consider
the first member—the Thesis—of each triad, we find that an
attempt to assert its validity, unreservedly and as it stands,
involves contradictions and is untenable. Yet we cannot unreservedly abandon the Thesis, for we have reached it, according
to Hegel, by a line of argument which cannot be impugned.
Thus we are driven on to the Antithesis, which also betrays
similar contradictions, which render it untenable, and so on to
the third member of the triad, the Synthesis, by the acceptance
of which as valid the difficulties are removed, since it contains
the Thesis and Antithesis in a modified and transcended form,
which removes their contradictions. The Synthesis in its turn
reveals fresh contradictions, and so we are driven on from triad
to triad until we reach the Absolute Idea, the Synthesis of the
last triad, in which alone no such contradictions are to be
found[1].

It follows from this that, according to the general principles
of Hegel's system, we can be certain, with regard to any category
in the system except the Absolute Idea, that the assertion of its
validity, though not completely false, is not completely true.

Hegel does not always carry this out consistently in detail.
His view of the absolute truth leaves some of the lower categories absolutely valid. In these cases the passage to the next
category consists in demonstrating, not that the category is not
absolutely true, but that it would not be true to deny the
existence of further categories. And this is a very different
thing. Still, as a rule, his demonstrations are directed to proving
that the lower categories are actually false, though not completely false. And there is no question that the general account
which Hegel gives of his system requires this to be so in the case
of every category.

---

[1] This account is very general, but not, I think, inaccurate. For the justification of this, and of my other statements as to Hegel's system, I would refer
to my *Studies in the Hegelian Dialectic*, and to my *Commentary on Hegel's Logic*.

In this point we shall depart from what was Hegel's principle, and also his usual practice. Each characteristic demonstrated in the course of our process will remain there at the end of the process. None of them, of course, will be the whole truth, but that will not prevent all of them from being quite true. We shall be led on from one stage to the next, not by any contradiction involved in asserting the first characteristic to be true, but by the contradiction between asserting the first to be true and denying the second to be true.

**49**. In the third place, Hegel professes to prove the validity of each of his categories without any data except the validity of the previous category, or of the two previous categories. It is doubtful how far this claim is to be taken literally. If taken quite literally, it is clearly wrong, for in the arguments—often long and complicated—which lead from one category to the next, it is obvious that Hegel relies on various self-evident principles of logical inference, and the like, and that he must do so.

I do not think he would have denied this. Probably the real meaning of his claim is that he believed himself to have dispensed with any premises except the previous category or categories. In an ordinary syllogistic argument, the validity of the mode employed is essential to the validity of the particular argument, but it would not be reckoned as a third premise, in addition to the major and the minor. It is quite clear, I think, that Hegel is not asserting *less* than this—that his claim is, at least, that the previous category or categories are the only premises.

It may perhaps be doubted whether he is altogether correct in this statement, and whether he did not in fact rely, perhaps legitimately, on other premises. But it seems certain that he professes to rely on no other premises. With the arguments in the present work, on the other hand, it will be found that other premises, besides the previous stage, are often required[1], and

---

[1] I do not think that the appeal to perception on the question whether anything does exist constitutes an additional difference from Hegel (cp. my *Studies in the Hegelian Dialectic*, Sections 18 and 79). But the appeal to perception to prove differentiation is an additional difference.

this makes another difference from Hegel's principles, whatever may be the case as to his practice.

**50**. In the fourth place, as we have already said, while logical necessity will be found to determine to a great extent the positions of the particular stages in our system, it will be found that it does not exactly determine the positions of some of them. It will be possible in some cases to demonstrate the validity of various stages in two or more alternative orders, and the order actually adopted will be chosen only on grounds of convenience.

Here again there is a marked difference from Hegel, who unquestionably believed that the order of the categories, as exhibited in the dialectic, was one which was in every detail logically necessary, and was the only order in which any of the categories could be demonstrated, or the Absolute Idea reached. It may perhaps be questioned, whéther, admitting the validity of all his categories, and of his demonstrations of them, some of the categories could not change places, but it is certain that he does not admit the possibility.

A final difference is that Hegel does not seem to be very clear as to whether his dialectic applies only to existence, or to all reality (using those words in the sense which we have given them, and not in Hegel's own). Generally speaking, the dialectic seems to apply only to the existent, but there are points in the argument where he seems to be speaking also of non-existent reality, recurring again later to the consideration of existence alone—an oscillation which does not seem to be clearly realized by him, or to be logically justifiable.

If we take all these differences together, it must be pronounced, I think, that our method is not characteristically Hegelian. No method could reasonably be classed as Hegelian which did not accept triadic division, and the partial falsehood of the lower categories. On the other hand it will stand much closer to Hegel's method than to that of any other philosopher.

**51**. In a defence of Hegel's system, it is necessary to include a general and preliminary justification of his method. For that method has two features which, at any rate at first sight, appear to be unknown, or even opposed, to our ordinary way of thought. These are the partial falsity of the lower categories (with which is connected the implication in the validity of one category of the validity of its contrary), and the reconciliation and transcendence of the contrary terms in the synthesis. Neither of these is so strange, or so alien to ordinary thought, as it appears at first sight, and for each of them, I think, a good defence can be made[1]. But a defence is certainly required.

In the case of our method, the position is different. The manner in which we shall advance, in an order more or less rigidly determined, from one characteristic of the existent to another characteristic of the existent, will present no special features in which it differs from the manner of argument adopted elsewhere in philosophy, and in other subjects. Whether it is correct in detail is another question, but there can be no reason to suppose that correctness in detail could be rendered impossible by any general fallacy of method.

Is any justification needed of the fertility of our arguments? In the case of Hegel's system it has been held that such a justification was necessary. Much more, it is said, is got out of the system than was ever put into it. All that we start with is the category of Pure Being, which is selected for the starting-point just because it is as abstract as possible, and contains the least content. And from this we pass to category upon category, the content of each category increasing as we go on, till we reach the most perfectly concrete content of all in the Absolute Idea. This, it is said, cannot be legitimate. No valid argument can have more in the conclusion than in the premises. The increase of content in the later stages of the dialectic must be due to the illegitimate introduction of those empirical elements which, it was professed, were to have been excluded altogether. This objection has been dealt with by Mr Bradley in a passage which I regard as by far the most important and illuminating comment ever made upon Hegel[2].

---

[1] That is, I think that there is no antecedent impossibility in the chief characteristics of reality being connected in this manner, and that, if they were so related, the Hegelian dialectic—or a dialectic of the same type—would be true. But it does not seem to me that, as a matter of fact, they are related in this manner.

[2] *Logic*, Book III, Part I, Chap. II, E.

I do not think that any such justification is required for our method. The fact that empirical data are introduced, not only at the beginning, but also at one point later on in the process, will not by itself remove the difficulty, for, by the time we reach the end of the process, we shall have reached a great deal which was not in the first stage, and is not due exclusively to the single element (the differentiation of the existent) which was added empirically after the first stage. But the fertility of the *à priori* process will not excite wonder or doubt when it is remembered that various synthetic propositions are evident *à priori*. And, consequently, when we have established that whatever exists is *B*, we may be able to establish that whatever exists is *C*, because it is evident *à priori* that whatever is *B* is also *C*. This explanation is not admissible in the case of Hegel's dialectic, because of his repudiation of all premises in each transition except previous categories. For "whatever is *B* is *C*" is as much a premise of our conclusion "whatever exists is *C*," as is the result of the previous stage of the process, "whatever exists is *B*." But we have not committed ourselves to any such limitation of the premises, and consequently the fertility of the process has nothing in it different from what is found in other arguments, and requires no special justification.

**52**. Passing from the comparison of our method with that of Hegel, we come to another point. Our method, and the results reached by it, are ontological and not epistemological.

From the time of Kant onwards, much of modern philosophy has been exclusively—or almost exclusively—epistemological. It has started from the fact of knowledge, or rather from the fact of belief. It has enquired what sorts of beliefs can be true, and under what conditions. From this it has arrived at conclusions about what can be known, and about what beliefs, though not strictly true, form a coherent system bearing a certain uniform relation to the truth. So far the conclusions of such a system deal with nothing existent except beliefs, but, in so far as it is held that certain sorts of beliefs may be true, and certain sorts of beliefs cannot be true, it is possible to draw conclusions, chiefly negative, as to the nature of existent things other than beliefs. But all conclusions of this sort are based on conclusions relating to beliefs, and such systems are therefore properly called epistemological.

Our method will not be epistemological. We shall not start from the consideration of beliefs only. We shall, on the contrary, endeavour to determine those general characteristics which apply to existence as a whole, or to everything that exists, whether these things are beliefs or not.

And thus, while the result which we shall reach will prove to be one which would be usually, and properly, called Idealism, it will be the idealism of Berkeley, of Leibniz, and—as I believe —of Hegel. It will not be the idealism of Kant, or of the school which is sometimes called neo-Hegelian. It will not, that is, be that idealism which rests on the asserted dependence of the object of knowledge upon the knowing subject, or upon the fact of knowledge, but the idealism which rests on the assertion that nothing exists but spirit[1].

**53.** We have now to consider the method to be adopted in the last three Books, in which we shall enquire what consequences of theoretical or practical interest can be drawn from the general nature of the existent with respect to various forms of the existent which are empirically known to us. This enquiry will fall into three parts.

In the first, which will occupy Book V, we shall have to consider various characteristics as to which our experience gives us, at the least, a *primâ facie* suggestion that they are possessed, either by everything that exists, or by some existing thing. Starting from our conclusions as to the general nature of the existent, as determined by the previous enquiry, we shall have to ask, to begin with, which of these characteristics can really be possessed by what is existent, and which of them cannot be possessed by it, in spite of any appearance to the

---

[1] Spirit is here used to include, not only individual spirits, but the parts and groups of such spirits. And the characteristics of such spirits, and of their parts and groups, being characteristics of the existent, would themselves exist.

The distinction in the text is the one which Kant has in mind when he says that Berkeley's idealism is empirical, while his own is transcendental. The terms which he uses are not, I think, as appropriate as the more ordinary terms, ontological and epistemological, but it seems clear that, in this passage, they are meant to express the same distinction.

contrary. And then we must ask further, which, if any, of those characteristics which are possibly true of the existent, can be known to be actually true of it—perhaps of more of it than the *primâ facie* appearance suggests.

The second part of the enquiry will depend upon the first. As a result of the first part we shall reach the conclusion that some characteristics, both positive and negative, which appear to be possessed by existence, are not really possessed by it. In Book VI, therefore, we shall have to enquire how such appearances can arise. And we shall have to enquire further whether there are any uniform relations which we can discover between different variations of the appearance, and different variations of the reality. (If, for example, time turns out to be an appearance, we shall have to enquire whether the apparent occurrence of the relation of earlier and later has itself any uniform relation to the occurrence of any relation among timeless realities.) If this is so, the variations of the appearance in question will give us knowledge about the variations of the reality of which it is an appearance[1].

In the third place, there are various questions, which are or appear to be of practical interest to us, of which it may be possible to learn something by means of the knowledge which we have gained of the general nature of the existent. These will be the subject of the third part of our enquiry, which will be contained in Book VII. Of these questions some are usually stated in terms of various characteristics which we shall have found reason to suppose are only apparently, and not really, possessed by the existent. In these cases we shall have to enquire what the realities are which correspond to the appearances spoken of in the questions, and we must then consider how the questions must be restated in order to apply to the existent world, and what answers to the restated questions would be correct.

---

[1] The appearance might then be called, in the words of Leibniz, a *phaenomenon bene fundatum*. In such a case the statement that the reality is as it appears to be is often said to be phenomenally true. This phrase, however, is misleading. It tends to make us forget the fact that such a statement, though it has a certain uniform relation to truth, is itself false, since it asserts the reality to be what in fact it is not.

**54.** In these three Books the argument will not form a continuous chain, as it did in the earlier enquiry. And it will also differ from the argument in the earlier enquiry by being less rigid. In that earlier enquiry we shall aim at absolute demonstration. Our results will either be fallacious through some error in the argument, or they will be certain. We may have occasion, at various points, to speak of probabilities, but this will be only incidental. The assertion of these probabilities will not form steps in the main line of the argument, and they will not affect the claim that the stages in that line have been absolutely demonstrated.

In the later enquiry it will be different. In the first part of it, indeed, some questions may be settled with absolute demonstration, but only such as are of a negative nature. It may be possible to show with perfect certainty that, having regard to the general nature of the existent as previously determined, some of the characteristics which we are considering cannot be true of the existent. But no positive results can be reached with perfect certainty. The most that we could do would be to show that the general nature of the existent, as determined in the first three Books, was such that nothing which we know or can imagine could have that general nature without having the characteristic in question. But this does not give more than a probability. For it is possible that that general nature might be found also in something which had, not that characteristic, but some other, which we have never experienced, and cannot now imagine. If, for example, we should prove that the existent must be without simple parts, and should then show that nothing which we know or can imagine could be without simple parts except spirit, it will not give us an absolute demonstration that all that exists, or indeed that anything that exists, is spiritual. For there may be some characteristic, which we have never experienced or imagined, which is as compatible as spirituality with the absence of simple parts. And it may be this other characteristic which is found in part or all of the existent.

In the same way, when we pass to the second and third parts of the later enquiry, all that can be shown is that certain solutions are possible, and that we do not know, and cannot imagine, any alternatives. But here again, our inability to know or imagine another solution might be due only to the limitations of our experience. It is possible that some characteristic, which could only be known empirically, and which we have had no chance of knowing empirically, might be the key to an alternative possible solution, and that that solution might be the one which was actually true. In problems of this sort, therefore, our arguments may possibly attain a high degree of probability, but can never hope for certainty.

# BOOK II

## SUBSTANCE

# CHAPTER IV

## EXISTENCE

**55**. We are about to consider what can be determined as to the characteristics which belong to all that exists, or, again, to existence as a whole. But there is one more preliminary question to be settled. Does anything exist?

It would be possible no doubt, without discussing this, to consider what characteristics are implied in the characteristic of existence, and then to say conditionally, that, if anything does exist, it has these characteristics[1]. But the whole practical interest and importance of our enquiry depends on the answer to the question "does anything exist," and it is with the consideration of this question that we shall start.

All that concerns us now is whether anything exists. It does not matter how much exists, or what kind of thing it is. All that is wanted is to determine the truth of the statement "something is." And that statement, of course, is true if any other statement asserting existence is true.

**56**. But *is* any statement asserting existence true? Could it not be the case that all judgments, actual or possible, which assert existence are false? We may answer any person who should put this question by an argument not unlike Descartes'. If the sceptic should say "I deny that anything exists," or "I doubt whether anything exists," does not this assertion involve his own existence, and so prove that something does exist? If, like Hume, he should deny the reality of the self, then his statement will take the form that the existence of anything is

---

[1] In such an argument we could only determine those characteristics which were implied in the characteristic of existence, and so could not establish the differentiation of the existent by an appeal to perception. But, as was said in the last chapter (Section 45), such an appeal to perception, although the most convenient and convincing way of establishing the differentiation of the existent, is not the only way in which it can be established.

denied or doubted. And this will involve the existence, somehow and somewhere, of the denial and the doubt. If it should be said that the denial or the doubt is as illusory as the self, that involves the existence of the illusion. And if it should be said that the existence of this illusion is again an illusion, and so on, at the end of the chain there must come an illusion which is really an illusion, and which therefore really exists. And a similar argument is applicable in the case of a thinker who should simply contemplate the question whether anything does exist, without either affirming it, denying it, or doubting it.

**57.** I think that this is valid. Of course, like all other arguments, it finally rests on propositions taken as ultimately certain, which, if challenged, cannot be proved by further argument. If, for example, anyone should assert that his belief that nothing existed was only an illusion, and should then deny that this explanation involved that an illusion existed, I do not see how he could be refuted. But I am confident that he would be wrong. And I believe that this would be generally—and, indeed, I should suppose, universally—accepted.

It might be said that the proposition that something exists is itself very generally accepted, and that if there are persons sufficiently sceptical to doubt or deny it, it is useless to attempt to refute them by arguments which the sceptic, if he carries his scepticism sufficiently far, may also doubt or deny. The answer to this is that the utility is shown by experience. Experience shows that some people who begin by thinking it possible that nothing exists, cease to think it possible when it is pointed out to them that, since they are thinking of the possibility, their thought of the possibility exists.

The advantage of starting from the denial or doubt that anything exists, rather than from any other assertion, denial, or doubt, is, of course, only *ad hominem*. The proposition that something exists could be proved in just the same way from the affirmation, or the denial, that two and two made four, or that they made five, since each of these would involve that the affirmation or denial itself existed. But we were considering how to deal with a possible sceptic on the subject of existence, and we could not be certain that he would be making any assertion about the sum of two and two, while we are certain that he will either doubt or deny that something exists.

**58.** We may notice that the proposition "nothing exists," which we have rejected is not self-contradictory. "No proposition is true" is a self-contradictory proposition, for, if it were true, then it, together with all other propositions, would not be true. But the truth of "nothing exists" is not inconsistent with itself, though it is inconsistent with the assertion of itself, or even the contemplation of itself, by any person. Thus "something exists" is not a proposition of which we can be certain simply by pure logic, as we are of the proposition "something is true."

Again, the proposition "something exists" is not self-evident. It is based, as we have said, on the fact that it is involved in any proposition asserting that any particular thing exists. Now, as was said in the last chapter, the evidence that any particular thing exists, always consists in perception. We can have no reason for believing $X$ to exist, unless we either directly perceive $X$ itself, or else perceive $Y$, whose existence involves the existence of $X$. Thus our belief in the proposition "something exists" depends upon perception. If, for example, a man who is contemplating the question whether something exists is convinced that it does by the argument given above, it will be because he perceives by introspection an existent state of his mind—the contemplation of the question whether something exists.

But, although its denial is not self-contradictory, and its truth is not self-evident, the statement that something exists is about as certainly true as any statement can be. It is, of course, possible for a judgment based on a perception to be erroneous, because it is possible for the judgment to misdescribe what is perceived. But such an error could not invalidate this particular judgment. For, as we have seen, if any judgment that $X$ exists is erroneous through such a misdescription, then that misdescription must exist, and thus the judgment that something exists would still be true.

# CHAPTER V

## QUALITY

**59**. Something, then, exists. And now we can go further. For existence is not a term which has no reference beyond itself, so that it would be sufficient to say that the nature of that which exists is that it is existent. To say that something exists inevitably raises the question what this something is. And that question must be answered by asserting something of it other than its existence.

The force of this argument will be missed unless we remember that "something" must not be taken in its literal sense. "Something" is the most abstract and indeterminate term that we can get, but if taken literally it is not indeterminate enough, for it would mean, in that case, some *thing*. And, if we say of the existent that it is a thing, in the ordinary sense of the word, we are saying much more of it than simply that it exists. We must take "something" here as perfectly indefinite—the abstract subject of predication. The German *etwas* is less misleading, though even this, at any rate in Hegel's use of it, is too definite for our present purpose.

And it must also be remembered that it is not merely positive qualities which we should, in this case, refrain from predicating of the existent. Not only the possession of this or that quality, but the non-possession of these qualities, would give the existent a nature besides its existence. And the same is true of relations. Nor could the existent be a substance without possessing a nature—substantiality—beyond its existence. If we stop with existence, and refuse to go any further, the existent is a perfect and absolute blank, and to say that only this exists is equivalent to saying that nothing exists.

We should thus be involved in a contradiction, since, starting with the premise that something existed, we should arrive at the conclusion that nothing exists. We must therefore abandon the hypothesis which leads to this contradiction—the hypothesis that the existent has no nature beyond its existence.

We can arrive at the same conclusion in another way. If nothing is true of the existent except the fact that it exists, then it will not, for example, be true of it that it is square. But, then, by the Law of Excluded Middle, it will be true of it that it is not square. And so, after all, something will be true of it besides its existence.

**60.** We must, then, pass beyond our first stage. It remains true that something exists, but, of that something, something besides its existence must be true. Now that which is true of something is a Quality of that something. And therefore whatever is existent must have some quality besides existence, which is itself a quality.

Quality must, I think, be considered indefinable. We have just said that whatever is true of something must be a quality. This, however, cannot be taken as a definition of quality, since we are not sure that all qualities are true of anything. If nothing were red, red would still be a quality. But can we define quality as that which is true or false of anything? There is no quality of which this is not true, and it might be thought that this gave us a definition of quality, since, in Chapter II, we defined truth and falsity in a manner which did not introduce the conception of quality.

But this would be a mistake. What we defined was "true," a term applicable to beliefs and assumptions, but not to qualities. This is quite different from "true of," a term which is applicable to qualities, but not to beliefs or assumptions. There is the same difference between "false" and "false of." If we say to define "true of" and "false of," we can only say, I think, that $X$ is true of $A$ when a belief which asserts that $X$ belongs to $A$ is a true belief, and that $X$ is false of $A$ when a belief which asserts that $X$ belongs to $A$ is a false belief. Now to say that $X$ belongs to $A$ is equivalent to asserting that $X$ is a quality of $A$. And thus our definition of quality would contain a vicious circle.

If we are endeavouring to discover whether something is or

is not a quality, it is no doubt useful to put our question in the form "is it true or false of anything." But to do this is not to replace the term "quality" by its definition. It is only to enquire whether the subject of which we speak possesses a characteristic which qualities, and only qualities, do possess.

Since quality is indefinable, all that we can do is to point to examples of qualities. It is not so easy as it might seem to be sure what things are qualities. Something which at first sight looks like a quality may turn out to be really a relation, while something which might be supposed to be a relation may really be a quality dependent on a relation. But in some cases there is no doubt. Goodness, happiness, redness, sweetness are qualities.

**61.** Something does exist, then, and it has some other quality or qualities besides existence. But it is also certain that there are qualities which it does not possess.

This is certain because there are qualities which are incompatible with each other. Squareness and triangularity are incompatible, and so are red and blue[1]. This is sufficient to prove that whatever exists does not possess certain qualities. If it is square, it is not triangular; if it is triangular, it is not square. If it is neither, then there are at least two qualities which it does not possess.

This non-possession of a quality has also a positive side. We gain knowledge about anything as truly when we deny the quality $X$ of it as when we affirm the quality $Y$ of it. It is true that to know that $A$ is not a triangle tells us much less about it than we learn about $B$ when we know that it is a triangle, because the differences of nature compatible with not being a triangle are so much greater than those compatible with being a triangle. Still, to know that $A$ is not a triangle does tell us something about $A$. And, within a field already positively

---

[1] It might be said that the evidence for this is only empirical. But I think it is not. That what is red cannot be blue is a universal proposition which is not proved by induction, but is evident to anyone who knows what red and blue mean. And therefore it is not empirical. It is true that we should never have had the concepts of red and blue without sense-perception. But without sense-perception we should never have had the idea of a straight line, and this does not make geometry empirical.

limited, the negation of one quality may imply the affirmation of another. If anything is a human being, and is not male, it must be female.

The positive side of the non-possession of a quality can be conveniently expressed by converting the denial of a quality into the affirmation of its contradictory. Instead of denying that a triangle, or a spirit, has the quality of squareness, we can affirm that it has the quality of not-squareness. The difference between "this is-not square" and "this is not-square" may seem trivial. But for our purpose it has significance, since the second, unlike the first, emphasises the positive aspect of all denial.

**62**. Whatever exists, then, has a plurality of qualities. Indeed, everything that exists will have as many qualities as there are positive qualities. For it has, in each case, either the positive quality or its corresponding negative quality. We are, further, certain that among them will be more than one negative quality. For, of the three negative qualities, not-square, not-triangular, and not-circular, it is clear that everything must have at least two. It is also clear that whatever exists will have more than one positive quality. For existence is itself a positive quality, and since whatever exists possesses a plurality of qualities, positive or negative, it will be true of it that it is many-qualitied. And this is itself a second positive quality[1].

**63**. Qualities may be divided into those which admit of analysis, and can therefore be defined by a statement of that analysis, and those which are not capable of analysis, and are therefore indefinable. The latter may be called Simple Qualities. The former fall into two classes, according to the nature of the analysis, which I propose to call respectively Compound and Complex Qualities.

By Compound Qualities I mean such as can be analyzed into an aggregate of other qualities. Any two qualities taken together form a compound quality. Red and sweet is a compound quality, though it has no special name. And so is square and triangular, though we know that nothing can possibly have

---

[1] "Many-qualitied" is a quality and not a relation, though it implies, no doubt, a relation to each of the many qualities.

this particular compound quality. The most obvious examples of compound qualities are to be found in the species of natural history. If, for example, we should adopt the old definition of man as a rational animal, then humanity is a compound quality, consisting of animality and rationality. The qualities of which a compound quality is composed may be called its parts.

A Complex Quality is one which does not consist of an aggregate of other qualities, but which can be analyzed and defined by means of other characteristics, whether qualities or relations, or both. Thus, if we defined conceit as the possession of a higher opinion of oneself than is justified by the facts, conceit would be a complex quality, since it is capable of analysis, but not of analysis into an aggregate of qualities. Every negative quality is complex, for it can be analyzed into two terms, of which one is negation and the other is the corresponding positive quality, and it is not an aggregate of those terms. Since a complex quality is not an aggregate of the characteristics which enter into its analysis, it is better to call them elements, and not parts, of the complex quality.

**64.** The immediate parts or elements of a compound or complex quality need not be simple qualities, but may themselves be compound or complex. The relation of "analyzable into" is such that, if $X$ can be analyzed into $Y$ and $Z$, and $Z$ can be analyzed into $V$ and $W$, then $X$ can be analyzed into $V$, $W$ and $Z$[1]. Thus, whenever in any definition we find a compound or complex term, we can replace that term with its own definition, and this process can go on until the definition of the original term is expressed entirely in terms which are simple characteristics.

But are we certain that this end will be reached in the case of every compound or complex quality? Is it possible that there may be qualities such that every term in their analysis may again be analyzed, and that the terms thus reached may again be analyzed, and so on endlessly, so that no simple terms are ever reached—or at least, no analysis into terms all of which are simple.

[1] That is, the relation is transitive. Cp. Section 84.

This, however, is not possible. If we ask what any particular quality is—what we mean when we predicate it of anything—the answer, in the case of any quality which is not simple, is that this depends on what the terms are into which it can be analyzed. And, therefore, if in any case the analysis could go on endlessly, what the quality is, and what we mean when we predicate it, would depend on the final term of a series which had no final term. Thus it would be nothing in particular, and we should mean nothing by predicating it. This is impossible in a quality. The series of analyses, then, cannot be endless, but must end in an analysis consisting entirely of simple characteristics.

This does not mean that the analysis of a quality may not be infinitely differentiated. If, for example, there are an infinite number of simple qualities, then there would be a compound quality consisting of all these, and such a quality would be infinitely differentiated[1]. And a complex quality might also have an infinitely differentiated analysis. Such qualities could not be known by a human mind, but they might nevertheless be real. What is impossible is that there should be an analysis which never ends in simple characteristics.

Since any two or more qualities form a compound quality, all the qualities possessed by any particular thing form a compound quality. And this compound quality may be called the Nature of that thing.

---

[1] A compound quality which consisted of all simple qualities could never be existent as a quality, since nothing can have all simple qualities (*e.g.* both red and blue). But it would be existent as an element in the corresponding negative quality, which would be a quality of all existent things.

# CHAPTER VI

## SUBSTANCE

**65**. Whatever exists, then, has qualities. These qualities will themselves be existent, and will have qualities, and so on without end. But, at the head of the series, there will be something existent which has qualities without being itself a quality. The ordinary name for this, and I think the best name, is Substance.

**66**. This conclusion has sometimes been challenged. It has been maintained that, in cases in which the qualities are commonly said to be predicable of substances, we shall, if we take the right view, be able to dispense with the conception of substance, and use only the conception of qualities. The group of qualities which are, in the ordinary view, held to be predicated of a substance, may, it is maintained, exist without such a predication.

But is it denied that any quality is predicable of anything, or is it admitted that all qualities are predicable of something, and only denied that any of them are predicable of substances? If the first alternative is taken we reach an absurdity, since in that case we could not say of the group that it was a group, or that it was existent, nor of the qualities that compose it that they were qualities, or that they were existent. The theory, therefore, is incompatible with its own truth.

But if we take the other alternative, of what can we say that those qualities are really predicated which, *primâ facie*, are predicated of a substance? It would, I think, be generally admitted that we cannot answer this question by saying that each such quality is predicated of itself. It would not be asserted, for example, that, when I say that Smith is happy, what I really mean is that the quality of happiness is happy.

But can each of the qualities be predicable of the group of qualities, of which it is one of the members, which would, in the ordinary view, be called the nature of the substance? If this were the case, then, whenever, in ordinary language, we predicate a quality of a substance, we could substitute the nature of that substance as the subject of our predication. And this is not possible. We predicate of Smith, for example, that he is happy. Let us take wisdom, goodness, consciousness, and happiness as constituting his whole nature. Now when we say that Smith is happy, we certainly cannot substitute for Smith any or all of those qualities. We do not mean that wisdom, or that goodness, or that consciousness is happy. Each of these three propositions has a definite meaning, and none of these meanings are what we mean by the assertion that Smith is happy. In the same way, we cannot mean that the aggregate of wisdom and goodness and consciousness is happy, or that any system formed by them, whatever the nature of the relations which unite the system, is happy.

What has been said above becomes more evident when we consider that in some cases, such as the one which we have taken as an example, while the proposition about the substance may be true, the propositions about the qualities must be false. It may be true that Smith is happy. But it cannot be true that happiness, or wisdom, or goodness, or consciousness, or any aggregate or system formed by them can be happy, because nothing but conscious beings can be happy, and no quality, and no aggregate or system of qualities, can be a conscious being.

Thus the attempt to substitute the qualities for the substance must be given up. It is true that the actual nature of the existent is always enormously more complicated than the example we have taken, which was limited to four qualities. But the increase in the complication would do nothing to remove the difficulty.

It is true, also, that the nature of anything is a unity as well as a plurality. But we cannot take this unity as that of which the different qualities can be predicated. However close may be the unity which is compounded of goodness, wisdom, and consciousness, it will remain true that it cannot be happy, and that, even if it could be happy, we should not assert its happiness when we asserted the happiness of Smith, although Smith might be good, wise, and conscious.

**67.** That of which the qualities of the existent are predicated, then, cannot be themselves, or one another, or the unity of them. But must it in any case be a substance? Could it not be in every case, as it admittedly is in some cases, another quality?

This, however, is impossible. For no quality is existent in its own right. The only case in which an assertion about a quality can be an assertion of existence is that in which the assertion links the quality with something else that exists—as when we say that courage was a quality of Nelson. And if there was nothing to link it with except other qualities, there would arise a vicious infinite series. For the first term, with which we begin our series, must be connected with something else that exists. If this something else must also be a quality, it can only get its existence by connection with a third existent thing, which, being also a quality, can only get it by connection with a fourth, and so on. And thus the connection of the first term with the existent would depend on the last term of a series which had no last term. It is therefore impossible to hold that nothing exists but qualities. There must be something which exists and has qualities without being itself a quality.

A similar argument will show that that which is existent and has qualities without being a quality cannot be in every case a relation. For a relation, like a quality, cannot be existent in its own right, and a vicious infinite series would arise in the same way as with qualities.

Something must exist, then, and have qualities, without being itself either a quality or a relation. And this is Substance. We shall see in the next chapter that all substances have relations, and shall thus arrive at the result that something exists which has qualities and is related without being itself either a quality or a relation. This is the traditional definition of substance, and it is the one which I propose to adopt[1].

---

[1] Strictly speaking, it would be sufficient to define a substance as that which exists and has one or more qualities without being itself a quality or a

It is to be noticed that, although a substance is not a quality, yet a substance will possess the quality of substantiality. For we can, of course, assert of a substance the fact that it is a substance, and this is to predicate of it the quality of substantiality. The existence of this quality, however, does not render it possible to reduce the existent entirely to qualities. For this particular quality would not be true of any existent, unless that existent was not itself a quality.

**68**. To the conclusion that substance exists it has been objected that a substance is nothing apart from its qualities, and that therefore a conception of substance, as distinct from its qualities, is impossible, and the name itself is a meaningless word. But this is erroneous. It is, of course, quite true that a substance is nothing apart from its qualities. And if we were to try to form a conception of a substance which had no qualities, the undertaking would be as hopeless as an attempt to form a conception of a triangle without sides. But it does not follow that, because a substance is nothing apart from its qualities, it is not anything in conjunction with its qualities. And it does not follow that, because we cannot form a conception of a substance which has no qualities, we cannot form a conception of a substance with qualities.

If the argument were valid at all, it would be just as fatal to the qualities of the existent as to its substance. For a quality can only exist as the quality of something else which exists. And we have seen that it is untenable to suppose that this something else is not, in some cases, a substance. The qualities of the existent are therefore just as impossible without the substance, as is the substance without the qualities. And so, if substance is to be rejected on the ground of this argument, we should have also to reject existent qualities—a consequence not foreseen by the supporters of the argument, who wish to reject substances, but to keep existent qualities.

The fallacy which we have just discussed is of a type which

relation. But every substance has more than one quality, and stands in more than one relation. (Indeed, as we shall see later, every substance has an infinite number of qualities, and stands in an infinite number of relations.) No inconvenience will follow therefore from keeping to the usual form of the definition, as given in the text.

is not uncommon, and which is generally worked out with the same inconsistency as here. *A* and *B* can only exist in relation. Then of one of them, say *A*, it is asserted that, since *A* without *B* is nothing, *A* is nothing at all. And *B*, being left by itself, is now asserted to be the sole reality in the matter, and to be self-subsistent. But it does not follow that *A* is nothing at all, because it would be nothing out of relation to *B*. And, if the argument were fatal to *A* it would be just as fatal to *B*.

**69**. An objection of a rather similar sort has been put forward by Dr Stout. "What then," he says, "is the subject itself as distinguished from the attributes? It would seem that its whole being must consist in being that to which its attributes belong. But how can the whole being of anything consist in its being related to something else. There must be an answer to the question,—What is it that is so related[1]?"

It may be admitted that the whole being of a subject cannot consist in its relations to its attributes—or, in our terminology, that the whole being of a substance cannot consist in its relations to its qualities. But, not to mention other elements which enter into the being of a substance, and confining ourselves to its qualities only, we must note that when we have said that a substance is related to its qualities, we have not mentioned the most important point. The substance is, no doubt, related to its qualities. If Smith is happy, then there is a certain relation between the substance Smith and the quality of happiness. But this is not all. He is not only related to the quality of happiness. He is happy. And it is the latter which is fundamental. The fact that he is happy is the primary fact, and the fact that he is related to the quality of happiness is only derivative. For if the fact of his happiness could be reduced to his relation to the quality of happiness, then, on the same principle, his relation to the quality of happiness ought to be reduced to the two relations between that relation and its two terms— Smith and happiness. And so we should have started on such an infinite series as has caused Mr Bradley to deny the reality of all relations[2].

---

[1] *Proceedings of the Aristotelian Society*, 1914–15, p. 350.
[2] Cp. Section 88.

Thus we may reply to Dr Stout's question as to what it is which is related by giving the qualities of the substance. Smith, who is related, is happy, he is also a man, and so on.

**70**. From another point of view the criticism has been made that we ought to substitute the conception of subject for that of substance. In this criticism the word subject is not used in its logical meaning of that which has predicates (as was the case in the passage from Dr Stout which we have just considered) but in its epistemological meaning of a conscious self which has knowledge. Now it may be the case—I shall try to show in Book V that it is the case—that nothing exists but spirits and parts and groups of spirits, together with their qualities and relations. But this would not justify us in discarding the conception of substance. Of such spirits, and parts and groups of spirits, many things would be true, besides the fact that they were substances, but still they would be substances, since they would have qualities and be related, without being themselves either qualities or relations.

This objection is usually made by thinkers who rank themselves as followers of Hegel. And it is true that Hegel's philosophy affords some excuse for it. The conception of a knowing subject involves one of the highest categories of his dialectic, while the category of substance comes much lower. It would follow, according to Hegel's principle of the partial falsity of the lower categories—a principle which we have not accepted—that it is always in some degree erroneous to call anything by the name of substance.

But the modern critics of substance of whom I have spoken seem to go a good deal further than could be justified by Hegel's principle. For, by that principle, every lower category is partially true of reality, and is absolutely true of it except in so far as the subsequent course of the dialectic has shown and transcended some error. Thus the category of substance would be true of reality except in those points in which it had definitely been shown to be false. These critics, however, apparently hold that, if any being has been proved to be a subject, we are entitled to sweep away at once all consequences inferred from its being a substance, in the same way that, if any figure were proved to be a square, we should be entitled to sweep away all consequences based on a previous erroneous belief that it was a triangle. And this would certainly not be justified by Hegel's principle.

**71.** Would it not have been possible, it might be asked, to have reached the conception of substance earlier? Could we not have proceeded to it direct from the conception of existence? For, after all, existence is itself a quality, though we did not use the latter name until we had deduced the possession by the existent of other qualities besides existence. And from this alone we might have deduced substance. For there cannot be simply existing existence. It cannot exist in itself any more than any other quality. If there is existence, there must be something, other than the quality of existence, which exists. And does not this take us on at once to the category of substance?

These questions must, I think, be answered in the affirmative, but this does not condemn the course we have taken. For our method, as has been pointed out in Chapter III, may sometimes have alternative paths open to it. If from $A$ we are entitled to proceed to a result including both $B$ and $C$, there is nothing surprising in the possibility of proceeding, in some cases, either from $A$ to $B$, and so to $C$, or else from $A$ to $C$, and so to $B$.

I believe that it would have been possible to have introduced substance earlier, and to have postponed quality till after we had reached substance. But the course which I have followed seems to me to be equally valid, and much more convenient. For this there are two reasons. In the first place, it is much easier, though not less illogical, to confound a substance with the only quality which is ascribed to it than to confound it with a plurality of qualities, all of which are ascribed to it. For it is obvious that, if qualities were only predicated of themselves, nothing could be both red and not-blue, since red and not-blue are not the same quality. Thus, in proportion as we realize that many qualities must be predicated of the same subject, it becomes clearer that the subject cannot be the quality predicated. And we see that, as a matter of history, it has often been the realization of the unity over against the plurality which has directed men's attention to the existence of substance.

And, in the second place, to show the necessity of substance we had to show that we cannot substitute, for the substance of which any quality is predicated, the other qualities which belong to that substance, or the aggregate of its qualities, or any system formed of them. And this point does not naturally arise until it has been demonstrated that there is such a plurality of qualities.

72. The conception of substance will be of cardinal importance throughout the rest of our enquiries, and it will be essential to keep closely in view the definition which we have adopted. Otherwise confusion may arise, for by that definition many things are classed as substances which would not usually be called so. The name of substance is often confined to that which, among other characteristics, is either timeless or persistent through time, or is more fundamentally one than many, or is held to be a unity of special importance. A sneeze would not usually be called a substance, nor would a party at whist, nor all red-haired archdeacons, be considered as a single substance. But each of the three complies with our definition, since each of them has qualities and is related, without being a quality or a relation; and each of them would therefore be called a single substance, although each of the two latter are obviously also an aggregate of several substances, and, as we shall see later, the first (and indeed every other substance) is also such an aggregate.

It might be said that our use of the term with so wide an extension is inconvenient and undesirable, since it differs so much from the common usage. But I think, as I said above, that our definition of substance is the one which would be most generally accepted, and that the difference of usage comes from inconsistency only.

# CHAPTER VII

## DIFFERENTIATION

**73.** Substance, then, exists. But the further question arises—do many substances exist, or only one? To this question we must now apply ourselves. It may be put more shortly—is substance differentiated? I propose to use the word differentiation to indicate plurality of substance only, and not to apply it to plurality of aspects or qualities. For example, since a person is a substance, I should say that a college was differentiated, because it is made up of persons. But I should not say that a person was differentiated because we can distinguish in his nature the two aspects of substance and qualities, nor because he possesses a plurality of qualities. If, on the other hand, a person turned out to consist of several substances, he would be said to be differentiated.

The question whether substance is differentiated must be distinguished from the question whether *every* substance is differentiated. If there were no simple substances, then every substance would be differentiated, and, *à fortiori*, substance would be differentiated. But supposing that there were a number—finite or infinite—of simple substances, then substance would be differentiated, since there would be more substances than one, but every substance would not be differentiated, since there would be simple substances.

It would, I suppose, be generally held that substance, in the sense in which we have defined the word, is differentiated. Indeed, the only people who uniformly deny it would be the Eleatics, and a few Oriental pantheists[1]. But can the view, so generally admitted, be proved?

In order to prove this it will be best, as I said in Section 45,

---

[1] It is not uniformly denied by Spinoza. For his Modes are, by our definition, substances. And it cannot be said that he *uniformly* denies all reality to the modes.

to make one more appeal to perception. Such an appeal, as was pointed out in that Section, is not strictly necessary. For I shall argue later that it is certain *à priori* that no substance can be simple, and this, as we have just seen, would prove that substance was differentiated. But the view that no substance can be simple, though I believe it to be correct, is novel and controversial, and a proof of the differentiation of substances by an appeal to perception, if not so symmetrical, seems more likely to command general assent.

**74.** It is evident that, if the existent is at all like what we normally judge it to be, substance must be differentiated. In the first place, unless it is the case either that solipsism is true, or that I myself have no reality, it must be the case that both I and something else exist, and this would prove that substance was differentiated. Nor would this result be altered if we held with Hume, or with Mr Bradley, that the self was not real, provided we held, as each of those writers do, that there is a separate reality which is mistakenly supposed to be a self.

Solipsism, however, has been defended. There is, I think, good reason for rejecting it. But those reasons do not become evident until we have gone considerably further in our enquiries than the point we have yet reached, and it would therefore not be safe to rely here on the differentiation of substance into myself and something else.

**75.** Even, however, if solipsism were granted, the normal position—if we can speak of a normal solipsism—would still hold substance to be differentiated. For, if time is real, then my states at each successive moment of time will be substances, since they will have qualities and be related without being qualities or relations. And so my existence at more than one moment of time would prove substance to be differentiated[1]. Or if time should be held to be unreal, even then the states, which we erroneously believe to be in time, would still be separate states, and so would prove differentiation.

[1] Even if such separate states should only occur when they were separated by a change in the nature of the self, substance would still be proved to be differentiated. For I certainly do change sometimes, and a single change in myself would be sufficient to prove that substance was differentiated.

But it is well to go further in our search for clear evidence of differentiation. For the reality of time has been denied, and I shall try to show in Book V that it ought to be rejected. And although, as has just been said, the rejection of time would still leave as separate substances those states which appear to be in time, it would be better if we could find some instance which would prove differentiation by a simpler process.

We can find such an instance in the differentiation of our field of perception which is manifest, if not at all moments, yet at most. When I experience the sensations of redness and of shrillness simultaneously, I am directly aware of the existence of two separate perception-data. And my perception-data are substances. They may be ephemeral in time, they may be peculiar to me, and unshared by anyone else, they may be parts of me. But they have qualities and are related, and are neither qualities nor relations. So they are substances, and if there are more than one of them, substance is differentiated.

This would be sufficient. But it is interesting to notice that we can go further, and that the perception of a single datum proves the differentiation of substance. For, besides the perception-datum, there is also the perception. If, as I believe to be the case, the perception is a mental state, then that and the datum are two substances. If, on the other hand, as is sometimes maintained, the perception is a relation of which the datum is one term, then the other term must also be something existent—presumably the self—and, once more, two substances must exist.

**76.** Can we go still further and say that not only all perception, but all thought, involves the differentiation of substance? If we could do so, we should, among other things, be able to say that the assertion of the proposition that substance was not differentiated would be sufficient to prove that the proposition was false. Whether all thought involves a differentiation of substance is a question whose answer depends on our theory of thought. I cannot make a judgment or an assumption without being aware of at least two things. If, for example, I affirm or consider the proposition that substance is undifferentiated, I must be aware of what is meant by substance and by undifferentiated. If such awarenesses are parts of me—and I think that they are so—then there is a differentiation of substance, since parts of a self are substances. But if, as has been held, a judgment or an assumption can be a relation of the self to various non-existent terms, then a judgment or an assumption need not imply the existence of any substance other than the self.

But even if a thought as such does not involve the differentiation of substance, my knowledge that I have a thought does involve it. For that knowledge is based on a perception, of which the thought which I know that I have is the datum, and, like other perceptions, it involves that substance is differentiated.

Without bringing thought into the question, however, the differentiation of substance is certain. It is self-evident to every man that he has perceptions. And even if nothing existed outside himself, and even if he had only one perception, this would, as we have seen, be sufficient to prove that substance was differentiated.

**77.** Substance, then, is differentiated. The proof of this on which we have relied is, as we have seen, empirical. We have based our belief that substance is differentiated on our knowledge of the existence of some particular differentiation—a single one would be sufficient to prove our point—and this can only be known empirically. But since, as we have seen, the existence of a single perception is sufficient to prove differentiation, the position of any person who should doubt or deny differentiation would involve that he should doubt or deny all perception. And such a position would be almost equivalent to complete scepticism. It would not be easy for anyone to doubt or deny perception without admitting that he knew that he doubted or denied it. And his knowledge of his doubt or denial could only be obtained from perception.

Since substance is differentiated there is a plurality of substances. But nothing in the arguments by which we have reached this conclusion prevents us from holding that all that exists is also a single substance. Indeed, it is clear that it must be a single substance. For if we take all that exists, it is clear that it has qualities, and it is not itself a quality or relation. Indeed, it is a result of the definition of substance which we have adopted—a result not always realized by those who adopt it—that all parts of substances and all collections of substances are themselves substances. It seems desirable to mention this point here, to avoid misapprehension, but its introduction into the chain of our argument must be postponed until we have developed further what is involved in the nature of a single substance.

# CHAPTER VIII

## RELATIONS

**78**. We have now a plurality of substances, and it is therefore evident that there will be Relations among substances. What relations there will be is a question to which much of the rest of this work will be devoted, but that there are some relations is beyond doubt. All substances will be similar to one another, for they are all substances. And all substances will be diverse from one another, since they are separate substances. (By diversity I mean what is sometimes called numerical difference, and not dissimilarity, the relation of which to diversity will be considered in Chapter x.) And substances which are similar to each other, or diverse from one another, stand to each other in the relations of similarity and diversity.

Relation, like quality, is indefinable. We can only show what we mean by it by giving examples. When we say that $A$ is greater than $B$, is equal to $B$, is the father of $B$, is to the right of $B$, loves $B$, is ignorant of $B$, we are asserting a relation in which $A$ stands to $B$. We cannot define a relation as that in which something stands to something, or which holds between something and something, for in order to give these phrases the meaning which would make them true of relations, we should have to define them as the sort of standing or holding which occurs when things are related. And thus our definition of relation would be circular.

**79**. Relations can have more than two terms, as when $A$, $B$, and $C$ are all equal. And, again, it is possible for a relation to have only one term, at any rate in the ordinary sense of the word. For a subject can have a relation to itself. Every substance has the relation of identity with itself. And some substances are equal to themselves, despise themselves, are their own trustees or their own cousins.

Thus we cannot say that every relation has more than one

term. Yet that which stands in a relation, even if the relation has only one term, has a certain aspect of plurality. For a relation always connects something with something. Even when it only connects something with itself, the term so connected with itself is—to use a metaphor which is not, I think, misleading—at both ends of the relation, and this does involve a certain aspect of plurality, though not, of course, a plurality of substances. This may be more obvious if we notice that it is impossible to express any relation without either having two terms, or using one term twice. It may be the case that $A$ loves nobody but himself, but this must be expressed by saying either "$A$ loves $A$," or "$A$ loves himself." It cannot be expressed by saying simply "$A$ loves," which only means that $A$ loves someone, without specifying whom.

It might tend to simplicity in considering relations to self if we used the word term differently, so that we should say, for example, that in self-love there were two terms, although both terms were the same substance. But it seems more convenient on the whole to take one thing as being always only one term; and to speak of relations to self as relations with only one term.

**80.** The difference between relations and qualities is sufficiently clear, though, since both terms are indefinable, it is impossible to define the difference between them. We may say that the qualities are qualities *of* something, while relations are not relations *of* anything, but between something and something. This, however, though it may help us to realize the difference, will not give us a definition, since "of" and "between," as used here, could only be understood with the help of the conceptions of quality and relation.

If what we have said is correct, it follows that relation is a conception which is indispensable in describing existence. For the existent has relations, and, since the conception of relation is indefinable, it will be impossible to substitute for it any other conceptions which can be taken as its equivalent.

Strenuous efforts have been made by various philosophers to dispense with the conception of relation in their theories of existence. The most usual form which these efforts have assumed is an attempt to substitute, in all cases, assertions of qualities for assertions of relations. The theories which have been put forward for this purpose have not confined themselves to saying that relation, though valid of existence, was not ultimate, but definable in terms of quality, so that statements about relations could be translated into statements about qualities. They have held that the conception of relation is positively invalid—one which is never rightly applicable anywhere. At the same time they do not go so far as to say that all statements which assert relations are absolutely and simply false—that the statement, for example, that London is larger than Cambridge is no more true than the statement that Cambridge is larger than London. But they say that such statements are confused and inaccurate versions of statements about qualities, and that such a confused and inaccurate version of true statements about qualities is nearer the truth than a similarly confused and inaccurate version of false statements about qualities. The statements about qualities are sometimes taken to be about a quality in each of the substances of which the relation was asserted—in this case Cambridge and London. Sometimes they are taken to be about a quality of some whole which includes both substances.

The chief reason which has been given for the rejection of relations is that there is nowhere for them to be. They are not, it is clear, in either of the terms without being in the other. Nor are they in each of them, taken separately. They are, it is said, *between* the terms, and not *in* them. Then, it is asked, is there anything *in* which they can be? And, when this is answered in the negative, it is concluded that they are impossible[1].

**81.** But this is invalid, because it assumes that a relation is impossible, unless some one thing can be found, in which it is or inheres like a quality. It takes, as the test of the possibility of relations, the question whether they can behave exactly as qualities behave, and when it is admitted that they cannot, it

---

[1] This is the line of Lotze's argument, and substantially of Leibniz's also. Mr Bradley's objections are different, and lead to a different conclusion. He does not, like Leibniz and Lotze, endeavour to reduce relations to qualities, but rejects qualities and relations alike. (Cp. Section 88.)

concludes that relations are impossible, and that, in a true view
of reality, judgments of relation would be replaced by judgments of quality.

There is, however, no justification for the assumption that
a relation is impossible, if it cannot inhere in something as a
quality does. To the question "in what is a relation?" we may
fairly answer that it is not in anything, but that it is between
two or more terms, or between a term and itself, and that the
conception of "between" is as ultimate as the conception of
"in," and has as much claim to be regarded as valid. Both are
ultimate, neither contains any contradiction, and the justification of our use of both lies in the fact that it is impossible to
state anything whatever without asserting or implying the
reality both of qualities and of relations. That this is impossible,
both as regards qualities and as regards relations, we have
already seen. In the case which immediately concerns us, the
relations of substances to substances, since substance does
exist, it must be identical with itself, and, as has already been
pointed out, since more than one substance exists, they must
be similar to one another, and diverse from one another.

And it must be noted that the propositions asserting those
relations will be absolutely true. It is not merely that we get
nearer to the truth by asserting them than by denying them.
There cannot be any substance unless it is absolutely true that
it is identical with itself, and there cannot be more than one
substance unless it is absolutely true that they are similar and
diverse.

**82.** The conception of relation, then, must be accepted as
valid of the existent. But it might be admitted to be valid, and
yet denied to be ultimate and indefinable. It might be said
that it really was true that substances were in relations, but
that the fact expressed in this way could be expressed in terms
of qualities only, without bringing in relations. But this also is
false. No fact which can be stated in terms of relations between
substances can ever be stated in terms which omit the conception of relation. (I use the phrase "between substances" to
include "between a substance and itself.")

There are three facts which have, I think, led to some doubt on this point. In the first place, a relation may no doubt be *based* on a quality in each of its terms. But this does not mean that it can be *reduced* to those qualities. If $A$ is larger than $B$, this relation may depend on the fact that $A$ covers a square mile, and $B$ covers an acre. If $A$ irritates $B$, this relation may depend on the political opinions of $A$ and the sensitiveness of $B$. But a statement of the size of $A$ and a statement of the size of $B$ are not equivalent to a statement that $A$ is larger than $B$, though the latter may be a certain and immediate conclusion from them. And a statement of $A$'s opinions and of $B$'s sensitiveness are not equivalent to a statement that $A$ irritates $B$, though this may follow from them by the laws of human nature.

In the second place, it is true, as we shall see in the next chapter, that the existence of any relation between two substances involves the existence of a quality in each of those substances. "$A$ admires $B$" is a statement of a relation between $A$ and $B$. But its truth implies the truth of the statements "$A$ is an admirer of $B$," and "$B$ is an object of admiration to $A$," which state qualities of $A$ and $B$. But we cannot state these qualities in terms which omit the conception of relation, since the first is the quality of being a person who admires $B$, and the second is the quality of being a person who is admired by $A$, and therefore neither of them can be stated without introducing the conception of admiration, which is a relation.

In the third place, a relation determines a quality of any whole which contains all the terms of the relation. We may say that it is a quality of this room, or of the universe, to contain a chair $A$ and a chair $B$, of which $A$ is larger than $B$. But then this quality cannot be stated except by using the conception "larger than," and therefore it cannot be stated without stating a relation.

**83**. Relations, then, cannot be replaced by qualities. Can qualities be replaced by relations? So far as I know, this view has never been taken. If it were to be taken, it would be necessary, as Mr Russell points out[1], to take the view that "exact likeness" is a simple relation, not analyzable into com-

---

[1] *Proceedings of the Aristotelian Society*, 1911–12, p. 9.

munity of qualities, and that there should be exact likenesses of various kinds. Then, instead of saying that *A* and *B* had both the quality of whiteness, we should say that *A* and *B* were two of the terms which stood to one another in an exact likeness of one particular kind.

There is, however, no reason that we should depart from the *primâ facie* view that there are qualities, since no reason has ever been given for doubting it. And the view that exact likeness is a simple relation, and independent of any community of qualities seems clearly false. We must therefore abide by the conclusion—which, as I said, I do not think has ever been challenged—that qualities cannot be replaced by relations.

**84**. Relations, like qualities, are either simple, compound, or complex. A Simple Relation is one which is not capable of analysis, and is therefore indefinable. A Compound Relation is one which can be analyzed into an aggregate of simple relations. A Complex Relation is one which does not consist of an aggregate of other relations, but which can be analyzed and defined by means of other characteristics, whether qualities or relations, or both.

All relations also fall into other classes, which have nothing correspondent to them among qualities. In the first place, every relation is such that what stands in it can only stand in it to itself, or cannot stand in it to itself, or can stand in it either to itself or to something else. For example, a substance can only be identical with itself, it cannot be its own father, and it can admire either itself or something else. Every relation then is either Reflexive, Unreflexive, or simply Not Reflexive.

In the second place, every relation is such that, if *A* stands in it to *B*, *B* must stand in it to *A*, or cannot stand in it to *A*, or may or may not stand in it to *A*. Thus if *A* is equal to *B*, *B* is equal to *A*. If *A* is *B*'s father, *B* cannot be *A*'s father. If *A* loves *B*, *B* may or may not love *A*. Thus we have the classes of Symmetrical, Asymmetrical, and simply Not Symmetrical relations.

In the third place, every relation is such that, if *A* stands in it to *B*, and *B* to *C*, then either *A* must stand in it to *C*, or cannot stand in it to *C*, or may or may not stand in it to *C*. If

$A$ is the ancestor of $B$, and $B$ of $C$, then $A$ is the ancestor of $C$. But if $A$ is the father of $B$, and $B$ of $C$, then $A$ cannot be the father of $C$. And if $A$ is the first cousin of $B$, and $B$ of $C$, then $A$ may or may not be the first cousin of $C$. Thus we have the classes of Transitive, Intransitive, and simply Not Transitive relations.

What do we know, so far, as to the occurrence of examples of each of these classes among the relations of substances? We know that the relations of identity, diversity, and similarity hold of substances. And, in addition to these, every substance has a relation to each quality which inheres to it, and to each relation of which it is a term.

It is clear that all three classes of the first group are represented. For identity is reflexive, diversity is unreflexive, and similarity is simply not reflexive, if we hold, as I think we must, that a thing can be said to be similar to itself.

In the next group, both diversity and similarity are symmetrical. The relation of a subject to its quality is asymmetrical, since a substance cannot inhere in a quality. We have as yet no reason to hold that simply not symmetrical relations occur, but we shall see later that the relation of determination does occur, and is of this class.

In the third group, similarity is simply not transitive. For, if $A$ is only similar to $B$ in respect of the characteristic $X$, and $B$ to $C$ in respect of the characteristic $Y$, the similarity of $A$ to $B$ and of $B$ to $C$ neither involves nor excludes the similarity of $A$ to $C$[1]. But specific similarity is transitive. If $A$ is similar to $B$ in respect of $X$, and $B$ is similar to $C$ in respect of $X$, then $A$ is similar to $C$ in respect of $X$. We have not yet reached a case of intransitive relation, but one will occur in the next chapter, when we shall get a series of derivative characteristics, in which $X$ will be the next term above $Y$, and $Y$ the next term above $Z$, while $X$, of course, cannot be the next term above $Z$.

---

[1] In point of fact, $A$ and $C$, whatever they are, will be similar, since they will both be real, existent, and substances. But this does not follow from the similarity of $A$ to $B$, and of $B$ to $C$.

# CHAPTER IX

## DERIVATIVE CHARACTERISTICS

**85.** We saw in the last chapter that the fact which is most simply expressed by "$A$ admires $B$" can also be expressed by "$A$ is an admirer of $B$," or "$A$ has the quality of admiring $B$." This, as we saw, did not enable us to dispense with the conception of relation, but it is nevertheless an important fact. With it we pass to the conception of Derivative Characteristics.

So far, however, we have only found one class of derivative characteristics, namely derivative qualities. The occurrence of any relation involves the occurrence of a quality in each of its terms—the quality of being a term of that relation.

A relation in which a substance stands may generate in this manner not only one quality but many qualities. If $A$ admires $B$, $C$, and $D$, this places $A$ in only one relation—the relation of admiration. But there will be three derivative qualities generated in $A$. He will possess the qualities "admirer of $B$," "admirer of $C$," and "admirer of $D$." It may be convenient to say that, while admiration and equality are relations, the admiration of $A$ for $B$, and the equality of $A$ and $B$, are Relationships. We can then say that each relationship generates a quality of each substance which is a term of that relationship. $A$ has the quality "admirer of $B$," and $B$ has the quality "object of $A$'s admiration."

Such qualities, though involved by the relations, can be clearly distinguished from them. For the quality, unlike the relation, is predicated, and predicated of a single substance, even when, as in the case we have taken, the relation is not reflexive. The relation is between $A$ and $B$, but the quality is predicated of $A$ alone. The difference is less obvious if we take such a relation as "greater than," because the ordinary form in which that relation is expressed is "$A$ is greater than $B$," which is not grammatically different from the form in which we should express the quality of $A$ which is generated by the relation. But the difference between the quality and the relation comes out clearly when we take such a relation as "$A$ admires $B$," where the natural statement of the derivative quality would be "$A$ is the admirer of $B$."

Derivative qualities, like all others, are included in the nature of the substance, as that has been defined by us. And therefore, although the nature of a substance consists exclusively of qualities, it will involve all the relations and relationships in which the subject stands. Complete knowledge of the nature of any substance, if it were possible, would give us all information which in any way applies to that substance.

**86.** It follows that, if time and change are real, and if a proposition of the form "$A$ is *now* $X$" has a definite meaning, the nature of a thing will change when any of its relationships change, even if nothing has taken place which would, in ordinary language, be called a change in that thing. If $A$, who was thinner than $B$, becomes fatter than $B$, then the nature of $B$'s body will change, though it is neither fatter nor thinner than it was before. For previously it was fatter than $A$'s body, and now it is thinner than $A$'s body, and this change of relationships involves a change of qualities, and so a change of nature.

Further, it follows that, when any substance changes, all substances must change. If $A$ and $B$ are any two substances, they must be related—by similarity and diversity, if in no other way. If $A$ changes, then the object to which $B$ stands in certain relations has changed. Even if $B$ keeps the same relations to the changed $A$, the object to which it has them will now have a different nature, and thus the relationship will have been changed. Instead of having the relations $XY$ to a substance with the nature $PQR$, it will now have them to a substance with the nature $PQS$. And this will mean that a derivative quality in $B$ has changed, and therefore that $B$'s nature has changed.

Moreover, the nature of the past will change. In 1900 the coronation of Queen Victoria was the last British coronation. In 1903 it had ceased to be so—a change of nature which occurred more than sixty years after the event. This seems startling and paradoxical, but I cannot see that there are any real difficulties about it, except those general difficulties which belong to the nature of time. I shall try to show in Book V that nothing does change, but, if anything at all could change, I see no further difficulty in the past changing in the way mentioned above.

The qualities which arise in this manner out of relationships are as real qualities as any others. But, since they differ from other qualities in so important a point, it is desirable to have a separate name for them. I propose to call the qualities which are generated in this way Relational Qualities, and to call those which are not so generated Original Qualities.

**87.** Besides generated qualities there are also generated relationships. In the first place, every quality generates such a relationship. For if a quality is possessed by a substance, that generates a relationship between the substance and the quality. And, secondly, every relationship generates such a relationship. For if a substance stands in a relationship, it is clearly in a relation to that relationship, as well as to the term with which the relationship connects it. If, for example, $A$ is equal to $B$, then $A$, besides being related to $B$, is related to the relationship between itself and $B$, since to be a term in a relationship is to be related to it.

I should propose to class the relations thus generated, together with relational qualities, under the general name of Derivative Characteristics. All qualities and relations which are not generated in this manner, I should call Original Characteristics.

It is to be noticed that there are two sorts of derivative relations, and only one sort of derivative qualities, since derivative relations are generated both by qualities and relations, while derivative qualities are generated only by relations.

**88.** We can now see that every characteristic of a substance generates an infinite series of characteristics of that substance. If we start with an original quality, there is the derivative relationship between the substance and the quality, the derivative quality of standing in that relationship, and so on without end. If we start with an original relationship, there is the derivative quality of standing in that relationship, the derivative relationship between the substance and that quality, and so on again without end. Moreover, whenever, in one of these series, we come to a relationship, that relationship generates, besides the quality derivative from it, a relationship derivative from it, and from each of these an infinite series arises, which again divides into two at each member which is a relationship. All the qualities in these infinite series are parts of the nature of the substance possessing them, and that nature therefore is a compound quality with an infinite number of parts.

These infinite series, however, are not vicious, because it is not necessary to complete them in order to determine the meaning of the earlier terms. The meaning of an earlier member in this series does not depend on a later, but, on the contrary, the meaning of any later term depends on that of an earlier term. The fact that $A$ is good starts an infinite series of qualities and relationships. But the meaning of "$A$ is good" does not depend on the meaning of the propositions asserting these qualities and relations. Such an infinite series, therefore, is not a sign of error[1].

It is true, no doubt, that the occurrence of these qualities and relations becomes of less and less interest and importance as we go down the series. It may be very important that $A$ is good. But the additional fact that $A$ has the quality of being a term in the relationship of inherence between himself and goodness could scarcely be interesting to any sane man, except as an example of a derivative quality. But a fact does not cease to be a fact because no sane man would be interested in it.

**89**. The qualities which make up the nature of any substance fall into two classes in respect of their importance. The first class consists of original qualities, and of those derivative qualities which are immediately derived from original relationships. The second class contains all other derivative qualities. The distinction lies in the fact that all in the second class are

---

[1] I venture to suggest that this consideration removes the force of Mr Bradley's argument for rejecting the validity of the conceptions of quality and relation.

generated, directly or indirectly, by those in the first class, and that, when we know those of the first class, it is unnecessary to enquire into those of the second, since they can be deduced, if knowledge of them should ever be wanted, by the application of the formulae of generation given above. We may name these two classes Primary Qualities and Repeating Qualities—in doing which we shall, of course, be giving "Primary" a different and wider meaning than that which we have given to "Original," since the primary qualities will include both the original qualities and those derivative qualities which are directly generated by original relations.

**90**. It may be objected that, if our argument is valid, the nature of every quality and relation, as well as of every substance, will be a compound quality with an infinite number of parts. For all qualities and relations have qualities and relationships, and these will generate infinite series in the same way that characteristics of substances do. Now, it may be said, it is impossible that the nature of qualities and relations should contain infinite series of characteristics. For then we should not know what a quality or relation meant until we had apprehended the whole of the infinite series, which we are unable to do. But if we do not know what any quality or relation means, we have no right to make any assertion which speaks of qualities or relations. And thus we should be reduced to an absurdity, since this assertion itself speaks of various qualities and relations.

But this objection is invalid. It would be valid if the characteristics of a characteristic were parts or elements of that characteristic. But the characteristics of a characteristic are no more parts or elements of it than the characteristics of a substance are parts of that substance. They are, indeed, parts of its nature, but that is a very different thing.

This may be made clear by examples. It is a quality of redness that it is the colour of doctors' gowns. It is a quality of triangularity that it is an object of thought to a particular school boy at a particular time. These qualities are parts of the nature of the qualities of redness and triangularity. But they are not parts of the qualities redness and triangularity themselves. Redness is a simple quality, and has no parts or elements. And the parts of triangularity are those which are given in its definition, which do not include its contemplation by a particular school boy.

When a characteristic is not simple, but has parts or elements, we do not know the meaning of the characteristic unless we know the meaning of the parts or elements. If humanity means the quality of being both rational and animal, we shall not know the meaning of humanity unless we know the meaning of animality. If what is meant by conceit is the possession of too good an opinion of oneself, we shall not know what conceit means unless we know what opinion means. But this does not prevent our knowing what characteristics mean, as long as their parts or elements are not too numerous to be grasped by our minds. So long as the parts or elements of the characteristic itself comply with this condition, we can know what it means, although its nature will contain an infinite series of qualities.

**91.** The number of qualities in the nature of any substance will, as we have seen, be infinite. But this is due to the fact that the number of repeating qualities will be infinite. It remains to consider whether the nature of any substance, or of all substances, contains an infinite number of primary qualities. So far we have no ground for pronouncing any opinion on this point.

We shall, however, see reason later to adopt the view that the number of substances is infinite. Now each substance is related to every other substance. For it has, at least, to every other substance the relation of similarity, since they are both substances, and the relation of diversity, since they are not the same substance. Since each substance stands in this relation to an infinite number of other substances, it will have an infinite number of original relationships, and therefore an infinity of primary qualities derived from them.

The qualities thus proved to be infinite in number are, as we have just said, derivative, although they are primary. As to the number of original qualities possessed by any substance, it is impossible, as far as I can see, to say anything.

**92.** We have now dealt with qualities, substances, and relations, and have found it impossible to dispense with any one of the three in our account of existence. But it may be worth while to enquire why quality occupies, in common opinion, a more secure place than either relation or substance. Many systems of philosophy have rejected the conception of substance, or the conception of relation, while retaining the conception of quality, but, as far as I know, no system has ever rejected the conception of quality and retained either of the other two. (Some, indeed, have rejected general qualities, while retaining relations and substances. But, however mistakenly and inconsistently, they have retained qualities which are not general.)

In the first place, we must ask what reasons can be found for the belief that characteristics stand on a firmer and more certain footing than substances. I think that there are three.

The first is that it is frequently held that characteristics are the only things which we perceive—that is, which we are directly aware of as existing. This is a mistake. The perception-data which we perceive are substances. They may not be persistent or independent. They may be events or states in our minds. But they have qualities and are related, and they are not qualities or relations. And therefore, by our definition, they are substances.

The cause of this mistake is, I think, that, in the case of those perception-data which are sense-data, we are accustomed in ordinary life to believe in corresponding qualities in external objects. I have a sense-datum of yellow, and this leads me to believe, rightly or wrongly, in the existence of an external object which is yellow. Now, as a rule, the existence of the sense-datum has no intrinsic interest for me, while the existence of the object, which it leads me to believe in, has often great interest for me. It is a matter of considerable interest to me whether the coin in my hand is a shilling or a sovereign, or whether the animal I meet is a dog or a lion, and it is only as leading me to a conclusion on these points that the sense-datum of yellow interests me at all. And since the only interest of the sense-datum of yellow lies in the characteristic of yellowness which it leads me to attribute to the external object, it is not wonderful that the sense-datum should be confused with the characteristic.

The second reason is that every substance is directly connected with characteristics, while every characteristic of the existent is not *directly* connected with substances. For some of them are characteristics of characteristics. This does not affect the fact that substance is indispensable. But it may give characteristics an appearance, though a mistaken appearance, of greater independence than substance.

The third reason is that we can know nothing of the nature of a substance except by knowing that it has certain characteristics. Even to know that it is a substance, and that it exists, is to know that it has the characteristics of substantiality and existence, nor should we ever have reason to believe that a particular substance existed, unless we had reason to believe that it had other characteristics besides these. But we can know a great deal about the nature of a characteristic without knowing what existent substance it belongs to, or whether it belongs to any at all. And, indeed, as we have seen, we can have knowledge of its nature, even if we know that it does not belong to anything existent. A mathematician knows many qualities which belong to the quality "to be a rigid body," though he has good reason to believe that no rigid body ever exists. This does not, of course, make substance less essential than characteristics, for it does not affect the conclusion that something does exist, and that, if anything exists, substance must exist. Nor does it affect, as we have seen, the validity of our conclusions as to the relation of existence and reality. But it does tend to give characteristics a false appearance of being independent of existence, and therefore more fundamental than substances, which are clearly not independent of existence.

These reasons may account for the belief that characteristics are more indispensable than substance. But why should qualities be taken as more indispensable than relations? Why should relations be condemned because they cannot inhere in anything as qualities do, while no one condemns qualities because things cannot stand in them as they do in relations? I think that the answer, in some cases, is to be found in the great objection which many thinkers entertain to admitting that what is really separate can be just as really connected. The assertion of relations involves this admission, except in the case of reflexive relations. All other relations require at least two terms, which must be really separate, since they are two, and really connected, since they are related. The assertion of a quality, however, does not involve such an admission, and thus the thinkers who are unwilling to make the admission take refuge from relations in qualities[1].

---

[1] Of course, when two substances have the same quality, we get real separation and real connection. But then we can assert the quality of one substance without asserting it of the other, while the relation cannot be asserted of one of the terms taken separately.

# CHAPTER X

## DISSIMILARITY OF SUBSTANCES

**93**. The question now arises whether two substances can have exactly the same nature, or whether the fact that they are two different substances involves that there must be some difference in their nature. If there was no difference between the nature of two things, they would be exactly similar, so that our question may be put in the form whether Diversity implies Dissimilarity—using dissimilarity to exclude exact similarity only, and as compatible with partial similarity.

We may note, to begin with, that, if there is to be any difference in their nature at all, there must be some difference among their primary qualities. For the formula by which the infinite series of repeating qualities is generated is such that there can be no difference in repeating qualities which does not arise from some difference in primary qualities.

Primary qualities may be either original qualities or qualities immediately derived from original relationships. There seems no reason for denying that it would be possible for two substances to be diverse without any difference in their original qualities. It is, of course, possible that all substances may differ in their original qualities. It is even possible that every substance should have some simple original quality which no other substance has. And, to take a supposition which seems less improbable, it is possible that the aggregate of original qualities in any substance should differ, in some at least of its constituents, from the aggregate of original qualities in any other substance. But we have no reason to suppose that this must be the case. If diversity does require difference of nature, that requirement could be satisfied by a difference of relational qualities, caused by a difference in original relationships.

We must not forget that the question is about exact similarity, and that exact similarity involves that there should be no difference in *any* relationship, however external and indifferent that relationship is commonly supposed to be. Two things are not exactly similar if one of them is known to me and the other is not. Nor are they exactly similar if one of them is ever perceived or thought of by me without the other (even if at other times I perceive or think of them simultaneously). For then one has, and one has not, the quality of being cognized by a particular person at a particular time. Nor are they exactly similar if they are ever distinguished by names or numbers, however arbitrarily applied. For then one would have the quality of being called $P$ by a particular person at a particular time, and the other would have the quality of being called $Q$ by him at that time.

**94.** Can there, then, be two things which are exactly similar? I think that the answer must be that there cannot. The connection between diversity and dissimilarity is, no doubt, synthetic. "$A$ and $B$ are two things," and "$A$ and $B$ are dissimilar," are not two ways of stating the same fact. But it seems clear to me that diversity implies dissimilarity—that two things cannot have the same nature. If we make the experiment of removing in thought all difference of nature from two substances, we shall find that, when we have succeeded, we are no longer contemplating two substances, but one. And this does not, as I conceive, come from the impossibility of our distinguishing the two substances—which would not prove there were not two—but from the recognition of the impossibility of diversity without dissimilarity. The nature of a substance expresses completely what the substance is. And the same complete expression of what a substance is cannot be true of each of two substances. The substance is made this substance by its nature, and, if the nature is the same, the substance is the same.

It would not, I imagine, be denied by anyone that there is one dissimilarity of relations which must exist between diverse substances. If $A$ and $B$ are diverse substances, then $A$ is identical with $A$ and diverse from $B$, while $B$ is neither identical with $A$ nor diverse from itself. But if our contention in the last paragraph is right, there must be some other dissimilarity between diverse substances, besides this one. For this dissimilarity depends on a diversity which has been previously established, and cannot therefore be the dissimilarity which is necessary to permit diversity.

**95.** The view that diversity requires a dissimilarity not dependent on itself is the view which has, I believe, been adopted by the majority of philosophers. But it has been denied, and we must consider what causes have led to the denial.

In the first place, the denial seems to be due in some cases to the adoption, more or less explicitly, of the erroneous conception of the Thing-in-itself. (I use this phrase here rather in Hegel's sense than in Kant's[1].) It is held that the substance has an individuality apart and distinct from its nature, and that therefore two substances, while they have the same nature, could be diverse in respect of this distinct aspect, in much the same way that two heads can be fitted with the same hat. But this is untenable. For when we try to explain what we mean by this distinct aspect of the substance—indeed, when we assert that it exists—we can only do so by asserting qualities of the substance. And these qualities are part of the nature of the substance, not something apart and distinct from that nature. It is therefore impossible to distinguish the substance from its qualities in such a way as to allow the substances to be different while their natures are the same.

As against this, it has been suggested to me that the assertion that a substance has an individuality apart from its nature is proved by the fact that such a judgment as "this is near that" may have a definite meaning. Such a judgment certainly does not gain a definite meaning by its terms being so precisely described that each description could apply only to one thing in the universe. Indeed "this" and "that" are each applicable to every object in the universe. And yet there is no ambiguity for me in such a judgment, if I am perceiving the substances which I designate as "this" and "that," or if I have perceived them and now remember them. Hence it is argued that there must be in each substance an individuality which is independent of its qualities, and which is revealed to us when we perceive the

---

[1] Cp. my *Commentary on Hegel's Logic*, Section 135.

substance—though, of course, it would be equally there whether the substance were perceived or not.

This argument, however, seems to me to be invalid. No doubt I can have unambiguous knowledge of $A$—knowledge which enables me to identify it—either by perception or by description. And in the first case I shall have unambiguous knowledge of $A$ which is not dependent on my knowledge of $A$'s qualities[1], just as in the second case I shall have unambiguous knowledge of $A$ which is not dependent on my acquaintance with $A$. But the fact that I can know the substance independently of its qualities does not prove that its individuality is independent of its qualities, so that it could be diverse from another substance from which it was not dissimilar.

The view that the individuality of the substance must be independent of any quality, which is such that the substance can be unambiguously known without knowing that quality, leads to an absurdity. For the qualities, without knowing which I can unambiguously know a substance by perception, include the quality "having an individuality independent of any quality." Therefore, if this view were true, the substance would have an individuality independent of any quality which would, among others, be independent of its possession of the quality "having an individuality independent of any quality." And this is absurd.

To avoid this it might be admitted that the substance could not have such an independent individuality and diversity, unless it possessed the qualities which are involved in it— substantiality, the possession of an individuality independent of any quality, and the consequent possession of a diversity independent of dissimilarity. But it might still be maintained that it has an individuality which, while dependent on some of its qualities, is not entirely dependent on its qualities, and that this individuality might be different in two substances which

---

[1] I doubt if we ever perceive a substance without knowing *some* of its qualities, since, after a perception, we are always able to make some judgments as to the nature of what we have perceived. (This subject will be discussed in Book V.) But I can have unambiguous knowledge of a substance by perception although my knowledge of its qualities falls very far short of an unambiguous description of it.

are exactly similar. But this admission would destroy the force of the argument. For I can perceive a substance without knowing that it has substantiality, or that it possesses an individuality independent of any quality, or that it possesses a diversity which is independent of dissimilarity. And if, nevertheless, its individuality is not independent of these qualities, we cannot argue that its individuality is independent of any other qualities merely on the ground that I can perceive the substance without knowing those other qualities.

**96.** This ground for rejecting our theory, therefore, must be regarded as inadequate. In other cases our theory is, I think, rejected owing to a misunderstanding of what it means. It has often been supposed that the dissimilarity required must be a dissimilarity of what we have called original qualities, exclusive of relational qualities. But this is a mistake, since all that is asserted is that diverse substances cannot be exactly similar both in their original qualities and in their original relations.

It is owing to this misunderstanding that it is urged against our theory that two exactly similar substances could exist at different times or places. It may be possible that there should be two substances at different times or places which were exactly similar in their original qualities, but they would have different relationships, and would therefore have different derivative qualities. Two substances at different times have different relations to each other, since one will be earlier than the other, and the other later than the first. And they will have different relationships to everything else in the time series. And two substances in different places will also have different relationships. If space is to be taken as absolute, then one substance will occupy one or more points of space, and these points will not be occupied by the other, which is in a different place. Then $A$ will have the relational quality of being the occupant of point $M$, and this quality will not be shared by $B$. If, on the other hand, space is to be taken as relative, it is clear that the two substances could not occupy different positions in space if there were no difference between their relationships to other substances in space.

**97.** There are other series of terms besides those of time and space, and it has been maintained, in the same way, that there could be diverse substances which were exactly similar, if those substances occupied different places in some such series. Whenever substances are counted or numbered we have, of course, such a series. And so important has this objection to our theory been considered that the expressions "numerically different" and "numerically diverse," are often used to express what we have called diversity.

This objection is due to the same misunderstanding. If two substances occupy different places in such a series their relationships are not the same. If $A$ and $B$ are at different points in the series, they will stand in different relations to any other term, $C$, in the series. If $C$ is in the same place in the series as $A$, it will not be in the same place as $B$. If $C$ falls between them in the series, then one of the two will be earlier in the series than $C$, and the other will be later. If $C$ is on the same side of $A$ and of $B$, then either $A$ must be nearer to it than $B$, or $B$ than $A$. And so the relationships and the relational qualities of $A$ and $B$ will be different.

And it makes no difference if the order of the series is determined by some consideration which, in ordinary language, would be called irrelevant to the substances which are its terms. I may think to-day of Fielding, Meredith, and Thackeray, in that order, merely because in looking at a book-case my eye has been caught successively by *Tom Jones, Evan Harrington,* and *Esmond.* But it will be true of Fielding that he is a man of whom, on a certain day, a certain person thought before he thought of Meredith, and it will be true of Thackeray that he is a man of whom, on the same day, the same person did not think before he thought of Meredith. And, although this is not an important difference in the natures of Fielding and Thackeray, it is a real difference.

Neither of the objections, then, which we have considered, is valid, and we must adhere to our view that diversity implies dissimilarity, and that all substances must be dissimilar to one another.

**98.** It may be said that, though we have shown that all substances must be dissimilar to one another, we must not assume that they must be dissimilar either in their original qualities or in their relations to other substances. May they not be dissimilar only in their relations to characteristics which do not belong to them? For example, if $A$ and $B$ are men, might not their dissimilarity consist exclusively in some difference of their relations to the characteristic of whiteness, or of rigidity?

But every such dissimilarity would involve a dissimilarity in the relations of $A$ and $B$ to other substances. If $A$ has the relation $Y$ to the characteristic $X$, while $B$ has not that relation to it, then, if any substance $C$ possesses the characteristic $X$, $A$ and $B$ will be in different relations to $C$. For $C$ will be related to $X$, and will therefore be in different indirect relations to things which stand in different relations to $X$. And though these relations will be indirect, they will be original relations between the substances. If, on the other hand, $X$ is a characteristic which no substance possesses, then every substance will possess the characteristic not-$X$. And, if $A$ and $B$ have different relations to $X$, their relations to not-$X$ will not be the same, nor, consequently, their relations to the substances to which the characteristic not-$X$ belongs.

**99.** The result which we have reached is the principle which is known historically as the Identity of Indiscernibles. It is true that when Leibniz, who invented the name, asserted that diverse substances must have dissimilar qualities, he meant that they must have what, in the terminology we have adopted, would be called dissimilar original qualities. But it must be remembered that Leibniz rejected relations altogether, and held that original qualities were the only characteristics of substances. And it seems to me that the essence of his contention in maintaining the Identity of Indiscernibles lay in the assertion that there was a dissimilarity of characteristics, and not in his denial that this might start in a difference of relations.

The name, however, is not a good one. For the principle does not assert that there are indiscernibles which are identical, but that there is nothing which is indiscernible from anything else. It would be better to speak of the Dissimilarity of the Diverse.

# CHAPTER XI

## SUFFICIENT DESCRIPTION

**100.** A substance cannot, of course, be defined, since it is particular. Definition is only applicable to characteristics, which are universals, and only to those characteristics which are not simple. It consists in stating the simpler characteristics —ultimately the absolutely simple characteristics—into which the characteristic defined can be analyzed. But, although a substance cannot be defined, it can be described. It is described, more or less, by every quality which it possesses, including the qualities derived from the relations in which it stands. (Characteristics, whether definable or not, can also be described by the qualities they possess.)

Description resembles definition in this respect, that by means of each we are enabled to distinguish that to which it is applied from anything else. Every characteristic which is not simple, and so admits of definition at all, has a complete definition which is not a definition of anything but itself. Indeed nothing but a complete definition is usually called a definition. We should not say that "rectilinear figure" was an incomplete definition of a triangle, but only that it was part of a definition.

On the other hand, an imperfect description is called a description. We describe Henry VII when we speak of him as an English sovereign, though that is a characteristic which does not distinguish him from Richard II or Elizabeth. And therefore we must make a distinction between a description and an Exclusive Description.

**101.** By an Exclusive Description I mean one which applies only to one substance, so that the substance is absolutely identified by the description. We must distinguish, again, between an exclusive description and a Complete Description. A Complete Description of a substance would consist of all its qualities, both primary and repeating, and would therefore, of course, consist of an infinite number of qualities. It follows from the results reached in the last chapter that a complete description must be exclusive, since no two substances have their natures completely the same, and a complete account of the nature of the one substance could therefore never be true of the nature of another. But an exclusive description need not be complete. "The most virtuous of all beings" could not be a complete description of any possible being, but it would be an exclusive description of any being of whom it was true, since it could not be true of more than one.

Descriptions are in terms of qualities. But a description by means of a quality derived from a relation sometimes introduces a substance. If I describe Henry VII as the father of a sovereign, I am describing him entirely by characteristics. But if I describe him as the father of Henry VIII, a substance comes into the description—the substance Henry VIII. And it is essential to the description. "Father of Henry VIII" is quite a different description to "father of a sovereign," for the latter describes many substances not described by the former.

It might seem as if a description which was partially expressed in terms of substances had no effect in increasing our knowledge of the substance described, unless each substance mentioned in the description was itself described. For if substances can be known without description, there is no need of description at all. If substances cannot be known without description, then the undescribed substance which forms part of a description is not known. And a description of anything in terms of the unknown is useless.

But this overlooks the fact that there are some substances of which I am aware by perception, and that a description of some other substance by means of these may describe something of which I am not aware in terms of which I am aware. I am not, for example, aware of my table, and when I describe it as "the cause of these visual sense-data," meaning the sense-data which I am perceiving while I make the description, I am describing it in terms of all of which, substances as well as characteristics, I am aware. And so this description may be exclusive although it does not contain exclusive descriptions of the sense-data.

**102.** I propose to distinguish between those exclusive descriptions which contain undescribed substances, and those which are entirely in terms of characteristics, by calling the latter Sufficient Descriptions.

A sufficient description might consist of a single simple quality. For if no substance but one had that quality, the substance which had it would be sufficiently described as having it. It might consist of a single complex quality. Or it might consist of a number of separate qualities, in which case it would itself be a single compound quality, which has the other qualities as its parts.

A sufficient description which is not a single simple quality may yet be comparatively simple as "the most virtuous of all beings." But it may also be infinitely removed from simplicity, for it does not cease to be a sufficient description because no mind is capable of grasping it. In some cases, as we shall see later in this chapter, such an infinite remove from simplicity would destroy the sufficiency of the description by introducing a vicious infinite. But if the description were of the type "$A$ has the quality $X$, the quality $Y$, the quality $Z$..." the list of qualities required for excluding everything but $A$ might be infinite without being vicious.

A substance may have more than one sufficient description. It might, for example, be the case that "the most virtuous of all beings," and "the most powerful of all beings" were descriptions of the same person.

**103.** Has every substance a sufficient description? There are very few cases in which we could know that any particular description is a sufficient description of any existent substance[1]. But there are many descriptions such that, if one of them is a description of any substance, it will be a sufficient description of that substance. Such, for example, is "the most virtuous of all beings," since it can only apply to one substance. But we are not certain that it applies to any substance. That virtuous beings do exist, indeed, we may perhaps affirm with confidence.

---

[1] We do know this in the case of the universe. Cp. Section 135.

But it is not absolutely impossible that two beings might be more virtuous than any others, and exactly equal to one another in virtue. In that case there would be nobody who was the most virtuous of all beings. And if we were certain it did describe somebody, we should not know whom it described. Even supposing that I happened to have met the man who was the most virtuous of all beings, I could not know him to be so, unless, either by my own investigations or by trustworthy report, I knew the limits of the virtue of all other virtuous beings.

Most comparatively simple descriptions which, if applicable to anything, would be a sufficient description of it are of this type. They are of the form "that which has most (or least) of the quality $X$." And the difficulties mentioned in the last paragraph occur in the case of each of them.

Descriptions by means of space and time have an appearance of being sufficient. "King of England in 1500" might be mistaken for a sufficient description of Henry VII. But if "England" is taken as the proper name of a particular substance, the description, though exclusive, will not be sufficient. The only other alternative is to take "England" as descriptive—as meaning a country whose official title is England, or which is habitually called by that name. And then we cannot be certain that at some time and place in the universe—perhaps in another planet—there may not be another country which is called England in the same way. And, if this should be so, we shall not have got a sufficient description of the country of which Henry VII was king, and therefore our description of him will not be sufficient. And similar difficulties occur about time; for 1500 years from the event which starts a calendar is not a sufficient description unless we can be sure that no other event which can be described in the same way ever took place or will take place. To date from the foundation of Rome, for example, would not be unambiguous, for we are not certain that in the course of the universe several cities of that name may not be founded.

It may be remarked in passing that many calendars *would* give sufficient descriptions of dates, if the beliefs of those who established them were true. Our present reckoning starts from an event which those who established the calendar believed to be an incarnation of God, and to be the only incarnation of God in the course of time. If this were true, "1500 years after the Incarnation" would be a sufficient description of a date. The same would be the case in the Mohammedan calendar, since that religion, I conceive, ascribes to its founder a unique position in the universe, and dates its calendar from an event in his life.

Moreover, if the same beliefs were true, it would be possible to make sufficient descriptions of places. Mecca, Medina, Jerusalem and Taif, could be sufficiently described by their relations to the life of Mohammed, who could himself be sufficiently described by his unique relation to God. And any other place could be sufficiently described by its relations to these four.

But if we do not accept any of these views of the unique character of certain persons and events, we can get no sufficient descriptions by means of space and time. It is true that, if time has limits, a date could be sufficiently described by its relation to these limits. But, even if time is limited in this way, it would be impossible for us, with our present knowledge, to know any such sufficient description.

There are, of course, many fairly simple *exclusive* descriptions by means of space and time. Such, for example, would be a description of Henry VII as the King of England in that planet in which I am making the description, 419 years before the time at which I am making it. But this is not a sufficient description, because it does not sufficiently describe the event of my making the description, but trusts to my immediate perception of it.

**104.** Thus there are but few cases in which we can know that a given description is a sufficient description of any particular substance. Are we sure that every substance *has* a sufficient description? Every substance must have an exclusive description, because no substance can have exactly the same nature as any other. But might it not be possible that $A$ could not be exclusively described without introducing the fact that $A$ had the relation $X$ to $B$? And this could not, as it stands, enter into a sufficient description, since it introduces a particular substance, while without it nothing could be a sufficient description, since every sufficient description must be exclusive.

But the fact that $A$ had the relation $X$ to $B$ may be capable of being stated in such a way that it could enter into a sufficient description. It may be the case, to begin with, that not only is $A$ the only substance which is in the relation $X$ to $B$, but it is the only substance which is in the relation $X$ to anything. In that case we can replace "having the relation $X$ to $B$" by "having the relation $X$ to *some* substance," which, on this hypothesis, will be equally exclusive, and, not introducing a particular substance, will be sufficient.

But if other substances than $A$ have the relation $X$ to substances other than $B$, we cannot make this substitution. If, however, we can find a sufficient description of $B$—for example "having the qualities $P$ and $Q$," we can get a sufficient description of $A$ by replacing "having the relation $X$ to $B$" by "having the relation $X$ to the only substance which has the qualities $P$ and $Q$."

If, again, no exclusive description of $B$ can be found which does not introduce a particular substance—*e.g.* "having the relation $R$ to $C$"—a sufficient description of $A$ is still possible. This may happen in two ways. Even if certain other substances besides $A$ have the relation $X$ to substances other than $B$, and even if other substances besides $B$ have the relation $R$ to other substances besides $C$, it may be the case that no substance besides $A$ has the relation $X$ to any substance which has the relation $R$ to any substance. In this case we can make our description sufficient by replacing "having the relation $X$ to $B$" by "having the relation $X$ to some substance which has the relation $R$ to another substance."

Or, in the second place, a sufficient description of $A$ will be reached if we can find a sufficient description of $C$—*e.g.* "having the qualities $S$ and $T$." For then we shall have an exclusive description of $A$ by including in it "standing in the relation $X$ to the only substance which stands in the relation $R$ to the only substance having the qualities $S$ and $T$." And this description will be sufficient.

If, again, $C$ cannot be exclusively described without introducing another particular substance—by saying, *e.g.*, that it has the relation $U$ to $D$—the same chances of reaching a sufficient description of $A$ will recur. We shall find a sufficient description of $A$ whenever either of two things happen—whenever, in the series of substances, $B$, $C$, $D$, etc., we reach one which has a sufficient description, or whenever the complex relation "having the relation $X$ to a substance which has the relation $R$ to a substance which has the relation $U$ to a substance which..." becomes so rare that nothing but $A$ stands in it to anything.

**105**. But supposing that neither of those things ever does happen, and that the series of substances involved in the exclusive description of $A$ never ceases? Shall we not then have a case in which a substance has no sufficient description?

This case, however, cannot occur because such an infinite series would be vicious. By the results in the last chapter, $A$ must be dissimilar to all other substances. The possibility of this depends on the existence of $B$, and the existence of $B$ depends on its dissimilarity to all other substances. And this depends on the existence of $C$, and this on its dissimilarity to all other substances, and so on. If this series is infinite, it is vicious. For, starting from the existence of $A$, each earlier term requires all the later terms, and therefore requires that the series should be completed, which it cannot be. If, therefore, the series is infinite, $A$ cannot be dissimilar to all other substances—cannot, in other words, have an exclusive description—and so cannot exist. Therefore, if $A$ does exist, the series cannot be infinite. And if the series is not infinite, $A$ has a sufficient description. Every substance, therefore, must have a sufficient description.

It is to be noticed that the necessity that a substance should have an exclusive description, on which we have based our demonstration that it must have a sufficient description, does not rest on the ground that, without an exclusive description, no one could know it as so to distinguish it from other substances. Such an argument would be invalid on three grounds. In the first place, there seems no necessity that every substance should be capable of being known so as to distinguish it from other substances, since they can be different substances without being known to be different. In the second place, an exclusive description may, as we have seen, consist of an infinite number of qualities, in which case it could not be known by minds like ours. In the third place, a substance when directly perceived is known as distinguished from other substances without any description of it being required. The necessity that a substance should have an exclusive description arises from the fact that two substances cannot be completely similar, and that a substance which is not completely similar to any other has necessarily an exclusive description.

# CHAPTER XII

## DETERMINATION

**106**. We have considered the relation of substances to their characteristics, and the question now arises of the relation of the characteristics of a substance to one another. It will be sufficient to consider the relations to one another of the qualities of a substance, since these will include the qualities of standing in its various relations, and thus the relations of relations to qualities and to one another will be dealt with indirectly. The most obvious point about the relations of the qualities of substances to one another is that, when $A$ possesses the qualities $X$ and $Y$, in some cases the proposition that it possesses $X$ implies the proposition that it possesses $Y$, while in some cases it does not.

I should say that Implication is an indefinable relation between propositions, and that $P$ implies $Q$ when (1) if I know that the relation holds between $P$ and $Q$, and know $P$ to be true, I am justified by this knowledge alone in asserting that $Q$ is true, and when (2) if I know that the relation holds between $P$ and $Q$, and know $Q$ to be false, I am justified by this knowledge alone in asserting that $P$ is false[1]. From this, of course, follows the proposition that $Q$ must be true or $P$ false.

**107**. We must distinguish implication from Inference. A judgment $N$ is inferred from a judgment $M$, when the person who makes the judgment believes that the proposition $P$, asserted in the judgment $M$, implies the proposition $Q$, asserted in the judgment $N$, and asserts $Q$ (that is, makes the judgment $N$) for that reason. Thus, in our statement about implication, we could substitute "justified by this knowledge alone in inferring" for "justified by this knowledge alone in asserting."

---

[1] The introduction of the knowledge of the relation in the above statement does not introduce a vicious circle, because the statement does not profess to be a definition of implication, which, as has been said, is indefinable.

But this does not reduce implication to inference, for $P$ implies $Q$ when we should be justified in asserting $Q$ to be true if we know $P$ to be true, and not when we do assert it for that reason. "No man should be enslaved" implies "no black man should be enslaved," even if every one believed the first, and no one had inferred the second from it. On the other hand, "all men should be voters" does not imply "all voters should be men," and would do so none the more, if everyone who believed the first had inferred the second from it.

Implication and inference, then, are not equivalent. Nor can implication be defined by means of inference. We have said that $P$ implies $Q$ when, if I know that $P$ does imply $Q$ and that $P$ is true, I am justified thereby in inferring that $Q$ is true. This leaves implication still indefinable. For, in the first place, we require the idea of implication to define inference. If a judgment $M$ caused a judgment $N$ for any other reason than that the proposition stated in the first was held to imply the proposition stated in the second, $N$ would not be said to be inferred from $M$. And, in the second place, $P$ implies $Q$ only when we are justified in making an inference. And if we ask when it happens that we are justified in making an inference, the only reply is that we are justified when there is an implication. Thus implication is not defined.

**108**. Corresponding to implication between propositions, there is clearly a relation between characteristics. If it is true that, whenever something has the quality $X$, something has the quality $Y$, this involves that, besides the relation between the two propositions "something has the quality $X$," and "something has the quality $Y$," there is a relation between the qualities $X$ and $Y$. I propose to call this relation Intrinsic Determination. (I insert "intrinsic" to distinguish it from another sort of determination which will be discussed later in this chapter.) The quality $X$ will be said to determine intrinsically the quality $Y$ whenever the proposition that something has the quality $X$ implies the proposition that something has the quality $Y$. The two qualities may be in the same thing or in two different things. The occurrence of blueness as a quality of anything intrinsically determines the occurrence of spatiality as a quality of the same thing. But if it is a quality of one person to be a husband, this determines the occurrence in someone else of the quality of being a wife.

If, on the other hand, the occurrence of $X$ does not intrinsically determine the occurrence of $Y$, we may say that $Y$ is Intrinsically Undetermined by $X$, or Contingent to $X$. (This, of course, does not imply that $X$ is contingent to $Y$, which may or may not be the case.)

From the results which we have already reached we can see that, in the nature of each substance, there are qualities which are connected by the relation of intrinsic determination, and also qualities which are connected by the relation of contingency. Every substance, for example, has the quality of having qualities, and the quality of standing in relations. And each of these qualities is intrinsically determined by the other. For everything which has a quality must stand in a relation—its relation to that quality. And everything which stands in a relation must have a quality—the quality of being a term in that relation.

On the other hand, since there is more than one substance, any substance, $A$, will have, as we saw in Chapter VII, the quality of dissimilarity to every other substance, for example to $B$. It will also have the quality of substantiality. And dissimilarity to $B$ is contingent to substantiality, for $B$ itself is a substance, while it is not dissimilar to itself.

Every quality of a substance, therefore, does not intrinsically determine every other. But intrinsic determination is not the only sort of determination which is possible. There is another kind of determination, which we must now consider.

**109.** Let us take $X$, $Y$, and $Z$ as representing all the infinite number of qualities possessed by some substance $A$, including those which are derivative from the relations in which $A$ stands. Each of them may occur in other substances, but, in so far as this particular occurrence of them is concerned, they only exist as qualities of $A$.

If now we enquire what $A$ is, a complete answer must be given by giving the nature of $A$, and this consists of its qualities. $X$, $Y$, and $Z$ are taken as a complete list of these, and thus the nature of $A$ is $X$, $Y$, $Z$. Let us suppose any of the qualities altered, either by addition or subtraction or substitution, so that the complete list would be represented by $W$, $X$, $Y$, $Z$, or by $X$, $Y$, or by $W$, $X$, $Y$. Thus the nature of the substance which had such qualities would be different from the nature of $A$. Therefore the substance in question could not be $A$.

But all that we knew of this particular occurrence of $X$, $Y$, and $Z$, of which we are treating, was that they occurred in $A$. And if there should be no $A$, but something different, $B$, the fact that they would have occurred in $A$ does not give us any reason to assert that they would occur in $B$. Thus, if one of the qualities of $A$ were not there, there would be no ground to assert that the others would be there. In the different substance $B$, which replaces $A$[1], the qualities $X$ and $Y$ might occur, for anything we know to the contrary, in spite of the absence of $Z$ or of the presence of $W$. But this is only possible in the same way in which $S$ and $T$, $U$ and $V$, or any other qualities (between which there was no intrinsic incompatibility) could occur. If any part of the nature of $A$ goes, the nature of $A$ as a whole goes. The substance which replaces $A$ might have some qualities in common with $A$, just as any other substance might have qualities in common with $A$. But we have no right to subtract $Z$, and then say "because we have only subtracted $Z$, and because there is no *intrinsic* determination of $Z$ by $X$ and $Y$, therefore $X$ and $Y$ remain." By subtracting $Z$, we have destroyed $A$, and $X$ and $Y$ were here only as parts of the nature of $A$.

No quality of a substance, therefore, could be different while leaving the others unchanged, and no quality of a substance is completely contingent to any of its other qualities. We may thus say that every quality of a substance will determine every other quality of that substance, but the determination will be of a very different kind from the intrinsic determination which we have already considered. In the first place, when one quality

---

[1] I do not mean by this that the absence of $A$ would imply the existence of $B$. This has not been proved, and could only be considered at a later stage. All that is meant is that we were invited to consider the hypothesis that some qualities of $A$ remained the same, while others were altered, and that the consequences of this, as pointed out above, would be that they would no longer be qualities of $A$, but of some other substance.

intrinsically determines another, the proposition that the first occurs implies the proposition that the second occurs, but there is no implication in this new sort of determination. We are not entitled to infer the occurrence of the determined from that of the determinant, unless the determination is intrinsic.

Secondly, intrinsic determination is universal. Whenever the one quality occurs the other will occur. But the second sort of determination only links one particular occurrence of one quality with one particular occurrence of the other.

Thirdly, since every quality of any substance determines all the others in this way, it is obvious that all such determination will be reciprocal, which is not the case with all intrinsic determination.

And fourthly, while intrinsic determination can exist between two qualities of different substances, we have so far only shown the second sort of determination to take place between qualities of the same substance, though this result will be extended in the next Book.

It will be convenient to have a separate name for this second species of determination, but it is not very easy to find one. We may perhaps call it, without impropriety, Extrinsic Determination, since it holds, not between two qualities as such, but between two qualities in virtue of the relation in which they stand to the same substance.

Since all qualities of a substance extrinsically determine one another, it follows that all characteristics of a substance intrinsically determine one another. For if any relationship in which a substance stands were different from what it is, then one of its qualities—the quality of standing in that relationship—would be different from what it is.

**110**. We must now consider some objections which can be raised to the results we have reached. In the first place, it may be said that it is notorious that some characteristics of a substance can often be changed, and often are changed, without changing the substance, or the other characteristics.

But the change of which we have been speaking is not a change in time which actually occurs, but a hypothetical change, which, if it did occur, would have made a substance

different from what it actually is, and which obviously, therefore, has not occurred. Of course, if change in time is real at all,
the same substance can be hot on Sunday and cold on Monday,
and be a poker on both days. But this does not affect the
question which concerns us here—the question whether, if it
had not been, as it was, hot on Sunday, it could have been
the same substance as the one which actually was hot on
Sunday.

In the second place it may be objected that the quality, for
example, which is possessed by Snowdon of being a mountain
cannot determine its quality of being to-day $M$ feet high. For a
substance which to-day was $M - 1$ feet high might be a mountain,
and consequently, it is said, we may be confident that Snowdon,
if to-day it were $M - 1$ feet high, would be a mountain.

It is, of course, quite true that a substance which was to-day
$M - 1$ feet high could be a mountain. But to argue from this
that Snowdon would be a mountain if it were to-day a foot
shorter than it is, would be to confuse intrinsic and extrinsic
determination. That anything should be a mountain does not
imply that it is exactly the present height of Snowdon. And,
therefore, if the present Snowdon, with its present height, did
not exist, there *might* be a mountain which possessed all the
qualities of Snowdon (including its position in space and time)
with the exception of its exact height and those qualities which
are intrinsically determined by its exact height. And thus, no
doubt, Snowdon's quality of being a mountain does not stand
to its quality of being $M$ feet high in the same relation as it
stands to its quality of being spatial. For whatever is not
spatial could not be a mountain.

But the difference is only that to be a mountain does intrinsically determine being spatial, while it does not intrinsically
determine being $M$ feet high. And this leaves our point undis-
turbed—that the two qualities of Snowdon, being a mountain
and being $M$ feet high, do extrinsically determine one another.
For anything which had not the quality of being to-day $M$ feet
high would not be the substance which we call Snowdon. And
it is therefore incorrect to argue that any such substance would
have the quality of being a mountain because Snowdon has such

a quality, and because that quality does not involve Snowdon's exact height.

I have purposely taken an example where the original substance has a proper name, as in such cases there is a peculiarity which has a tendency to obscure the issue unless it is realized. A mountain which differed from the actual Snowdon only in being a foot shorter, and in whatever was implied by that, would resemble it so closely in every characteristic in which we were interested, that we should certainly give it the name of Snowdon. And thus we might be led to suppose that the actual and the hypothetical Snowdon were the same substance, and that the hypothesis was only that this substance had different qualities from those it does have. But this would be wrong. A substance which had to-day a different height from that of the actual Snowdon could not be the same substance, since it would have a different nature.

In the third place, it may be objected that, if there were not the present Snowdon, we might have reason to believe that there would be a mountain with most of the important qualities of the actual Snowdon, though without its present height, because the existence of other substances, in which our hypothesis makes no change, might intrinsically determine the existence of such a mountain.

We cannot deal with this objection at present, because we have not yet arrived at the consideration of the relations in which any substance stands to any other substances in the universe. When we do so, it will be seen that the objection is not tenable[1].

**111.** In the fourth place, objections may be raised which depend on the adoption of the conception of the Thing-in-itself, in the Hegelian sense of the term. It is held that the substance has an individuality apart and distinct from its nature, and that therefore a substance could have been the same substance even if it had had a different nature.

This, it will be seen, is closely analogous to an objection to our doctrine of the dissimilarity of the diverse, which we have discussed earlier[2]. There it was argued that the individuality of

---

[1] Cp. Section 139.  [2] Section 95.

two substances would permit them to be different substances, though each had the same nature. Here it is argued that the individuality of a substance would allow it to be the same substance, even if it had had a different nature.

And, if it could be the same substance, then the removal of the quality $Z$ would not involve that $A$ should cease to be $A$. And consequently the removal of $Z$ would have no effect on the presence of $X$ or $Y$, unless they are *intrinsically* determined by $Z$. Otherwise, since our hypothesis has not removed them, they will remain qualities of $A$. Our only ground for supposing that there was no reason that they should remain if $Z$ were removed, was that the removal of $Z$ involved the removal of $A$. And this, it is said, we have now seen not to be the case.

**112.** Our answer to this argument will run on the same lines as our answer to the argument against the dissimilarity of the diverse. When we try to explain what we mean by this distinct aspect of the substance—indeed, when we assert that it exists—we can only do so by asserting qualities of the substance. And these qualities are part of the nature of the substance, not something apart and distinct from that nature. It is therefore impossible to distinguish the substance from its qualities in such a way that the substance would be the same if its nature had been different.

We saw, when we considered the previous argument, that an attempt was made to support it by the fact that such a judgment as "this is near that" may have a definite meaning. Such a judgment certainly does not gain a definite meaning by its terms being so precisely described that each description could apply only to one thing in the universe. Indeed "this" and "that" are each applicable to every object in the universe. And yet there is no ambiguity for me in such a judgment, if I am perceiving the substances which I designate as "this" and "that," or if I have perceived them and now remember them. Hence it is argued that there must be in each substance an individuality which is independent of its qualities, and which is revealed to us when we perceive the substance—though, of course, it would be equally there whether the substance were perceived or not.

But, as we saw before, this argument is invalid. No doubt I can have unambiguous knowledge of *A*—knowledge which enables me to identify it—either by perception or by description. And in the first case I shall have unambiguous knowledge of *A* which is not dependent on my knowledge of *A*'s qualities, just as in the second case I shall have unambiguous knowledge of *A* which is not dependent on my acquaintance with *A*. But the fact that I can know the substance independently of its qualities does not prove that its identity is independent of its qualities, so that it could be the same substance if its qualities were different.

The view that the individuality of the substance must be independent of any quality, which is such that the substance can be unambiguously known without knowing the quality, leads, as we have seen, to an absurdity. For the qualities, without knowing which I can unambiguously know a substance by perception, include the quality "having an individuality independent of any quality." Therefore, if this view were true, the substance would have an individuality independent of any quality which would, among others, be independent of its possession of the quality "having an individuality independent of any quality." And this is absurd.

To avoid this, it might be admitted that the substance would not have such an independent individuality unless it possessed the qualities which are involved in this—substantiality, the possession of an individuality independent of any quality, and the consequent possibility of being the same substance, even if its qualities had been different. But it might still be maintained that it has an individuality which, while dependent on some of its qualities, is not entirely dependent on its qualities, and that this individuality might be the same if the qualities of the substance had been different. But this admission destroys the force of the argument, as it did in Section 95. For I can perceive a substance without knowing that it has substantiality, or possesses individuality independent of any quality, or has the possibility of being the same substance with different qualities. And if, nevertheless, its individuality is not independent of those qualities, we cannot argue that its individuality is independent of any other qualities merely on the ground that I can perceive the substance without knowing those other qualities.

**113.** We are thus, I submit, entitled to accept the validity of extrinsic determination. And, in accepting it, we have not merely decided that, if any characteristic of a substance should be altered, its nature will be altered, and that this nature, therefore, would belong to another substance, and not to the first. There is also the further result that all the other characteristics are only given, in the original case, as characteristics of the first substance; and since that substance, if the new hypothesis is true, does not exist, there is no reason to suppose that those other characteristics would remain. The new substance, which the new hypothesis supposes, might have these characteristics, but there is no reason to suppose that it will. $B$ is a different substance from $A$. We know of $B$, by the hypothesis, that it has not the quality $Z$. But as to any other quality $Y$, we know no more than the abstract possibility that it *may* have it—unless the absence of $Z$ intrinsically determines the absence of $Y$—and that it may not have it—unless the absence of $Z$ intrinsically determines the presence of $Y$.

This result makes by itself but little difference to our view of the reality round us, since it still involves the consideration of the substance apart from all others, and thus still remains more abstract than our ordinary *primâ facie* view. But the conclusion we have reached here will have considerable significance when we come to the consideration of all substances taken together.

# CHAPTER XIII

## MANIFESTATION

**114.** We now pass to a different view of the relation which exists between the characteristics of a substance. We have seen that the characteristics of each substance are mutually dependent—a dependence which is due to the fact that a substance is a real unity, and that its nature, which is made up of all its qualities, including those derived from relations, is also a real unity.

But we have so far regarded the unity of this nature as what may be called a Compound Unity—a unity which is constituted by its differentiations. (The qualities of a substance, though, according to our definition of differentiation, they are not differentiations of the substance, are differentiations of the *nature* of the substance.) Put together the qualities $X$, $Y$, $Z$, and the rest, and they form the nature of $A$. That nature is a real unity, and so the qualities of $A$ are not indifferent to each other, but mutually dependent. But the most appropriate expression of this sort of interdependence is negative. The qualities are so connected that, if one is supposed to be withdrawn, the other cannot be taken as remaining.

But the relation between the nature of the substance as a whole and the particular qualities can be expressed just as well in another manner which is complementary to this. In all such relations, the individual substance to which the quality belongs is as essential as the particular quality which belongs to it, and the nature of that substance is as much a unity as it is a plurality. It is as legitimate, therefore, to take as our starting point that nature as a unity, as it is to take as our starting point the plurality of qualities. We can say just as correctly that the unity of the nature of $A$ is differentiated into the qualities $X$, $Y$, and $Z$ (taking these to represent the whole number of the qualities) as we can say that the qualities $X$, $Y$, and $Z$ are united into the nature of $A$.

I propose to express this by saying that the nature of the substance is manifested in the qualities of the substance, and that the nature of the substance is not only a Unity of Composition, but also a Unity of Manifestation. By Manifestation I mean nothing more than the relation between a whole and its parts, when the emphasis is placed on the unity of the whole rather than the plurality of the parts, so that the parts are regarded as due to the differentiation of the whole rather than the whole as due to the union of the parts. Manifestation is often used to mean, not only this, but also more than this, but I shall endeavour to show later, in discussing Organic Unity, that the increased significance thus attributed to it has no place in the general nature of existence, and for this reason I think it best to use the term to denote the simpler conception which does form a part of the general nature of existence.

Manifestation is a relation of a whole and its parts. We must say, therefore, that the qualities are a manifestation of the nature of the substance, and not of the substance itself. We shall see when we have reached the conception of organic unity that the substance itself is manifested in the substances which are its parts.

**115**. It must be noticed that the recognition of the qualities as manifestations of the nature of the substance does not displace our previous view that the nature of the substance is compounded of the qualities. It is no more true that the nature of the substance is a unity of manifestation than that it is a unity of composition. Our advance consists, not in passing from one to the other, but in passing from a position in which only one is recognized as valid to a position where both are recognized. This is true with regard to all the conceptions which we reach in the course of our enquiry, and not only of those two. But it is desirable to emphasize it here because it has so often been maintained that unity of manifestation gives a truer view of existence than unity of composition. (As this is chiefly maintained with regard to the manifestation of a substance in its

F

parts, it will be well to postpone considering it till we come to consider organic unity.)

**116**. It must also be noticed that any attempt to state the nature which is manifested in the qualities $X$, $Y$, and $Z$ (which we are taking as a complete list) can only consist in stating that it is a nature which has as parts of its manifestation one or more of those very qualities $X$, $Y$, and $Z$. We can, indeed, say of it that it is the complete nature of a substance, and that it is a unity of qualities. But this would not distinguish the nature of one substance from the nature of another. And if we were to try to distinguish it by saying that it is the nature of the substance $A$, we do not distinguish it unless we so describe $A$ as to distinguish it from all other substances. But this can only be done by ascribing to it one or more qualities and thus we should come round once more to describing the nature of $A$ by means of the qualities in which that nature is manifested.

Thus we must not look to the nature as a unity with the hope of explaining the qualities which manifest it. The manifestation is only one way of stating the fact that these are the qualities of $A$.

This looks at first sight as if the two ways of stating the relation of the nature of a substance to its component qualities were not, after all. equally valid. If we only know the unity by knowing the plurality of qualities, while we know each of the qualities without knowing the unity, does not this make the qualities more fundamental than the unity? And in that case is it not more expressive of their true relation to regard the unity as compounded of the qualities than to regard it as manifesting itself in the qualities?

But this is erroneous. The unity is as essential as the plurality. Qualities can only occur as qualities of something, and the substance is as essential to its qualities as they are to it. The substance would not be what it is without these qualities, but, on the other hand, this particular occurrence of the quality would not take place unless it were a quality of this substance. And as the unity which binds the qualities in one nature is due to their being qualities of one substance, the unity of the nature is as essential as the plurality of qualities.

The conception of manifestation, though valid, is not by itself of particular fertility. It does not change our view of the universe very much. But it is an essential step to the conception of organic unity, the use of which, as we shall see, does make a considerable difference to our view of the universe.

This concludes our treatment of individual substances. In the next Book we shall pass to the relations in which various substances stand to one another.

# BOOK III

## GROUPS

# CHAPTER XIV

## SIMILARITY OF SUBSTANCES

**117**. We must now proceed to a further consideration of the relations which substances bear to one another. In the last Book we learned that there was a plurality of substances, that they stood in relations to one another, that every substance was dissimilar from every other substance, and that every substance could (ideally, though not always for human knowledge) be so described in general terms that the description would be inapplicable to any other substance. What other relations can we determine as holding between them?

All substances are dissimilar. No two can have the same nature. But the nature of any substance can be analyzed into many qualities. Now there is nothing to prevent the nature of $A$ being partially identical with the nature of $B$, so that they have some qualities in common. In this case $A$ and $B$ themselves will be similar as well as dissimilar. And we can see, not only that this is possible, but that it is actual. For the qualities, for example, of substantiality, existence, and the possession of qualities, are qualities which belong to more substances than one. And, if there are more than two substances, as we shall see later that there are, the quality of dissimilarity to $A$ will be common to at least two substances, since it belongs to every substance but $A$.

**118**. A quality, then, may be common to several substances, and we know that some of them are. But the plurality of the substances connected with a quality is not completely analogous to the plurality of qualities connected with a substance. For we know that every substance has a plurality of qualities—and, indeed, an infinite number of qualities. It is true that all those qualities, which constitute the nature of the substance may also be taken as a single quality, but then that quality is a compound quality which contains an infinite number of parts.

On the other hand, while we know that some qualities do belong to more than one substance, we do not know that this is the case with all qualities. There are, to begin with, qualities which do not belong to any substance—such as that of being President of the Commonwealth of England in 1919. Then, as we have just said, the nature of each substance is one single quality, and we know that it can belong to no other substance. But even with qualities which, unlike these last, are either simple or only finitely compound or complex, we do not know of each of them that it applies to more than one substance, even if it does apply to one.

And, further, in the case of some such qualities we know that they cannot apply to more than one substance. We do not, I think, know this of any simple qualities. But it might nevertheless be true of them. I do not see that we can be certain that there is no simple quality which applies to one substance, and to one substance only.

And, in the case of finitely compound and complex qualities, we do know of many which could not apply to more than one substance. We shall see in Chapter XVIII that the quality of being a universe is one which, though not simple, is not infinitely compound or complex; and we shall also see that it does apply to one existent substance. and that it cannot apply to more than one. Again "the most virtuous of all dogs" is a quality which is not infinitely compound or complex, and which obviously cannot apply to more than one substance, though. it might apply to none, if dogs should not be susceptible of virtue, or if two equally virtuous dogs should excel all others in that quality.

**119**. Some substances, then, are similar to some others. And the same considerations which have proved this will also prove that every substance is similar to every other substance. For the qualities of substantiality, existence, and the possession of qualities are common to all substances, and this is sufficient to prove that every substance is similar to every other substance.

And we can also see that there are qualities which are common to two substances, but not to all. Such (if there are more than two substances) is "dissimilar to $A$," where $A$ is an existent substance[1]. What can we say about such similarities, which are confined to some substances only? This question leads us to the consideration of Groups.

[1] This quality can be expressed entirely in general terms by substituting for "$A$" the equivalent phrase "a substance with the qualities $X$, $Y$, and $Z$," where $X$, $Y$, and $Z$ form a sufficient description of $A$.

# CHAPTER XV

## GROUPS

**120.** By a Group I mean any collection formed of substances, or of collections of substances, or of both. The substances or collections which form the collection are called Members of the Group.

A group must be distinguished from a Class. A class is determined by a class-concept. This concept consists of one or more qualities, and everything which possesses these qualities is a member of that class. Thus the quality "to be a member of the class $P$," can be defined, the definition being "to possess the qualities $X$, $Y$, and $Z$." And by means of this definition we can determine whether any particular thing is a member of the class. But the members of a group are determined by denotation. $L$ is the group which consists of $A$, $B$, and $C$. Thus we cannot determine by a definition what are the members of a particular group. It is true that the quality of being a member of $L$ may be defined as the quality of possessing either the qualities $RST$, or the qualities $UVW$, or the qualities $XYZ$, where these qualities form sufficient descriptions of $A$, $B$, and $C$ respectively. But we cannot know this definition until we know what the members of the group are, and therefore we cannot determine what they are by means of this definition[1].

The fact that a group is not determined by a definition may be easily overlooked. For, as we shall see, for every group there are certain qualities which belong to every member of the group, and to nothing outside it. And it might be supposed that these qualities defined the quality "to be a member of the group." But this would be a mistake. The substances do not belong to the group because they have qualities in common,

---

[1] Another distinction is that a group, by our definition, must consist either of substances or of collections of substances, while there can be classes, not only of substances and collections of substances, but also of qualities and relations.

but because this particular group is the group which consists of those particular substances. And, indeed, we shall see that the only qualities of which we are sure that they are found in every member of the group, and in nothing outside the group, are qualities which depend on the inclusion of particular substances in the group, and could not therefore be used to determine what substances are included in it.

**121**. The difference between groups and classes produces several important consequences. It has been maintained, in the first place, that it is possible that a class should contain no members—that, for example, the Presidents of the Commonwealth of England in 1919 are a class. And, in the same way, it has been maintained that it is possible that a class should contain only one member—that, for example, the sovereigns of the United Kingdom in 1919 are a class. But a group is only determined by the members it contains, and it is therefore impossible that it should be without members. And, since a group has been defined as a collection of members, it must have more than one.

Secondly, certain criticisms have been made of the conception of classes, on the ground of the difficulties which arise about classes which are members of themselves. No such criticisms can apply to the conception of groups, since it is clear that no group can be a member of itself. A group $L$ is constituted of $A$, $B$, and $C$. Whatever $A$, $B$, and $C$ may be, it is clear that none of them can be $L$, for $L$ is all three of them. It is true, as we have seen, that a group may be constituted of members of which one or more are groups. $C$, for example, may be itself a group. But it cannot be the group $L$, for then $C$ would be identical with the group of itself with $A$ and $B$, which is impossible. And, again, $L$ may be grouped with $A$, $B$, and $C$. But this group, $M$, with its four members, will not be the same group as $L$, which is part of it.

Thirdly, the content of two different classes may be co-extensive. Cambridge colleges in which, in the year 1919, the Headship is not in the gift of the Fellows are a class. Cambridge colleges founded between the years 1515 and 1550 are another class. Each class contains only the same two members—

Magdalene College and Trinity College. But the classes are different[1]. The two colleges, on the other hand, form only one group, for there can be only one group with one set of members.

It is obvious that, whenever a class has more than one member, its members form a group—though, as has just been said, it may be the same group in the case of many different classes. The question whether the members of every group form at least one class will be discussed in Chapter xvii.

The members of a group may be so linked together as to be the members of some system of relations. And they may be linked so as to be members of more than one such system. *A* and *B* may be husband and wife, and *C* and *D* their son and daughter. And, on a particular day, *A* and *C* may be partners at whist against *B* and *D*. Here then are two separate systems of relations, each of which unites each of the four to the other three. But, however many such systems of relations hold between them, they form only one group.

**122.** It is to be noticed that, according to our definition, *any* combination of substances or groups is a group. Groups vary much, no doubt, in their importance to us, and in the utility of contemplating them. The group of the people of England, for example, or of the Presidents of the United States, or of all elephants, are much more important, and much more useful to contemplate, than the group formed of the table at which I am writing, the oldest rabbit now in Australia, and the last medicine taken by Lewis XV. And yet the latter is just as truly a group. All three members of it are substances[2]. They can be taken as some sort of unity—this is proved by the fact that it is true that there are three of them, for if they were not united together and separated from all other things they would not be three. It is not each of them which is three, but all together, and

---

[1] Mr Russell would treat these two classes as the same class. ("We wish classes to be such that no two distinct classes have exactly the same members." *Introduction to Mathematical Philosophy*, p. 184.) Since Mr Russell adopts this usage in dealing with mathematics, it is doubtless the best for his purpose. But I do not think it is the common usage, and it seems to me not to be convenient for philosophy.

[2] *I.e.* they are substances if they exist, and, *primâ facie*, they do exist. It is possible that we may hereafter reach the conclusion that one or more of them do not exist.

therefore that they are three proves that they are united. And
if they were not separated from all other things, the number
would not be only three. (If, for example, they were not
separated from Westminster Abbey, the number would not be
less than four.) And so they are a group.

There would, I think, be a tendency to admit that these
three substances could be *taken* as a group by any observer who
was led to contemplate them together, but to deny that, apart
from such observation, it was a group. Such a group as the
people of England might be admitted to exist objectively. But
of a fantastic group, such as that given above, it might be said
that it did not exist independently, as the substances which
compose it do, but only if and when observed.

This, however, is mistaken. The fact that the table, the
rabbit, and the medicine are three substances is not dependent
on their being observed as three. If no one ever thought of
them together, no one would ever know that they were three
substances, but they would be three substances all the same.
And, as we have seen, the fact that they are three proves that
they are a group.

I have spoken above of the groups of the people of England,
of all elephants, and so on. But "the people of England" and
"all elephants" are names of classes, not of groups. Their content can be determined by definition. The accurate expression
of what I meant would have been, for example, "that group
which has as members all those substances, and only those,
which fall within the class of elephants." But this expression
would have been inconveniently long. And even this might
have been mistaken for an attempt at a definition, though it is
really a description of the group, based upon its denotation.

**123**. We must distinguish between the members of a group
and the parts of a group. If we take the group of all the counties
in Great Britain, neither England nor Whitechapel are members
of the group, but they are parts, of which the group is the whole[1].
All members of a group are also parts of it. And, in addition to
these, there are also parts which are either parts of members,

---

[1] The relation of Whole and Part appears to me to be ultimate and indefinable.

such as Whitechapel, or groups of members, such as England[1].
And there are also parts which overlap different members, such
as the diocese of Ely.

The relation of part to whole is, of course, transitive. If $A$
is a part of $B$, and $B$ a part of $C$, then $A$ is a part of $C$. But
the relation of member to group is not transitive. If $L$ is a
member of the group $M$, and is itself a group of which $A$ is
a member, then $A$ is not a member of $M$, though it is a part
of $M$.

**124.** It is common to say that a whole consists of all its
parts. But this is not strictly accurate. Great Britain, for
example, consists of England, Scotland, and Wales. And it
does not consist of anything except England, Scotland, and
Wales. But these are not all the parts of Great Britain, for
Surrey is also a part of it.

We require a further conception—the conception of what I
propose to call a Set of Parts. A Set of Parts of any whole is
any collection of its parts which together make up the whole,
and do not more than make it up, so that the whole would not
be made up if any of those parts, or of their parts, should be
subtracted[2]. Thus England, Scotland, and Wales are a set of
parts of Great Britain. So are all the counties in Great Britain.
And so are England, Scotland, and the counties within Wales.
But Scotland and Wales are not a set of parts of Great Britain,
for they do not make up the whole. Nor are England, Scotland,
Wales, and Surrey, for the whole would still be made up if
Surrey were subtracted. Nor are England, Wales, and the district north of York, since the whole would still be made up if
that part of the district north of York which lies south of the
border were subtracted. One whole can thus have many sets
of parts, and every whole will have more than one set of parts,

---

[1] Such a group of members may be conveniently termed a Sub-group of the
original group.

[2] Cp. Dr Whitehead's definition of the composition of a sense-object. (*The
Organisation of Thought*, p. 159. "Call two sense-objects 'separated' if there is
no third sense-object which is a part of both of them. Then an object $A$ is composed of the two objects $B$ and $C$, if (1) $B$ and $C$ are both parts of $A$, (2) $B$ and
$C$ are separated, and (3) there is no part of $A$ which is separated both from $B$
and from $C$.")

with the exception of those wholes which consist of two simple and indivisible parts[1].

The relation between a whole and its set of parts is transitive. If England, Scotland, and Wales are a set of parts of Great Britain, and if one collection of counties is a set of parts of England, a second is a set of parts of Scotland, and a third of Wales, then the three aggregates taken together will be a set of parts of Great Britain.

The members of a group are a set of parts of that group. For when they are taken together, they make up the group, and if any of them, or any of their parts, were subtracted, the group would not be made up.

**125.** A group has, besides members and parts, something which I propose to call Content. By Content I mean that plurality which is identical in the different sets of parts of a group. England, Scotland, and Wales are one set of parts of Great Britain, the counties are another, the parishes and extra-parochial places are another. Not only are they separate sets of parts, but, in the case of these three sets, no part which is to be found in one set is to be found in either of the others. And yet we realize that there is a certain identity between them so that in taking the set of counties and the set of parishes we are not taking two realities, but the same reality over again. It is this that I mean by Content[2].

Two groups can have the same content. For the group whose members are the counties of Great Britain, and the group whose members are the parishes and extra-parochial places of Great Britain, are different groups, since they have not the same members. Two groups will have the same content if there is no part of the one which is not also a part of the other. And we shall see in the next Chapter[3] that in certain cases they

---

[1] Thus a compound idea which consisted of two simple ideas would only have one set of parts. But, as we shall see in Chapter XXII, there are no simple and indivisible substances. Every group, therefore, will have more than one set of parts, and, indeed, will have an infinite number of such sets.

[2] If a group consisted of two simple and indivisible members, it would have only one set of parts, and its content would not be distinguishable from that set. But, as was said in the last note, we shall see that there are no simple substances, so that this case is impossible for substances.

[3] Section 128.

may have the same content even if there is a part of the one which is not a part of the other. They will have completely different contents if there is no part of the one which is a part of the other. In all other cases they will have partially identical contents.

**126.** Can a group be formed of two members, one of which is a part of the other? It seems clear that it can. It is true that, since all the content is taken in that substance which is the whole, we add no additional content if we repeat part of it a second time. But in spite of the partial identity of content, there are distinct groups. The Kitchen Committee of the House of Commons is a group which is a part of the group of members of the House of Commons, since no one is in the Committee who is not also in the House. But they are distinct groups, which have different qualities. The members of the House group form a body which can vote taxes, which is not the case with the members of the Committee group. The members of the Committee group form a body elected by the House, which is not the case with the members of the House group. And, since they are distinct groups, there is a further group of which they are the members.

We may call such groups Repeating Groups, since they repeat part of the content. The number of such groups is infinite. For we saw in Chapter VII that there cannot be less than two substances. And if there are two substances, $A$ and $B$, there will be a group $L$, of which $A$ and $B$ are the members. And then there will be another group $M$, of which the members are $A$, $B$, and $L$, and so on endlessly.

As we pursue this infinite series, the groups soon become, in most cases, of very little practical importance. There may be some utility in contemplating the group which consists of the House of Commons and the Kitchen Committee, for, as the only two bodies having authority over certain matters, it may often be worth while to contemplate them together. But the group which has this group and the Kitchen Committee as its members could be of no practical importance. And the groups further on in the series would be, if it were possible, even less important. But things which are unimportant are none the less real.

A repeating group will have some sets of parts, each of which will contain the same part more than once. If the group $L$ has $A$ and $B$ as its members, and the group $M$ has $L$ and $A$ as its members, then $A$ and $B$ will be a set of parts of $L$, and $L$ and $A$ will be a set of parts of $M$. Since the relation between a whole and a set of its parts is transitive, $M$ will have a set of parts consisting of $A$, $B$, and $A$. These together make up $M$, and do not more than make it up, for if either $B$ or either of the two occurrences of $A$ was withdrawn, $M$ would not be made up. It is only in a repeating group that one part can occur more than once in the same set.

# CHAPTER XVI

## COMPOUND SUBSTANCES

**127.** Every group has qualities and stands in relations. We saw, in Chapter XIV, that there are certain qualities which all groups have in common. And it is obvious that some groups, at any rate, have qualities and stand in relations peculiar to themselves. The group whose members are all the Frenchmen living in 1919 has the qualities of being a nation, of being a republic, and so on. And it stands in certain relationships of similarity and dissimilarity, and in certain causal relations, to the group whose members are all the Frenchmen living in 1899. Since a group has qualities and stands in relations, and is not itself a quality or a relation, it is a substance.

Substances are parts of groups. Some substances, therefore, have substances for their parts. We may call a substance which has substances for its parts a Compound Substance. Our present position, then, is that some substances at least are compound. We shall see reason later to hold that all substances are compound.

**128.** Every group, then, is a substance, but is every different group a different substance? The group of the counties of Great Britain and the group of the parishes of Great Britain are different groups. But, as we have seen, they have the same content. Shall we say that they are different substances because they are different groups, or the same substance because they have the same content?

It seems clear to me that we ought to say that they are the same substance. There is only one difference between them—of two sets of parts, which they both have, one set is the set of members of one group, and the other is the set of members of the other group. This difference only applies to their nature as groups, and does not go beyond it; and, while it certainly prevents their being one group, does not affect the question whether they are one substance. On the other hand, the identity of the substance does seem to be bound up with the identity of content.

Nor is there any difficulty in one substance being several groups. "To be the group whose members are $X$ and $Y$" is a quality. "To be the group whose members are $T$, $U$, $V$, and $W$" is another quality. Every substance has many qualities, and there is no reason why it should not have both these, if the content of $X$ and $Y$ is identical with the content cf $T$, $U$, $V$, and $W$.

A compound substance, then, will be as many groups as it has sets of parts, since each of its sets of parts will be the set of members of a group. It will not have any set of parts of which it can be said that it is the set of members of the substance. For one set of parts can only be distinguished from the other sets, as being the set of members, by reference to a particular group. And a substance is not more specially any one of these groups than it is any of the others.

And, further, every compound substance is also an infinite number of repeating groups. For a compound substance has two or more substances as its parts. And, as we saw in the last Chapter[1], any group of two or more substances generates an infinite series of repeating groups. And, as all these repeating groups have the same content as the non-repeating group which generates them, they will be all identical with the same compound substance.

It was mentioned in the last Chapter[2] that in certain cases two groups will have the same content, although there is a part of the one which is not a part of the other. If, for example, $L$ has $A$ and $B$ as members, $M$ has $L$ and $A$ as members, and $N$ has $M$ and $A$, then $L$ and $N$ have the same content, but $N$ has a part $M$ which is not a part of $L$. We get a general formula for identity of content, if we say that two groups have the same content, if a set of parts can be found of each, such that there is no part in the one set which is not also a part in the other set. $N$, for example, has, as a set of parts, $A$, $B$, $A$, $A$, and $L$ has, as a set of parts, $A$, $B$. And there is no part in either of these sets which is not also a part in the other.

[1] Section 126.          [2] Section 125.

A compound substance, then, is identical with an infinite number of repeating groups, in each of which there are sets of parts which contain the same part more than once. We must not, however, say that the compound substance has sets of parts, each of which contain the same part more than once. $A$, $B$, $A$, $A$, for-example, is a set of parts of $N$, because, if any of the four parts were withdrawn, $N$ would not be made up. But that is because $N$ is a repeating group. If two of the occurrences of $A$ were withdrawn, no content would be withdrawn. And, since it is identity of content which makes the substance, the substance would be fully made up. The substance has, as its sets of parts, all sets of parts of non-repeating groups with which it is identical, but not the sets of parts of repeating groups.

A compound substance will have other substances which are its parts, and fall entirely within it—as in the case of the House of Commons and the Kitchen Committee. But there will be other substances again which fall partially within it, having a part in common with it, and a part which falls outside it. The House of Commons and the Privy Council, for example, overlap in this manner.

**129.** Any two or more substances, which do not contain, in whole or in part, the same content, form a compound substance. The number of compound substances is therefore infinite, except on one hypothesis. If a finite number of simple substances formed a set of parts of the universe, then the number of compound substances would be finite. In any other case it would be infinite. And we shall see later that the universe does not consist of a finite number of simple substances, so that the number of compound substances will be, in fact, infinite.

The conclusion that any two or more substances of different content form another substance will seem in many cases paradoxical. In other cases it will seem natural enough. To say that the group of French citizens at the present time is a substance has nothing surprising in it. For the group of French citizens at the present time is the French nation at the present time. And a nation is a unity so close and so important that it would generally be admitted that there is nothing strange in calling it a substance. But when we come to such a group as that mentioned earlier, which consists of a table now in Cambridge, a rabbit now in Australia, and a dose of medicine in France in the eighteenth century, then, it might be said, the unity is so slight that it is preposterous to call such a group a substance.

The answer to this objection is that our definition of substance said nothing about the closeness or the importance of the unity. A substance was defined as that which had qualities, and stood in relations, without being itself a quality or a relation. And since the most fantastic group answers to this definition, it must be called a substance.

Nor would it be a fair objection to our definition of substance that it leads to paradoxical results. For the word substance is applied so inconsistently in ordinary discourse that any definition, if adhered to consistently, would lead to results so strange as to appear paradoxical. And besides, if we were to reserve the name of substance for a unity which was close or important, it could not have been used till much later in the system. For we are not, as yet, in a position to determine what would be meant by a close unity. And it will not be till a still later point that it will be possible to determine what is really important. To define substance by means of a conception which can only be reached late in a system would be at least as great a departure from common usage as anything produced by the course we have taken. Moreover, we have had much to say, and shall have still more to say, of that which has qualities and stands in relations without being a quality or a relation. We must have some name for it. And, if we refuse it the name of substance, it is not easy to find it another.

**130**. Again, our use of the name may be regarded as inappropriate in some cases, not, as to those just discussed, on account of the intrinsic unimportance of the particular group in question, as from its unimportance as compared with its own members. It may be said, for example, that it is unreasonable to give the name of substance both to a bridge-party, and to the men who make up the party. The bridge-party is not a fantastic group, like that composed of the table, the rabbit, and the medicine. Its members must have various qualities in common, and the relations between them must be direct and obvious. But the men are so much more important, they are so much more persistent (even if it is held that they are not immortal), and they are so much less dependent on the bridge-party than the bridge-party is on them, that it might be held to be inappropriate to call both the ,men and the bridge-party substances.

The answer to this objection is the same as to the last. The definition of substance which we have adopted says nothing about importance, persistence, or independence, and the bridge-party complies with it as much as the men do.

Or again, the objection may be made, not that the compound substance is too unimportant, as compared with its parts, to be a substance, but that it is too important, as compared with its parts, to be taken as compounded of them. If a man, for example, is regarded as standing to his successive states in time as a whole to its parts, and if all the content of the man falls in time, he must be considered, not only as a substance, but as a substance compounded of his states in time, which must also be considered as substances. And it may be said that this is unreasonable. For, even on the assumption that the whole content of the man falls in time, there is much in the nature of the man which is not to be found in any of his states. How then can he be compounded of the states?

The answer here is that a substance which is made up of substances, and is therefore a group, must have many qualities which are not found in any of its parts (among others, the quality of being the whole, of which they are parts) and that among these qualities may be some of the greatest importance. For example, France is made up of individual Frenchmen. There is no content in the substance France which does not fall within this, that, or the other Frenchman. Yet France is a nation, and a republic, and no Frenchman is either. And, in the same way, there might be no content in John Smith which did not fall within this, that, or the other of his states in time, and yet he would have many qualities which were not qualities of any of those states, and it might well be that among them were those of his qualities which were of most importance both to himself and to his friends.

# CHAPTER XVII

## EXCLUSIVE COMMON QUALITIES IN GROUPS

**131**. We have seen that in certain groups there are qualities which are common to all their members. We may call them Common Qualities in the group. (A common quality *in* a group, which is a quality of each of the members, must be distinguished from a quality *of* the group. In many cases a quality which is common in the group is not a quality of the group itself. For example, when "to be an elephant" is a common quality in a group, it is not a quality of that group, since a group of elephants is never an elephant.)

Are there common qualities in every group? (Among common qualities are included, of course, the common derivative qualities which will arise if each member of the group stands in the same relation to anything.) It is clear that there are common qualities in every group, since there are some qualities—such as existence, substantiality, and the possession of qualities—which are possessed by all members of any group, and are therefore common in any group.

But there is a further question. We see that in some groups there are common qualities which are not shared by anything except the members of that group. Such, for example, is "to be an elephant" in the group which contains all elephants as members and which has no member which is not an elephant. We may call them Exclusive Common Qualities. Has every group one or more Exclusive Common Qualities?

**132**. Here, too, the answer must be in the affirmative. In the first place, if any group, *L*, has as members *A*, *B*, and *C*, it will be an exclusive common quality in the group that each member is a member of the group whose members are *A*, *B*, and *C*. This is, indeed, scarcely more than a tautology, but it does give an exclusive common quality.

And, again, there is at least one substance which is not a member of $L^1$. Now of any one of those substances, $D$, it will be true that all the members of the group will be diverse from it. And, being diverse from it, they must, as we have seen, be dissimilar to it. Thus every member of the group has the quality "diverse from and dissimilar to $D$," which is therefore a common quality in $L$, and which is not possessed by $D$.

If, however, outside the group $L$ there is also another substance, $E$, then "diverse from and dissimilar to $D$" will not be an *exclusive* common quality in $L$, since it will be shared by $E$, which is not a member of $L$. But an exclusive common quality of this sort can always be found. There are certain substances which are not members of $L$. Let us take $D$, $E$, and $F$, as representing a complete list of these. Then the compound quality "diverse from and dissimilar to $D$, $E$, and $F$" belongs to each member of $L$, and so is a common quality in $L$. And it is also an exclusive common quality in $L$, since it cannot belong to anything which is not a member of $L$. For anything which is not a member of $L$ must be either $D$, $E$, or $F$, and cannot, therefore, be diverse from all three of them.

Such an exclusive common quality as this, however, while it would exist could never be known by our present powers of knowledge. In order to know it, we should have to be able to give an exclusive description of every substance which was not a member of $L$. And, further, in order to know that the quality in question *was* an exclusive quality in $L$, we should have to know that we had included everything which was not a member of $L$—not only would our knowledge have to be exhaustive, but we should have to know that it was exhaustive. This is obviously far more knowledge than we can acquire. Indeed, though not omniscience, it would have to be infinite knowledge, if, as we shall find reason to believe later on, the number of existent substances is infinite. The fact, however, that every group has such an exclusive common quality is not necessarily

---

[1] A group which did not contain all existent content would clearly have a substance outside it, which was not one of its members. And one which did contain all existent content, would still have one substance which was not one of its members—namely itself. For a group is never one of its own members.

unimportant, even if in some cases we can never know what that quality is.

**133**. But some groups, at any rate, have exclusive common qualities which can be known by such powers of knowledge as we possess. We saw above that the Colleges of Magdalene and Trinity in Cambridge are the only members of two classes. And, consequently, in the group of which they are the members, there are two exclusive qualities, namely, "to be a Cambridge College in which, in the year 1919, the Headship is not in the gift of the Fellows," and "to be a Cambridge College founded between 1515 and 1550."

Thus the common qualities in groups are divided into two classes. The first includes those which can be defined (or, being simple, can be known without definition) without the introduction of exclusive descriptions of all the substances which are members of the group, or else of all the substances which are not members of the group. The second includes those which do require the introduction of some such descriptions. We know that in all groups there are exclusive common qualities of the second class. We know that in some groups there are exclusive common qualities of the first class. But we have not proved, and we have no reason to believe, that an exclusive common quality of the first class is found in every group[1].

It is evident that, although we can never know an *exclusive* common quality which is defined by descriptions of the substances excluded from the group, yet we can always find, in the case of any group, *some* common quality of that type. Thus the group which consists of Napoleon and the Great Pyramid has the quality common to both its members of being diverse from the Albert Memorial. But this is not an exclusive common quality in the group, since it is shared by Mount Everest.

**134**. Not every group in which there is an exclusive common quality of the first class has any importance for us, or can be usefully contemplated by us. But, on the other hand, it is safe to say that no group has any importance for us, or is worth

---

[1] We shall see reason, however, in Chapter xxviii, to believe that every substance belongs to at least one group in which there is an exclusive common quality of the first class.

contemplating (except as an example of unimportant groups), if it does *not* possess an exclusive common quality of the first class. In each group the members are joined to each other, and separated from all others. And there can be no importance for me in the fact that this and that substance are joined to one another, except in the possession by them of a common quality (which may, of course, be the quality of having a common relation to something—perhaps to myself). Nor is there any importance for me in the fact that they are separated from all others, except in their possession of a common quality, which no others have. And the quality which makes it important that the group should be marked out cannot be simply the fact that, when it *is* marked out, its members agree in the quality of being members of that group, or in the quality of not being anything which is not a member—that is, it cannot be a quality of the second class.

As the exclusive common qualities of the first class are the only ones which we ever know to be such, and the only ones which give a group any importance for us, it is, as a rule, of these only that we speak. It is therefore important to remember, when we say that in each group there is an exclusive common quality, that this is so far only proved about qualities of the second class.

# CHAPTER XVIII

## THE UNIVERSE

**135**. There can be no group which contains all other groups as its parts. For, as we saw above, every group generates an infinite number of repeating groups, of each of which it is a part, and which cannot therefore be parts of it[1].

But no such considerations render it impossible that there should be a substance of which all others are parts. For in a substance no content is taken more than once, and there is therefore nothing in substance analogous to repeating groups.

And, further, we can see that there *is* a substance of which all others are parts. We have seen that any two or more substances, which do not contain, in whole or in part, the same content, will form a compound substance. There is therefore a compound substance which contains all existent content. For any content which is not in any given substance, *A*, must be in some substance or substances outside *A*, and by adding these to *A*, we shall have a substance, *U*, which contains all content. For every compound substance other than *U* will contain some but not all of the content of *U*, and will therefore be a part of *U*. And, if there were simple substances, they would all be parts of compound substances, and therefore parts of *U*.

There is therefore a substance which contains all content, and of which every other substance is a part. This substance is to be called the Universe. From a formal point of view it is indifferent whether we take as a definition of Universe that a universe contains all existent content, or that it is a substance of which all other substances are parts, since possession of either of these qualities involves the possession of the other. The definition by content is perhaps the more fundamental, but

---

[1] Cp. Section 126. *A fortiori* there can be no group of which all other groups are members.

the definition by relation to other substances requires less explanation, and is therefore perhaps more suitable for general use.

Our definition is not of course a definition of *the* universe, which is a particular substance, and so does not admit of definition. The definition is of "universe," or, in other words, of the quality of being a universe. But it is clear, not only that there must be a universe, but that there cannot be more than one. If there were two, they would each contain all existent content, that is, they would have the same content. And there cannot be more than one substance with the same content.

Since "universe" can only apply to one substance, its application distinguishes that substance from everything else, and is therefore a sufficient description of it. For this reason we speak of the substance as *the* universe. And we saw[1] that in a set of parts of a substance no content can be taken more than once. If all content could have been finally analyzed into simple substances, those simple substances would have been a set of parts of the universe. In any case, the universe will have as many sets of parts as there are combinations of compound substances, such that each of those combinations contains all the content of the universe, and contains none of it more than once[2].

**136.** The fact that any substance other than the universe has a particular quality is an element in a fact about the universe. If it is a fact that John Smith is English and hates Thomas Brown, then it is a fact about the universe that it possesses the quality of having a part with the qualities of John Smith, and that among those qualities are the qualities of being English and of hating Thomas Brown[3].

It does not follow from this that the only true way, or the

---

[1] Cp. Section 128.

[2] The number of these sets of parts would have been finite if all content could have been finally analyzed into simple substances, and if these were finite in number. Since this is not so, they are infinite in number.

[3] The two facts are not identical, since the first is the possession of a quality by John Smith, and the second is the possession of a quality by the universe. But the first fact may be properly said to be an element in the second, since the quality of the universe is its possession of a part with the quality possessed by John Smith.

simplest or most ultimate way of stating a fact about such a substance is to state it as an element of a fact about the universe. It has sometimes been maintained that no assertion can be absolutely true unless its subject is the universe. Very probably this would never have been maintained if it had not been really the case that a fact about any other substance is an element of a fact about the universe. But the passage from this to the view that an absolutely true assertion can have no subject except the universe rests, as far as I can see, on a confusion between a statement which is not all the truth and a statement which is not absolutely true. If this confusion were not mitigated by inconsistency, it would lead to the conclusion that no assertion can be absolutely true, even if it is about the universe. For no one assertion, whatever its subject, can express all that is true.

And the statement which does not bring in the universe is as true as the other, and more simple and ultimate. It is as true, for, obviously, if it were not true that Smith had the quality of hating Brown, it would not be true that the universe had the quality of containing a Brown-hating Smith. And it is more simple and ultimate, because it does not bring in the universe, but only Smith, while the other statement has to bring in both Smith and the universe.

# CHAPTER XIX

## UNIVERSAL DETERMINATION

**137.** The result reached at the end of the last Chapter has important bearings on the question of extrinsic determination. It will be remembered that extrinsic determination was so called, not because it is the determination of one substance by another, but because it is the determination which holds between two qualities in virtue of the relation in which they stand to the same substance, while intrinsic determination is that which holds between two qualities as such.

At the end of the last Chapter we saw that, if any substance, $A$, other than the universe, has a quality $X$, the universe has the quality of containing a part with the nature of $A$, which has the quality $X$. We may call this quality of the universe $X'$. It is clear that the possession of $X$ by $A$, and the possession of $X'$ by the universe, intrinsically determine one another.

We saw in Chapter XII that all the qualities of any substance are connected with one another by extrinsic determination, so that it is unjustifiable to assert that any of them would remain the same if any others were different from what they are now. And the universe is a substance. It would therefore be unjustifiable to assert that, if $A$ had not the quality $X$, any of the qualities of the universe would remain the same. For if $A$ had not the quality $X$, the universe could not have the quality $X'$, and $X'$ extrinsically determines all the other qualities of the universe.

In the same way, it would be unjustifiable to assert that, if any of the qualities of the universe were not the same, $A$ would still possess $X$. For it could not possess $X$ unless the universe possessed $X'$, and $X'$ is in reciprocal extrinsic determination with all the other qualities of the universe.

Since we have defined a fact as the possession by anything of a quality, or the connection of anything with anything by a relation, we may express the results we have just arrived at by saying that every fact about every other substance extrinsically determines every fact about the universe, and that every fact about the universe extrinsically determines every fact about every other substance.

**138**. And, further, it would be unjustifiable to assert that, if $A$ had not the quality $X$, any quality of any other substance would remain the same. Take, for example, the quality $Y$, possessed by the substance $B$. The possession of this quality by $B$ stands in reciprocal intrinsic determination with the possession by the universe of the quality $Y'$. And, as we have seen, if $A$ had not the quality $X$, it would be unjustifiable to assert that any of the qualities of the universe, including $Y'$, would remain the same. And in that case it would clearly be unjustifiable to assert that $B$ would continue to possess the quality $Y$, since $B$ cannot be $Y$ unless the universe is $Y'$.

The occurrence, then, of any quality of any substance extrinsically determines every other occurrence of a quality of any substance. And if all the qualities of substances are thus determined, then the substances themselves are determined in the same way. For, as we have seen[1], the individuality of a substance is inseparable from the qualities it possesses, and, by determining what qualities occur, and in what combinations, it is also determined what substance possesses them. By determining, in other words, that a substance exists with a certain nature, we determine what substance exists.

Our conclusion is, then, that all that exists, both substances and characteristics, are bound together in one system of extrinsic determination[2].

**139**. We can now return to the consideration of the third objection to the view that extrinsic determination occurs between all the characteristics of a single substance, which was dis-

---

[1] Section 95.

[2] Characteristics include relations as well as qualities. But if all the qualities of a substance are determined, including the qualities of standing in certain relations, then the relations of the substances are determined.

Besides characteristics of substances, there exist also characteristics of existent characteristics. But if the characteristics of substances are determined, their characteristics will be determined also, and also the characteristics of those characteristics, and so on.

cussed in the last Book[1]. The objection was that, if there were
not the present Snowdon, we might have reason to believe that
there would be a mountain, with most of the important qualities
of the actual Snowdon, though without its present height,
because the existence of other substances, in which our hypothesis makes no change, might intrinsically determine the existence of such a mountain.

We can now see that the objection is untenable, because, if
the present Snowdon did not exist, the present universe would
not exist. We should therefore have no right to assume that
there would be any substances which would resemble the substances now intrinsically determining Snowdon to such an extent
that they would intrinsically determine the existence of a
mountain with many, or with any, of the important qualities of
Snowdon.

The supposition that anything should be different from
what it is, therefore, is one which we have no right to make. To
ask what would happen, or what would remain in the universe,
if I had sneezed yesterday once less often than I did sneeze, is
as hopeless and unprofitable as it would be to ask what would
happen, or what would remain in the universe, if twice three
were seven, or if things which were equal to the same thing
were not equal to one another. It is true that in these two
cases there is intrinsic determination—that a group numbers
twice three implies that it does not number seven—but the
question is as futile when the determination is only extrinsic.

This result will appear unduly paradoxical, unless we
remember that it does not deny our right to make the supposition that the same substance may have different characteristics
at different moments of time. All that is denied, in the case of
a substance existing in time, is our right to make the supposition
that, at any moment of time, it should have been different from
what it actually is at that moment[2].

**140**. It would have been possible to arrive at our conclusion
in a different way. Instead of connecting each substance with
each other substance by means of the connection of both with
the universe, we might have proceeded more directly. Every

---

[1] Section 110.                    [2] Cp. Section 110.

existent substance is related to every other existent substance And so, if $A$ should not have existed with exactly the nature $XYZ$, which it actually has, $B$ could not have had the quality which it actually has, of standing in the relation $W$ to something which has the nature $XYZ$. And this quality is connected by extrinsic determination with all the other qualities of $B$. Thus the occurrence of any quality in $A$ extrinsically determines the occurrence of every quality in $B$, and *vice versa*, and this can be extended to all other substances and their characteristics.

This method has the advantage of being more direct than the one which we have employed above, but it seemed better to use the method which lays stress on the connection of all other substances through the universe, because that connection is of such general importance, especially in connection with the conception of organic unity, to which we shall proceed in the next Chapter.

**141.** We have no right, then, to make any supposition about what would happen if anything were different from what it is. Will this introduce any difficulty with regard to general laws? It is very usual to state general laws hypothetically. "If a man's head is cut off, he dies." "If an Australian Archdeacon's head is cut off, he dies." "If anything is a rigid body, not operated on by forces, its centre of gravity will move with uniform velocity in a straight line." With regard to the first of these, there might seem to be no difficulty. Men's heads have been cut off. And so this law might be said to be equivalent to "Whenever a man's head is cut off, he dies." But this will not help us for the other two. For I do not know that any Australian Archdeacon has been or will be beheaded. And I have reason to believe that nothing ever has been or will be a rigid body, not operated on by forces. Thus, if they were to be stated in this hypothetical form, the law about the Archdeacons might turn out to be a statement about what would have happened if things had been different from what they are, and the law about rigid bodies certainly would be such a statement. And such statements are illegitimate. And yet it is impossible to deny that such laws as those about the Archdeacon and the rigid body are true.

But there is really no difficulty. For the proposition expressed in a general law is not primarily a statement about any individual, actual or possible. It is primarily a statement of the relation between two characteristics. The relation in question is, no doubt, of such a nature that, in the case of those general laws which deal with characteristics that occur in existence, we can infer that, in all cases in which the characteristic $X$ occurs, the characteristic $Y$ will occur also. But this is not the essence of the law. That consists in the connection of characteristics. And this connection can exist, even when nothing existent has these characteristics[1].

**142.** The interdependence of all existent characteristics, which we have now proved, is not, of course, equivalent to the determination of all characteristics by general laws. The determination of a characteristic by a general law means that the occurrence of some other characteristic $Y$ intrinsically determines the occurrence of $X$. The assertion that all characteristics are determined by general laws would mean that, for any occurrence of any characteristic $X$, an occurrence can be found of a characteristic $Y$, which is such that $Y$ intrinsically determines $X$[2]. And all that we have proved is that characteristics determine one another extrinsically.

Since we are not considering here a determination which is intrinsic, or which acts by general laws, we are not dealing with causality. We shall consider later what meaning should be given to this term. But the ordinary view of causality certainly includes, among other elements, the presence of general laws. $X$ is not held to be the effect of $Y$ unless it is connected with $Y$ by some general law. And we shall find reason to accept this view as correct. Extrinsic determination, therefore, is not causality.

The result which we have reached, however, seems to be very much the same as the results which Hegel conceived himself to have established in his categories of Causality and Reciprocity. In those categories he reaches the conclusion that

---

[1] It has been seen in Chapter II that this is not incompatible with the view that nothing is real except the existent.

[2] Cp. Section 217.

everything is determined by everything else, and he cannot mean that the determination takes place by general laws. For he does not, it seems clear, introduce the idea of general laws until he comes to the category of Universal Judgment, which is further on in the dialectic[1].

**143**. The objection has been raised to certain theories of reality that they make the universe a "block" universe, in which every part is rigidly connected with every other part. This objection is generally raised against theories which regard all parts of the universe as connected with all other parts by general laws. In that case, every part would certainly be rigidly connected with every other part. But the rigidity to which objection is taken would arise, even if determination by general laws were not complete. For, as we have just seen, no characteristic of any substance is extrinsically contingent to any other, and it is therefore not legitimate to say that $A$ might have possessed the characteristic $W$, instead of the characteristic $X$, without affecting the possession by $A$ of the characteristic $Y$, or by $B$ of the characteristic $Z$. And the connection here is just as rigid as the connection by general laws.

The objections to a "block" universe are, as far as I know, based entirely on judgments of value. It is asserted that such a rigid universe would be very unpleasant, or would be destructive to morality, and it is therefore said that a universe of such a nature is to be condemned as evil, to which it is sometimes added, on pragmatic grounds, that it is to be rejected as false. The value of contingency is a point on which opinions differ, and which does not concern us here. We have only to note that, if the absence of contingency *is* an evil, it is an evil which is inevitable and universal.

---

[1] The details of Hegel's treatment of causality, however, are very different from the conclusions at which we have arrived, especially his extraordinary view that cause and effect are identical.

# CHAPTER XX

## ORGANIC UNITY

**144.** We saw in Chapter XIII that the qualities of a substance could be taken, not only as the parts of which the nature of that substance was composed, but also as the manifestations of that nature, taken as a whole. We saw also, in the last Chapter, that the existence of each substance involved the existence of a quality of the universe—the quality of having that substance as one of its parts. This is true of other wholes besides the universe. If any substance, *A*, has a part, *B*, whose nature consists of the qualities *XYZ*, then it will be a quality of *A* to have a part whose nature is *XYZ*. And this quality of *A* may, by the result reached in Chapter XIII, be considered, not only as one of the parts of the nature of *A*, but also as a manifestation of that nature.

From this relation of the qualities of *A* and *B* there follows a relation between *A* and *B* themselves. A substance which is a whole may be considered as compounded of its parts. And this is the way in which we do, *primâ facie*, consider it. But since, as we have just seen, the fact of having a part of such a nature may be considered as a manifestation of the nature of *A*, the existence of the part may be taken as dependent on the existence of the whole. Instead of considering the parts as constituting the whole, we may—not more truly, but just as truly—take the whole as issuing in the parts. And so we may say that the parts are the manifestation of the whole.

We must distinguish between the manifestation of the whole and the manifestation of the nature of the whole. *A* is manifested in the substances which are the parts of *A*, while the nature of *A* is manifested in the qualities of *A*, which are parts of that nature (including, of course, the qualities of having as its parts *B*, and the other substances which are its parts). For, in the sense in which we are using the word manifestation, nothing can be manifested except in its own parts, and it is obvious that the parts of a substance are substances, while the parts of the nature of a substance are qualities.

To each part of $A$ there will correspond a quality of $A$—the quality of having that part. But for every quality of $A$ there will not be a correspondent part. For every substance has other qualities besides the qualities of having the parts which it has.

We saw in Chapter XIII that to the question as to any substance "What is the nature which is manifested in such and such qualities?" we can only answer by saying that it is the nature which is manifested in those qualities, because the nature of a substance consists of nothing else besides the qualities in which it is manifested[1]. But to the question "What is the nature of that substance which is manifested in such and such parts?" it is possible to return an answer which does not mention any of the parts, because we may answer by means of those qualities which have no reference to parts. Smith, Brown, and their fellow-citizens, are the parts of the British nation, and that nation could not be *completely* described without including the quality of having Smith as a citizen, and so of Brown and the rest. But we can say of the British nation that it is a great power, a limited monarchy, contains two established Churches, and so on, and in this way it might be possible to form a sufficient description without including any of those qualities which are qualities of possessing a particular part.

**145.** The new relation of the whole to its parts, which is reached at this stage, involves a fresh relation of the parts to one another. We saw in the last chapter that all the substances in the universe were interdependent, and the grounds on which we arrived at that conclusion would equally justify us in concluding of any whole, besides the universe, that its parts were interdependent. If any part were different, it would no longer be the same whole, and, if it were not the same whole, we should have no reason for holding that any of the other parts

---

[1] This would only be tautological if all the primary qualities of the substance were enumerated in the question—and their number is infinite, since the number of substances, and so of the relations of each substance to others, is infinite. To the question "what is the nature of $B$ which is manifested in $X$?" it may be answered "the nature which is also manifested in $YZ$."

would exist. But now we can go further. For the parts are now seen to manifest the whole, taken as a unity. No part could do this, if the others did not do so also. For, if any part were wanting, then the whole containing that part could not be manifested at all. Thus no part could manifest the whole, if the others did not do so also. And thus the parts may be said to co-operate in manifesting the whole.

The interdependence is not more complete than before, but it is more positive. We no longer say only that, if one of the parts were different, the whole would be different, and we should have no ground for supposing that the other parts would remain. We say also that the parts have a common function to perform—the manifestation of the whole—and that, while each of them performs it in a different way, yet none could perform it unless the others were performing it also. To the idea of mutual indispensability is now added the more positive idea of mutual co-operation.

**146.** The more positive relation of the whole to the parts, and of the parts to one another, which we have now reached, is sometimes expressed by saying that the whole is in every part. The phrase seems to me unfortunate. It is not desirable in philosophy to use any phrase which, in its literal sense, is false, unless it is quite obvious that it is only used metaphorically. It does not seem quite obvious in this case that the phrase is only used as a metaphor, while, if it is not used as a metaphor, it is false, since no whole can be, in the literal sense[1], within any one of its parts.

And the phrase does, I think, lead to confusion. In the case of a whole whose parts were conscious beings, each of whom perceived the whole, or judged it to exist, it might be said that the *idea* of the whole was in every part, and this (if we limited the statement to the one set of parts who were conscious beings) would be literally true. And when it is said that the whole is in each of the parts—which can only be true as a metaphor—it is

---

[1] I do not take "literal" as equivalent to "spatial." It seems to me that such words as in, out, whole, parts, greater, smaller, can be used as literally of what is non-spatial as of what is spatial. The statements that my thought is in my mind, and that Meredith was in the Order of Merit seem to me as literally true as the statement that the grave of Nelson is in St Paul's.

sometimes, I think, assumed that every whole of which this may be said metaphorically is one of which it would be literally true that the idea of the whole is in every part. And this leads to error, since the metaphor is applied to many wholes whose parts are not conscious beings, and it is only when the parts are conscious beings that the idea of the whole can be in each of them.

But while the expression that the whole is in the parts is unfortunate, we must admit that it is not unnatural that it should have arisen. When it is realized that the whole cannot be manifested at all, unless it is manifested in each particular part, then each part is seen to perform a unique function in relation to the whole. It is, indeed, no more essential to the whole than all the other parts are, but that it should be just what it is, and nothing else, is essential to the whole[1]. And since the whole, to which the special nature of this part is essential, is taken as a unity, it is not surprising that attempts should have been made to express the relation by saying that the whole is in each part.

**147.** Again, it is sometimes said that in such a whole as this the nature of the whole is expressed in each part. This, also, is not literally true. The nature of the whole is expressed —or, so we have called it, manifested—in all the parts taken together, but not in each separately. And in this case, also, it seems undesirable to use the expression, even as a metaphor. But, in this case also, there is some excuse for the expression having been adopted, since the unique function of each part in assisting to manifest the whole might not unnaturally be confused with the expression of the nature of the whole by that part alone[2].

**148.** Every substance which has parts is manifested in this

[1]
> "Thy voice seemed weak. It dropped.
> Creation's chorus stopped."
>         BROWNING, *The Boy and the Angel.*

[2] We shall see later (Section 286) that there is a possible form of unity of which it would be more appropriate to say that the whole was in every part, or that each part expressed the nature of the whole, than it is with a merely organic unity. But, even with this further unity, the expressions would not be literally true.

way in its parts. If we recur to our example of a fantastic substance, the nature of that substance includes the quality of
having as one of its parts the oldest rabbit in Australia. And
therefore the substance itself is manifested in the rabbit. This
does not seem so natural an expression as when we say that my
body as a whole is manifested in my heart, or that a picture as
a whole is manifested in its various details, but the manifestation
is there in the first case as much as in the other two. (The
reason why the expression seems more natural in the second
and third cases will be considered later in the chapter.)

Since substances which are wholes overlap each other, the
same substance will be a manifestation of various overlapping
wholes. William Pitt in 1800 is a manifestation both of the
Privy Council in 1800 and of the House of Commons in 1800,
since it is a quality of both of them to have Pitt as a member.

**149**. I have entitled this chapter Organic Unity, because it
seems to me that our present position is very like that which
has generally been given by philosophers the name of organic
unity, or of Inner Teleology. It is, I suppose, beyond doubt
that by these names—which, when they are both used, are
taken as synonyms[1]—there is always designated a differentiated
unity in which the position of the whole in relation to the parts
is stronger than in a unity which is merely mechanical, and in
which the relation of the parts to one another binds them
together more closely than is the case in a mechanical unity.

The name of organic unity has been given to this conception,
not because it is held to be peculiar to the organic life which is
studied in biology, but because it is held to be especially prominent and obvious in that organic life. This, I think, is true. If
our arguments have been correct, all wholes are organic unities
in this sense. But some wholes exhibit the special character-

---

[1] Hegel uses Teleology as the name of one category, and Life as the name
of another, immediately succeeding Teleology. The conception of organic unity
is introduced under the category of Life. But the full conception of inner
teleology is not attained till the last subdivision of Teleology, while the conception of organic unity comes in the first subdivision of Life. And the passage
from one of those subdivisions to the other is, according to Hegel's method, a
collapse into immediacy," which reaches no fresh result, but only restates a
result previously reached.

istics of organic unity far more obviously than others do. Most of the unities in which these characteristics are specially obvious fall into two classes—biological organisms, and objects which are recognized as beautiful. Why is this so? Why does a horse, or a Persian rug, or the sky during a beautiful sunset, appear more obviously an organic unity than a heap of stones, or a yard of plain canvas, or a sky which is not specially beautiful? I conceive that the reason is that in the cases of the first class a small alteration will change a characteristic of the object to which we ascribe high importance—importance not only for a personal need of the observer at the moment, but importance which stands high when judged by objective standards of value. If a heap of stones was slightly increased in size, it would be different, but the difference is not one which we should regard as important, except for some special purpose. But a very slight change in a living body may make it diseased, or kill it; and a very slight change in a beautiful thing may make it ugly. And these are qualities which we regard—rightly or wrongly does not matter here—as important when judged from objective standpoints.

Now the essential feature of an organic unity is that the parts manifest the whole—that, since the whole as a unity is what it is, the parts must be what they are. This, as we have seen, is really the case with all wholes, and therefore all wholes are really organic unities. But their organic nature only becomes obvious when it becomes obvious that a set of parts only slightly different would be a manifestation of the nature of a whole which was different in some important characteristics. This is not the case with the heap of stones—the addition or subtraction of a stone, or the interchange of two of the stones, would make it a different whole, but not different in any important characteristics. But life and beauty are held by us to be important characteristics, and slight changes in the parts may destroy them. And thus it is obvious with wholes which are living or beautiful that the parts are manifestations of the nature of the whole, since different parts would be so obviously inconsistent with the whole being the same.

There are, no doubt, other cases in which the organic nature of the whole is obvious although the whole possesses neither life nor beauty. But there are no large and well-defined classes of wholes in which organic unity is obvious, except the classes of biological organisms and beautiful objects.

**150**. This, then, is the justification of the name of organic unity. It is not however without its inconveniences. For the association of the philosophical and the biological conceptions by the use of the same name has caused some philosophers to assert certain propositions about the one, which could only be justifiably asserted about the other.

In the first place, the explanation of biological facts by the ordinary principles of physical science, which are sometimes called "mechanical" principles, has not progressed as far as the explanation of the facts relating to inorganic matter. An organic nature, in science, has thus become associated with a failure, at any rate for the present, of mechanical explanation. And so it has sometimes been supposed that, in putting forward the philosophical conception of organic unity as a fundamental principle in the explanation of the universe, we are asserting that the universe is not capable of mechanical explanation, or, at any rate, that, in so far as existence is successfully described in terms of organic unity, it cannot be successfully described in terms of mechanical determination. And this, as we have seen, is erroneous. It is not less correct to regard the whole as compounded of the parts than to regard the parts as a manifestation of the whole. Both are true. The superiority of our position when we have reached organic unity does not lie in the superiority of what we have reached last, but in the fact that we have reached both.

In the second place, the analogy with biology may lead us to limit unduly the scope of the conception in another direction. Even if it is admitted that it applies to all existence—that is to say, that all substantial content falls within some organic unity, it would often be denied that all substances were organic —for example, the substance, mentioned before, which consists of a table, a rabbit, and a dose of medicine. And this, I think, is suggested by biology. For although a sheep is a biological organism, and so is a shepherd, yet a flock of sheep, or a sheep and its shepherd, or the group formed of the left legs of all sheep, are not biological organisms. But this restriction is unjustified when applied to our conception. For all these groups are substances which have parts, and we have seen that every substance which has parts is an organic unity.

**151.** In the third place, it must be noted that organisms as conceived by biology are less complete unities than the organic unities which are contemplated under our present conception. For in these organic unities the wholes are seen to be as fundamental as their parts, while in biology the wholes are not as fundamental as their parts.

The units of matter which make up a biological organism can exist, and in every case have existed, and will exist again, outside that organism. If, indeed, it were the case that they could only exist as parts of other organisms, the fact that the same piece of matter could be successively in many organisms might only balance the fact that in the same organism one piece of matter can be succeeded by another. But the fact that the same matter which exists in an organism can, and at other times does, exist without being a part of *any* organism, while an organism cannot exist without some pieces of matter as its parts, does, it would seem, make a biological organism more dependent on its parts than its parts are on it.

There is another respect in which the material units are more fundamental than the biological organisms which they compose. Biology deals with events in time. Now the higher organisms have a nature which involves their death and dissolution within a certain time from their birth, and even if death is not inevitable for some lower organisms, still they can die, and in many cases do so. With the matter which makes up the organisms it is different. Not only does it not necessarily cease to exist, but there is no known cause which could bring its existence to an end.

The confusion produced by the association in this case does not work in the same manner as in the first and second cases. In those the result was that elements from the biological conception were illegitimately introduced into the philosophical conception. Here, on the other hand, what generally happens is, I think, that philosophers have been led mistakenly to conclude that the parts are not more fundamental than the whole in a biological organism, because they are not more fundamental than the whole according to the philosophical conception of organic unity.

Indeed, this has often gone further. For many philosophers have regarded the whole as being, according to the philosophical conception of organic unity, more fundamental than its parts, and this has led them to hold that the wholes are more fundamental than the parts in biological organisms. Their reason for supposing that, in the philosophical conception the whole was more fundamental than the parts, was, I think, largely due to misleading associations connected with the name of inner teleology, which, as we have said, is frequently used as a synonym for organic unity.

**152.** These associations tend to a confusion between inner teleology and teleology in the ordinary sense, which, to distinguish it from inner teleology, is sometimes called external. It is true that writers who speak of inner teleology generally begin by stating, and even emphasizing, the difference between it and external teleology. But, in the course of the argument, the associations aroused by the noun have often been too strong for the adjective. In external teleology the occurrence of the facts which are teleologically explained is accounted for by their position as means to the end which has been adopted by some conscious being. In this case the end—the purpose of that conscious being—exists as something quite distinct from the facts which are its means. It is itself a separate fact—a volition in the mind of the conscious being who entertains the purpose. Now, even when it is realized that in inner teleology there is no separate fact to explain and unify the plurality, there is often a tendency to forget that the aspect of unity—which, when the conception is spoken of as inner teleology, is spoken of as the end—is nothing but the unity of the whole which is formed by the plurality of separate facts which realize that end. It is often supposed to be something more than just this unity, though less than a separate thing. What, under these conditions, it could possibly be, is not easy to see, nor is it made very clear by those who support the position. But it seems to be sometimes taken as being a principle from which the nature of the facts which constitute the plurality united by it might in some way be deduced[1]. And, if it is held to be this, it is naturally considered to be more fundamental than the plurality of parts which is deduced from it.

**153**. The name of teleology is also misleading in another way. It suggests that the organic unities to which it is applied must necessarily possess value. In the case of external teleology an end is often—though not always—aimed at because the person who adopts it judges it to be good. And, in any case, the attainment of an end gratifies desire, and so tends to give pleasure, which is generally regarded as good. Thus external teleology has a certain connection with value, though, even if it were the case that nothing was aimed at which was not believed to be good, many things would be aimed at which, in point of fact, are not good. But there is no connection with value in the case of inner teleology. The whole manifested in the parts may be evil and not good, or it may have no value at all, positive or negative.

There seems, however, in the case of some writers to be a confusion in this respect between the two kinds of teleology. To begin with, they exaggerate the connection which exists between external teleology and value, by maintaining that no man wills anything unless he believes it to be good. And from this they conclude that the end in inner teleology must also be directed towards the good, while from the fact that it is immanent they conclude that, unlike the ends of external teleology, it cannot fail to be realized, and from the fact that it is not in any one's mind they conclude that it must be really good, and cannot be mistakenly supposed to be good. Thus they arrive at the conclusion that the connection of inner teleology with value is closer than that of external teleology, when in reality inner teleology has no such connection at all.

We may remark in passing, however, that, while a substance

---

[1] This view derives no support from Kant, who teaches that the unity in inner teleology can only be expressed as the unity which does unite those parts. Nor is it supported by Hegel, who never held, as he has so often been accused of holding, that a plurality could be deduced from a unity.

does not necessarily possess value because it forms an organic unity, yet the conception of organic unity may have an important bearing on the judgments which we form as to the value of the universe. Before we reached organic unity, a part of a whole was regarded mainly as determined by the other parts, for, although it is no doubt determined by the whole, the whole was regarded as a compound of those parts. But in organic unity each part is regarded as determined by a whole which is not merely compounded of the parts, but is manifested in them. And the relation of each part to the others is that it is not only determined by them, but that it co-operates with them in manifesting the whole. Now a conscious being is a part of the universe, and it may very well make a considerable difference to the way in which he contemplates the universe, whether he regards himself mainly as determined by other parts, which are external to him, or as determined by the whole of which he is himself a part[1].

**154.** Thus neither the name of organic unity nor the name of inner teleology is without its inconveniences. But some name we must have, and it does not seem possible to find one which is better than organic unity. The name of inner teleology is in a different position. It is, I think, more misleading than organic unity, while it has not the advantage which the other has of pointing to an empirical subject-matter which illustrates the conception with special clearness. It seems therefore desirable to lay it aside.

---

[1] Mysticism may be based on either conception, but the difference between the two conceptions may perhaps be the explanation of the difference between different forms of mysticism which are very dissimilar in important characteristics. I am inclined to think that the difference between Spinoza's Second and Third Knowledge—and, consequently, the distinction he draws between ordinary love of God and intellectual love of God—is based on two ways of regarding the relation of God to the modes, of which the first does not, and the second does, involve what we have called organic unity. But Spinoza's meaning is so obscure that I make the suggestion with great diffidence.

# CHAPTER XXI

## SUMMARY OF RESULTS

**155.** We have now discussed at some length the relations of wholes and parts. The results which we have reached apply through the whole of the universe. For the universe itself is a whole, and every other substance is a part, while many, if not all, of these other substances are both wholes and parts. Thus our results apply to all substances.

But the effect which they produce is limited. In the first place we have not demonstrated the existence of anything in the universe which can fairly be called order.

A whole may be more or less ordered. And we should, I think, say that any whole was ordered in proportion as it possessed any one of three characteristics, each of which is compatible with the other two. The first of these is that its parts should determine one another in accordance with general laws. We may call this Causal Order. The second is that its parts should be connected with one another by such a relation that the parts in question should form a single series. We may call this Serial Order.

The third may be called Order of Classification. To define this it is necessary to define first what I should propose to call a Classifying System. The parts of a whole may be said to form a Classifying System when there is such an arrangement of parts within parts as to fix the place of each part in the whole with reference to other parts, and when each group of parts formed by the arrangement possesses some exclusive common quality other than that which arises from its denotation[1]. And a whole may be said to possess Order of Classification if its parts can be arranged in a classifying system, and if that system is of such a nature that it is based on common qualities which are of fundamental importance to the parts which possess them. The

---

[1] Cp. Sections 132–133.

greater the extent to which the system carries the classification, the more perfect will be the order.

We saw, when we were dealing with universal determination, that we had not yet reached any conclusions as to the extent to which facts are determined by general laws, and therefore we can say nothing so far as to causal order. Nor have we found any reason to suppose that there is any relation between all or most substances by means of which they can be arranged in a single series. Serial order is not therefore to be asserted of the universe, at any rate at present.

**156**. There remains order by classification. This is the sort of order which is formed in the animal kingdom, when its members are grouped into species, genera, families, etc., and also in the subject-catalogue of a library. No whole can be completely ordered by means of order of classification only. Order of classification may, for example, group species into genera, but, except by an introduction of sub-genera, it cannot give the species any definite position within the genus. Even if sub-genera are introduced, each of them must contain more than one species, if they are to be instrumental in establishing order by classification. And the order of classification will not be able to determine the mutual positions of the species in each sub-genus. Unless a serial order should be found to exist between them, their mutual positions would remain unordered. But a whole which had as much order of classification as the animal kingdom, or as a good subject-catalogue, would certainly be called an ordered whole, though the order would not be complete.

A whole, as we have said, would not be considered to be ordered because it formed a system by classification unless the classification were based on fundamentally important qualities. If a library were divided according to the material used in binding the books, and these groups were subdivided according to the number of pages in each volume, we should have a classifying system, but its existence would not, I think, be held to justify us in calling the library an ordered whole.

**157**. A whole is only to be considered as ordered by classification when the classification unites things in so far as they are like, and separates them in so far as they are unlike. And this can only take place when fundamentally important qualities occur in such a manner in the parts of the whole that a reasonably definite system can be established by taking them as criteria. Now we have as yet no reason to believe that such qualities do so occur in the parts of the universe as to establish a reasonably definite system by their means. It is true that, when we observe subordinate wholes, we often find that a grouping by one possible criterion appears far more reasonable and profitable than grouping by some other. It is far more sensible to adopt sex or religion as a principle for classifying the human race than to divide it into those who have, and those who have not, an even number of hairs on their heads. Division by sex or by religion may be relevant to many questions in which a reasonable man might feel a practical or theoretical interest, whereas division by the number of hairs cannot, as far as can be seen, have the least relation to any question in which any reasonable man could take the slightest interest.

But it does not follow from this that we have reached even a fragment of a system which would introduce order into the universe. In the first place, we should have no reason to assert that the substances which possess sex or religion formed a complete set of parts of the universe. And if they did not, this system of classification would not extend over the whole universe, nor should we have any reason to believe that there would be any complementary system of classification which would arrange the remaining part.

And, in the second place, the fact that one system is, and another is not, relevant to questions in which a reasonable man can take any practical interest, will not help us unless it can be established that the questions in which reasonable men take practical interest are matters which are fundamentally important in the nature of the universe. And, even if this is true, we have not proved it yet. Our theoretical interest, indeed, may be said to be directed mainly to what is fundamentally important in the nature of the universe. But our knowledge is very incomplete, and the fact that one system appears to us to rest on more fundamentally important qualities than another, may be due to our ignorance. An observer whose knowledge was limited to a map of England might well condemn as capricious and useless a classification of English towns which should place Cambridge nearer to Oxford than to Ely. Yet greater knowledge might enable him to see that such a classification had considerable significance.

We have failed, then, so far to find—if the metaphor may be permitted—any grain in substance. It can be divided and united in as many ways as there are possible combinations of substances, the number of which we shall see reason in the next chapter to regard as infinite. And of all these ways in which it can be arranged, we have no reason to suppose that any one expresses its nature better than any other.

**158.** And, besides this, there is a second problem, of somewhat similar nature, on which we have as yet no light. When we look at those parts of the universe which are known to us empirically, we find that there are cases in which the conception of unity of composition seems far more appropriate than the conception of unity of manifestation. In the case of the fantastic whole previously considered, it is, no doubt, equally true to say that the table, the rabbit, and the medicine are manifestations of the whole, as it is to say that the whole is composed of the table, the rabbit, and the medicine. But the second statement seems much more expressive of the real nature of the whole. And even in cases where the reality is not, from our point of view, so arbitrary, it often happens that unity of composition seems the more natural conception to use. We should certainly think of a heap of stones as composed of the stones rather than of the stones as manifestations of the heap. On the other hand, there are cases, such as the successive states of a human consciousness for example, where it seems at least as natural to take them as manifestations of the whole—in this case the man—as it would be to take the man as compounded of them[1].

---

[1] Some philosophers would maintain that, in this last case, manifestation is *more* appropriate than composition. But I cannot think of any case where the superior appropriateness of manifestation would be so universally admitted as the superior appropriateness of composition is admitted in the cases mentioned

**159.** Such examples as these suggest very strongly that there are certain cases in which the nature of the differentiated unity is better expressed by composition than by manifestation, even if we are unable to define the limits within which the two classes of cases fall. But we have no right to be certain that this is so. It is true that in some cases, as was said above, manifestation seems much less appropriate than composition. But we can never be certain that, if we know more about the whole in question, manifestation might not seem to be equally appropriate. A unity is not necessarily trivial or superficial because it appears so to us. For, as we have seen, a group is determined by denotation, and it is quite possible for us to know of what members a group consists, and yet to be ignorant of the most important relations between its members.

From this it follows that it is quite possible that, when a unity appears to us to be trivial and superficial, the judgment is due to our ignorance, and not to any r al triviality or super-ficiality in the group. A group whose members were the shopmen to a particular greengrocer in London, the policeman on a particular beat in Liverpool, and the porter of a particular club in Melbourne, looks, when described in this way, a group of very superficial importance, and one to which the conception of manifestation would be quite inappropriate. Nor would there be any reason to think that such a description was not an exclusive description which completely identified the group. For it might well be the case that the description it contained of each man was an exclusive description of that man, and in that case it would itself be an exclusive description of the group. And yet, though the description is exclusive, it might completely ignore relations of the members which made the unity very far from superficial. All three men might be brothers, and their mutual affection, and the influence which each exerted on the others, might be such as to render their mutual relations the most important and significant characteristics in the life of each of them.

above. The fact that composition thus appears to have a stronger position than manifestation is perhaps connected with those relations between a whole and its parts which will be discussed in Chapter xxiii.

**160**. And thus the information which we have reached so far about the nature of substance is deficient in two respects. Existent content falls within many substances, and the greater number of these (indeed, as we shall see later, all of them) are groups which overlap each other in great complexity, and each of which may be taken either as a unity of composition or as a unity of manifestation. Now, in the first place, if none of these divisions are more fundamental than others, we have no reason to believe that existence is an ordered whole, and, while some of them certainly seem to us more fundamental than others, we have no reason to believe that any of them really are so. And, in the second place, while there is much to suggest that some groups are more appropriately expressed as unities of composition, while some are equally well expressed as unities of manifestation, we can find no demonstration that this is really the case.

Can we find any fixed points in all this complexity? At present, I think, we can find only one—the universe. If there were simple substances, which, of course, would not be groups, they would also be fixed points, but the existence of simple substances has not been proved, and we shall see in the next chapter that there is reason to disbelieve in it. But the universe does exist, and its position among substances is unique and important, for it includes all content, and it includes all substances other than itself. It has thus, objectively, and not merely from the point of view of our interests, a position much more fundamental than that of most substances, if not of all.

And from the point of view of our own interests, also, the determination of the nature of the universe as a whole is not unimportant. For example, since the universe is a substance, we now know that it is an organic unity. And the category of organic unity has its chief importance for mysticism because it applies to the universe as a whole. The essence of mysticism is to emphasize unity, and though it can be based, and has been based, on unity of composition, yet the closer unity which is reached in the category of organic unity affords it a more favourable basis. And the conception of organic unity only reaches its full importance when we recognize, not only that the universe contains such unities, but that it is also itself such a unity. Only, therefore, when the conception of organic unity is applied to the universe as a whole, does that conception become really important for mysticism. If, for example, as I suggested above, the explanation of Spinoza's Third Knowledge, and the consequent intellectual love of God, is to be sought in the difference between organic unity and unity of composition, it is only in the application of the conception of organic unity to the universe as a whole that the explanation is to be found.

But this one fixed point of the universe, while, as we have said, important in itself, does nothing to introduce order among the different substances which are its parts. If we are to find any order, we must look further.

# CHAPTER XXII

## INFINITE DIVISIBILITY OF SUBSTANCE

**161**. At the end of the last chapter we were left with the result that the parts of the universe were combined in wholes which overlapped one another with enormous complexity—perhaps with infinite complexity. No principle had been discovered which enabled us to assert that among all such combinations of substantial content, any were more intricate or fundamental than the rest. The universe itself, indeed, was found to be in a unique position. But this goes a very little way towards introducing order into the existent.

Another question now arises. Every substance, except the universe, is a part of another substance. And many substances are both parts of other substances, and wholes of which other substances are parts. But is this true of all substances, or are there some which are parts without being wholes? In other words, are there any simple substances?

If no substance is simple, then every substance has content, since content has been defined as that plurality which is identical in different sets of parts of a whole. And, conversely, if a substance has content, it has parts, and so will not be simple. Thus our question may also be put—has every substance content?

**162**. It is clear that a substance is not simple if it is divisible at all, even if there are certain ways in which it is not divisible. In other words it must be indivisible in every Dimension.

The conception of dimension is applicable, not only in space, but wherever a series can be found. The terms of any series form a field of one dimension. Wherever there is a series such that each of its members is again a series, we have a field of two dimensions. The members of this field are each in some one position in one series, and in some one position in the other. If each of these members is again a series, we have a field of three dimensions, and so on[1].

[1] Cp. Russell, *Principles of Mathematics*, Section 354.

We shall speak of a substance as possessing a dimension wherever it forms either a series or a term of a series in that dimension. Thus we shall say that a line possesses the dimensions of breadth and thickness as well as the dimension of length; and that an individual moment in the time series possesses the dimension of time. This is a departure from the ordinary usage of geometry, which would say that a line possesses no spatial dimension, except length.

When dimension is defined in this way, it is clear that, while it is applicable to the dimensions of space, it is also applicable elsewhere. If what is three-dimensional in space is also in time, then it has time as a fourth dimension. For when we have got any member of the three-dimensional field of space—anything which occupies some one position in each of the three spatial series—the states of that thing at the different moments of time form another series.

Again, a pleasure may be said to have at least two dimensions. For a pleasure lasts for a certain time, and has at each moment of that time a certain intensity—the same or different. And therefore, by our definition of dimension, it has two dimensions just as much as a figure which has a certain length horizontally, and at each point of this has a certain particular height—the same or different.

**163**. Are any substances simple? We must begin our enquiry by noticing that the question cannot be decided by arguments drawn from our perceptions. Whatever we perceive is a substance, and, if we perceived anything which we knew to be simple, we should know that there were simple substances, though it would not be certain that all compound substances consisted of simple substances. But, in point of fact, nothing that is perceived is simple.

We perceive, to begin with, sense-data, which are apprehended by means of the external senses. And we also perceive, by introspection, events in our own minds, which we have classed with the sense-data under the more general name of perception-data. Now in the first place there appears to be reason to think that every perception-datum has extensive quantity, in the form of what has been called extensity. In this case every perception-datum will have parts[1]. But the extensity of all perception-data has been denied. Nor is their extensity necessary to prove our present assertion.

For, as we have seen, time is a dimension of whatever exists in time. And everything which exists through several parts of time will have, as its own parts, itself as existing in each of those parts of time. "St Paul's Cathedral in the nineteenth century," and "St Paul's Cathedral in 1801," are both names of substances. But they are the names of different substances, since many assertions are true of St Paul's in the nineteenth century which are not true of St Paul's in 1801, and *vice versa*. And the second substance is part of the first. If we take the substances which are named "St Paul's in 1801," "St Paul's in 1802," and so on to "St Paul's in 1900," they will together include all the content which is included in "St Paul's in the nineteenth century."

Now every perception-datum which I perceive lasts for a finite time. Stimuli which follow one another at a certain rate, give us separate perceptions of separate and successive sense-data. But if they follow on one another more rapidly they give us a single sense-datum, in which there are no successive parts which are separate sense-data. Thus there is a minimum duration for a sense-datum, and all sense-data last through a period of time. So also do the perception-data which are not sense-data. Now if the perception-datum lasts through a period of time, it is divisible in the dimension of time. If time has no simple parts, the perception-datum will have no simple parts. If every period of time has an infinite number of simple parts, the perception-datum will have an infinite number of parts which will not be further divisible in this dimension. If a period of time has a finite number of simple parts, the datum will have a finite number of parts which will not be further divisible in this dimension. But, in any case, every period of time is divisible into parts, and therefore every perception-datum will be divisible into parts.

---

[1] I do not mean that whatever has quantity has parts. Some relations have quantity, but they are not divisible into smaller relations. My assertion is that all substances which have extensive quantity have parts.

**164**. It might be objected that a perception-datum does not always change while it is perceived, and that if there is no change there will be no successive parts. But this would be incorrect, for the nature of anything which exists through time cannot be exactly the same at two different moments of time. At the later moment its temporal relations to various events in the past and future will be more or less different from what they were at the earlier moment. And a difference in relations involves a difference in relational qualities.

We must remember also that a substance is not necessarily simple because it cannot be divided into parts which have the same nature as itself in any particular respect. A college, for example, in spite of the fact that it does not consist of colleges, is not a simple substance, since it does consist of human beings. In ordinary life this distinction is clearly recognized. But in philosophical discussion there is sometimes a tendency to assume that a sense-datum, for example, is simple if it cannot be analyzed into sense-data, and to ignore the fact that the shortest possible sense-datum is compound in respect of the still shorter parts of which it consists.

**165**. It would be universally admitted that each of us perceives sense-data and also, by introspection, various events which take place within himself. I think that, in addition to this, it is possible for a man to perceive himself, and that most men do so frequently, though not always. The correctness of this view will be discussed in a later part of this work[1]. At present it is sufficient to point out that, if a man does perceive himself, he does not by doing so perceive anything which is simple. In the first place each self has many parts which are simultaneous. At many moments, if not at all moments, the field of consciousness is differentiated. And if, as I believe to be the case, the perceptions, judgments and volitions of a self are parts of that self, this would prove that the self was not simple.

But the view that perceptions, judgments and volitions are parts of the self which experiences them has been denied. And it is not necessary for our present purpose to decide the question[2].

---

[1] Book V.

[2] This also will be discussed in Book V.

It is certain, at any rate, that any perception I have of myself is of that self as existing through a certain duration of time. And the self which is thus perceived is therefore not simple, since it consists of as many parts as there are parts of time through which it exists[1].

Our argument, then, for holding that we perceive nothing simple rests on the fact that all we perceive is divisible in time. It would not be invalidated if we came to the conclusion that time has simple parts. For we are not here trying to show that what is perceived in time has no simple parts, but that what is perceived in time has no simple parts which are perceived. Nor would it be invalidated by a demonstration that time was unreal. For, even if time should prove to be mere appearance, yet whatever appears as an event in time would really exist, though it would not really be an event, or temporal. And thus the plurality which was the basis of our argument would not disappear.

**166**. Our result, so far, is merely negative. There is nothing in our perception of substances to give us any reason to believe that there are simple substances. But this leaves it possible that even the substances which we perceive consist of simple substances which we do not perceive. It may still be the case that all compound substances—and à fortiori that some compound substances—consist of simple substances.

**167**. We come back, then, to the main question. Can a substance exist without content, and so be simple? It seems to me that it cannot—that there can be no substance without

---

[1] If, owing to its duration in time, the perceived self cannot be simple, à fortiori the self as a whole cannot be simple, since that exists through a duration of which the duration of the self perceived in any one perception is only a part. In order not to exaggerate the significance of our denial of the simplicity of the self, it must be remembered that, by the assertion that A has B and C as its parts, we do not assert that A is less of a unity, or less important, than B or C. For all our interests, theoretical and practical, it may be the whole which is important, and not its parts. And if any of the substances in the universe can be shown to be more ultimate and fundamental than others, it may be A, and not B and C, which rank highest in this respect.

It must also be remembered that, when we assert that a self has parts, we are not asserting that its parts could exist, like the parts of human bodies, or of other material compounds, sometimes as parts of that self, and sometimes not as parts of it. And the objections made to the assertion that a self has parts are sometimes due to a failure to see this.

content, and therefore none without parts, so that there can be no simple substance.

The result thus reached is of great importance. The impossibility of simple substances is, in itself, a matter of considerable theoretical interest. But its consequences, as it seems to me, have still greater interest—not only theoretical but practical. (The rest of this work will consist to a large extent of a deduction of these consequences.) Our decision on this point, therefore, requires the most careful consideration.

The proposition that no substance can exist without content is clearly synthetic. We do not mean by substance that which has no content. We defined it as that which has qualities and stands in relations without being itself a quality or a relation. In saying that it has content, we are not asserting over again that it is substance, but asserting a fact about substance.

And the proposition is, I think, self-evident and ultimate. It is self-evident, because it does not need proof; and it is ultimate because it cannot be proved from any proposition more clearly self-evident. All that each of us can do is to regard it carefully, and to see whether he does accept it as self-evident. It does not follow that exposition and discussion will be useless. They may clear away misapprehensions, make the meaning of the proposition clearer, suggest consequences of its truth or falsehood which may make its truth or falsehood more clearly evident. But a positive proof is impossible.

**168**. There are, it must be admitted, several considerations which should make us hesitate before we accept the view that every substance must have content and parts. In the first place, while the proposition, as we have just said, is put forward as self-evident and ultimate, it is certainly not universally accepted as such. Indeed, as far as I know, the assertion that it is self-evident and ultimate has never been made before. This does not show that the assertion is wrong. Among self-evident and ultimate propositions there are some—the Law of Excluded Middle, for example—which are, as a matter of fact, so obvious that they are universally accepted as self-evident and ultimate. But there are others whose self-evidence and ultimate truth, though just as real, does not suggest itself till after long and careful examination and analysis of the facts of experience. Our assertion, therefore, need not be mistaken because it is new. But, on the other hand, the rash acceptance of propositions as self-evident and ultimate has been a fruitful source of error. And undoubtedly we take a very heavy intellectual responsibility when, without the universal concurrence of mankind, we assert of any proposition that, though it cannot be proved, it ought not to be doubted.

**169**. There is a second risk of error which also requires careful attention. It seems clear that we do not know what a simple substance would, in the ordinary phrase, "be like"— that is, we do not know what other qualities it would, or could, have, except those which were implied in its being a substance, and in being without content. For, as was shown above, we never perceive a simple substance, and, as far as I can see, it is quite impossible to imagine a simple substance. But the limits of our imagination are not the limits of possibility. We cannot therefore argue from the impossibility of imagining simple substances to the impossibility of their existence. And we must be on our guard against making the mistake of confusing the two impossibilities, and of supposing that we see clearly the impossibility of a simple substance, when in reality all we see is our failure to imagine a simple substance.

**170**. There is a third risk of error of the danger of which, so far as it affects myself, I am profoundly conscious. With the help of the result which we are now discussing, I believe it possible, as I shall explain in the later Books of this work, to reach conclusions which, to me at any rate, seem very desirable. Without this result I do not see how any conclusions can be reached which are nearly so desirable. The history of philosophy shows with weary repetition how easy it is to accept a proposition as true, if its truth is held desirable, on evidence which would never have been deemed sufficient if its correctness had not been desired. All that I can say is that I have never forgotten this danger, and that I have done all that I could to guard myself against it.

**171**. But, after taking account of all these grounds for hesitation, it does seem to me that we must accept the proposition that a substance must have content and parts. As far as I can see there is a positive connection between the two qualities—the quality of being a substance and the quality of having content and parts. Just as our belief in the law of Excluded Middle rests, not on the impossibility of imagining a statement which was neither true nor false, but on the recognition of the positive necessity that whatever is a statement should be either true or false, so in this case also we are not dependent on the failure of our imagination, but on the recognition of an immediate implication of one quality by the other.

The matter can be put in different ways, and although these furnish no proof of our contention—which we have admitted to be incapable of proof—still they may make the matter clearer. We may ask ourselves whether a substance could be made without a filling of some sort, and whether there could be any filling for a substance except a set of parts. Or we may reflect that if a substance had no parts there would be nothing inside it, and we may ask ourselves whether the conception of a substance with no inside is tenable.

Another way in which we may regard our problem—and one which I think does make it clearer—is with reference to internal structure. By internal structure I do not mean anything which implies any high degree of organization or unity, but a quality which inevitably belongs to any whole of parts. The parts of such a whole will necessarily have some relations to each other, and the fact that it has these related parts is what I mean by its having internal structure. A simple substance could, of course, have no internal structure. And it seems to me that when we endeavour to separate the two qualities of substantiality and internal structure we find them connected in such a way that the separation is impossible, since the removal of the second implies the removal of the first. The peculiar sort of reality which a substance must have, if it is to be real at all, depends on possession of internal structure.

**172.** Another point which must not be forgotten is that a simple substance could have no history, and no duration. For it must be undivided in any dimension, and, for anything which exists in time, time is a dimension. I think that some of the writers who appear to have no difficulty in accepting the possibility of simple substances have ignored this point, and, while they fix their attention on the absence of *simultaneous* differentiation, make no attempt to exclude successive differentiation. If they realized that their substance, besides having no simultaneous parts, could only exist for one simple and indivisible moment of time, they might revise their judgment about the possibility of simple substances[1].

**173**. And we must also remember that the question is about the possibility of a simple substance—that is, one which has no parts at all. A substance which has any parts is not simple, although its parts are so closely attached to one another that there is no known force which can separate them. Nor is it even simple if the nature of its parts is such that it can be seen *à priori* to be impossible that any of them should exist except as parts of that whole, or that the whole should exist without any one of them. If these things are true, the whole will be more closely united than it would otherwise have been, but it will still be compound and not simple.

Now in some cases I think that this has been forgotten, and that it has been asserted that simple substances were possible, when the conception in the thinker's mind was not really one of a simple substance, but of a compound substance closely united.

**174**. It seems to me then, that it is self-evidently and ultimately true that every substance must have content and parts,

---

[1] I am not suggesting that a substance cannot exist at a single and indivisible moment of time. It is clear that, if there are single and indivisible moments of time at all, there must be substances—which would in ordinary language be called states of more persistent substances—each of which exists only at one of these moments. And, as I shall try to show in my second volume, there seems good reason for holding that the series which appears to us as the time-series is made up of simple and indivisible terms. It will follow that when the series appears to us as the time-series, these terms will appear as simple and indivisible moments. And thus there will be substances each of which will, *sub specie temporis*, exist only at one of such moments.

My point is that there cannot be a substance which is absolutely simple and has no parts in any dimension, and that some people fail to see this because they have not excluded the idea of successive parts from the conception which they are forming, and therefore are not really contemplating the conception of a simple substance. The true solution is, as I shall argue in the second volume, that there are substances which are indivisible in the dimension of apparent time, but that, in other dimensions, they are divisible into parts of parts to infinity.

and that there is no simple substance. But it has been admitted that this is by no means so certain as, for example, the self-evident and ultimate truth of the Law of Excluded Middle, or of Euclid's first axiom. And if we could find any circumstances which raised a strong presumption against the proposition being true at all, we might find reason to doubt our conclusion that it is self-evidently and ultimately true. Can we find anything which would raise such a presumption?

In the first place, is there any reason to suppose that the hypothesis that the proposition was true would involve a contradiction? I do not see any way in which it could be supposed that it did involve a contradiction, except one. If every substance has parts, then every substance has an unending series of sets of parts, since each part in any set will be a substance which has parts, and the parts of the parts will form a fresh set of parts of the original whole. It might be said that this infinite series was vicious. This point will be discussed in the next two chapters.

**175**. In the second place, is there any presumption raised against our view by the fact that there are simple character-istics? It is beyond doubt that there are simple characteristics. Red, for example, is a simple quality. And, further, it is beyond doubt that there are no compound characteristics except such as are composed of simple characteristics. Every quality and every relation must mean something, so that when it is asserted that anything has that quality, or stands in that relation to anything, the assertion may be significant. And the meaning of a compound characteristic depends on the meanings of its parts. A compound characteristic, therefore, which had no simple parts, would involve a vicious infinite regress. Its meaning would depend on the meaning of some set of its parts. But, whatever set might be taken, the meaning of each term in it would depend on the meaning of a set of its parts, and so on infinitely. The meaning of the original characteristic could only be fixed when the end of the series had been reached, and terms had been found whose meaning did not depend on anything beyond themselves. And as the series would have no end, there would be no such terms in it. Such a compound characteristic, therefore, would have no meaning, and so could not be real.

But the occurrence of simple characteristics gives no presumption in favour of simple substances. For it is evident that, if there were simple substances, the relations between them and compound substances would be very different from those between simple and compound characteristics. We cannot be aware of a compound characteristic without being aware of the simple characteristics of which it consists. This follows from what was said above, since to be aware of a characteristic is to know its meaning[1]. But we can be aware of a compound substance without being aware of the simple substances which compose it. For the awareness of a substance is perception, and we can perceive a compound substance without perceiving any simple substances as its parts. Indeed, as was shown above, we never do perceive simple substances, and therefore, whether they exist or not, we are not aware of them. Simple substances, then, if they did exist, would be in relations to compound substances so different from those which hold between simple and compound characteristics, that the reality of simple characteristics gives no presumption for the existence of simple substances.

Indeed I think that the consideration of simple characteristics should rather strengthen our belief that we judged rightly in regarding the impossibility of simple substances as a self-evident truth. For it seems to me that the possibility of a characteristic being both real and simple can be seen to depend on its being a characteristic; or, as it might otherwise be expressed, of being a universal, or being significant. I do not mean that the possibility of its being a real and simple characteristic depends on its being a characteristic—which would be tau-

---

[1] We can, of course, have an exclusive description of a compound characteristic without being aware of the simple characteristics which compose it. Humanity, for example, is a compound quality. And if I know of humanity only that it is the chief subject discussed by a certain writer in the twentieth chapter of his first book, I shall have an exclusive description of humanity without being aware of any of the qualities which compose it. But then I shall not be aware of humanity. I shall have a description of it which applies to nothing else, but I shall not be aware of it, since I shall not know what it means.

tologous—but that the possibility of its being real and simple depends on its being a characteristic. This would support the view that a substance cannot be both real and simple. It is not much more than a fresh expression of our original proposition; but, as we have said, it is by such restatements that we may hope to throw light on the contention that a proposition is ultimately true.

**176.** In the third place, do we find in what is taught us by science anything which could give us a presumption in favour of simple substances? Supposing that views which were generally accepted in science did involve the existence of simple substances, we should have to enquire into the precise metaphysical significance of those views, and to consider whether, in rejecting simple substances, we should really come into conflict with science, or only with the uncritical metaphysics of scientists. But it is not necessary to consider this question, because there is nothing in any of the teachings of science which involves the existence of simple substances.

It has never been suggested, I think, that anything in the science of psychology rendered probable the existence of simple substances—in the sense in which we have used this phrase. If any science demands it, then, it must be physical science, and the simple substances must be—or appear as—matter. Nothing can be simple, as we have seen, if it has extension in space, since then it must be spatially divisible. Does physical science suggest that anything which is spatially indivisible does exist?

It might be said that physical science asserts that the truths of geometry are applicable to existent matter in space, and that this involves that something exists of which the conception of a spatially indivisible point is true.

This, however, would not show that the substance which was spatially indivisible was a simple substance, since it might be divisible in some other dimension. The objects of physical science have the dimension of time as well as those of space, and I do not know that there is anything in science which would make it difficult to hold that, in the dimension of time, every part was divisible into other parts to infinity.

I do not, however, wish to press this point, because, as I

said above, I believe that the time series is composed of simple parts. But there might be differentiation in other dimensions. For example, there is perhaps no inherent impossibility in spatial relations existing between minds, and, if there were such relations, it might also be the case that there were no spatial relations between the parts of any mind, and that the mind, therefore, was not spatially divisible, while it had spatial relations. Such a mind would therefore, among other qualities, have the quality of being a geometrical point. But it would not be a simple substance, for it would have non-spatial parts. And the possibility would remain that none of its parts were simple in this dimension.

Science does not assert, of course, that this is so, but there is nothing in the hypothesis which is incompatible with any scientific result. And if this were the only alternative which would avoid simple substances, we should be entitled to accept it, since we have found reason to believe simple substances to be impossible.

**177.** There is, however, no necessity to adopt this hypothesis, for, even without it, we should not be compelled to accept simple substances. There is nothing in science which compels us to believe that anything spatial contains parts which are not spatially divided.

And this conclusion does not depend on the view that space is only an illusion, and that whatever appears to us as in space is really non-spatial. I believe this to be the case. But we need not rely on it in order to avoid simple substances. Even if space were absolutely real, there would be no reason to hold that the contents of space had simple parts.

It is true that geometry deals with points, which are spatially indivisible, and that geometry has a certain relation to what exists in space. The assertions of geometry—for example, that two sides of a triangle are always longer than the third side—do give us valid information about everyday objects. If three streets, when correctly drawn on a map, are not to be distinguished from the drawing of a triangle, we can be sure that, in walking from one corner to another, we shall have further to walk if we go through two streets than if we go through one.

But we have no reason to think that the assertions of geometry are *exactly* applicable to what exists in space. Our reasons for believing that they are applicable at all are only empirical—we see that, in point of fact, they are applicable. And the only conclusion which can thus be justified is that the axioms of geometry are approximately true of the existent. We cannot tell if they are exactly true of it, for our powers of observation are limited, and, however closely we can observe, there will always be variations which would be too small to be observed, and which no observation will assure us are absent.

If existent space had no simple parts, it would contain no points, lines or planes[1]. But since it is infinitely divisible it will contain parts which are smaller, narrower and thinner than any given part. It will contain, therefore, parts whose size, breadth, or thickness are too small to be observed, by any finite powers of observation. No observation therefore can tell us whether existent space is such that it has no simple parts, or whether it is such that geometry is exactly applicable to it. And thus science does not demand that what is spatially existent shall have simple parts[2].

**178**. But, it may be objected in the fourth place, though the conclusions of science do not require that any substance should be simple, yet the conceptions of science are such that their occurrence refutes our contention that no substance can be simple. For, it may be said, geometry gives us a perfectly clear conception of a point, and one which involves no impossibility. Now a point, which is defined as having no parts, would be simple. But a point is a substance, since it has qualities and stands in relations, without being itself a quality or a relation. And thus, it would be urged, we have a clear conception of a certain sort of simple substance which involves no impossi-

---

[1] Strictly speaking, perhaps, nothing but the points would be necessarily excluded. But it is not probable that space would have simple parts in respect of one of its dimensions, and yet have no simple parts with respect to one or both of the others.

[2] Sections 176 and 177 were written before the publication of Dr Whitehead's *Principles of Natural Knowledge*. On this subject Dr Whitehead speaks with a competence and a knowledge which I am far from possessing. That my conclusions should agree with his has much strengthened my confidence in them.

bility. And this refutes the contention that there is an intrinsic impossibility that a substance should be simple.

This objection, however, is unjustifiable. A point is no doubt a substance. But to be a point is a quality. A substance which was a point would have other qualities besides this quality of punctuality. And they might be such that it was divisible in other dimensions, in spite of being a point. It might be divisible in time, if it persisted through time[1], or in some such way as was mentioned in Section 176. Since a substance which was a point could be divisible in this way, the fact that we have a clear conception of a point does not prove that we have a clear conception of an indivisible substance.

Of course many people have had a clear conception of a geometrical point who did not realize that a substance which was such a point need not be simple. But this does not affect the argument. Anyone has a clear conception of a geometrical point who knows the definition of such a point and is aware of the simple characteristics which enter into that definition. The clearness of his conception will be the same, whether he draws from it the right conclusion that a substance which is such a point need not be simple, or the wrong conclusion that such a substance must be simple, or whether he draws no conclusion on the subject at all.

**179.** Finally it might be said that the novelty of our view, while not actually proving it to be false, did raise a presumption against it. If it is really a self-evident and ultimate truth that no substance can exist without content, is it probable that the impossibility of simple substances, which follows from it so directly, should not have been accepted long ago, very generally, if not universally?

But it must be remembered that, though ultimate truths are logically prior to all others, they are not always the truths which occur to us first when we contemplate any particular subject. And there would be nothing very suspicious in the

---

[1] The question whether there are simple parts in the time series is not relevant here. I am endeavouring to disprove the contention that the quality of being a geometrical point involves the quality of being indivisible. And this would be disproved by the possibility of its being divisible in time, even if it were divisible into indivisible parts.

fact that substance had been discussed for many years without one particular ultimate truth about substance being discovered. And it becomes still less suspicious when we remember that many questions may be raised and settled about substance without determining the possibility of simple substances.

Looking back on the history of modern philosophy, we shall find that Leibnitz did, in effect, reject simple substances; for though he called his monads simple, he treated their perceptions as their parts, and, since a monad perceived the perceptions of any other monad in perceiving that other monad, the perceptions, and so the monads, were differentiated into parts of parts to infinity. Schelling's theory of substance, if I understand it rightly, also involved that there were no simple substances. Kant's views as to the nature of noumenal substance, which were based exclusively on ethical grounds, seem to leave it quite open whether there were or were not any simple substances. Neither Descartes nor Spinoza can be taken as being on either side of the question. Material substance for Descartes, and all substance for Spinoza, were infinitely divisible, but it was of no importance to their systems whether substance was divided into an infinite number of simple substances, or whether every part of it was again divisible. And although Descartes called selves simple, he did not affirm them to be simple in the sense in which we have used the word, since he admitted that they possessed simultaneous differentiations and successive states. Fichte and Lotze, again, do not deal with the problem at all.

It is rather difficult to say what Hegel's position was on this question. If I am right in my interpretation of his system, he regarded the universe as having a set of parts, each member of which was a self, which was conscious of all the other selves[1]. If they were also conscious of the parts of those other selves, and if the consciousness was perception rather than judgment, this would involve that there was no simple substance[2].

I believe that Hegel did regard the selves as being conscious of the parts of the other selves, and that he regarded this con-

[1] Cp. my *Commentary on Hegel's Logic.*
[2] For a proof that the impossibility of simple substances would follow from these premises, cp. below, Section 236, where a similar hypothesis is discussed.

sciousness as perceptual in its nature. But I should doubt if he ever drew the conclusion that there could be no simple substances.

The result, I think, is that in the whole line of great philosophers from Descartes to Lotze, only the British Empiricists affirmed the existence of simple substances[1]. All of the others, if they have not denied the existence of simple substances, have not affirmed the existence of such substances, or even failed to find them impossible, but have never raised the question at all.

If we turn to the philosophy of the present day we find very little ontological discussion of substance. This is largely due to the great extent to which that philosophy has based even its ontological conclusions on purely epistemological considerations. When the attention of philosophers has been directed so little to the subject, it need not arouse surprise if we find reason to believe that more remains to be said about it.

**180**. Our conclusion, then, is that there are no simple substances, and that every substance has parts within parts to infinity. Every substance is thus infinitely divisible. But this infinite divisibility is of course of a different type from the infinite divisibility generally asserted of time and space. It is generally held that time and space have simple parts, but that the number of these simple parts in any time or space, however small, is infinite, because no parts in the series are next to one another. But in the type of infinite divisibility which we are considering here, it is possible—though not necessary—that there should always be next terms, and it is possible therefore that the number of terms in each set of parts should be finite. The necessity of infinite divisibility comes in through the fact that beyond any set of parts, $A$, there is always another, consisting of the parts of the parts of $A$.

**181**. Can we say, then, that the sets of parts of any substance form an infinite series? This is only correct if we make

---

[1] In the senses in which they themselves used the word substance, Locke did not assert the existence of simple substances, while Hume denied the existence of all substances. But the ideas of Locke, and the impressions and ideas of Hume, would be substances according to our definition. And when one of these is what Locke or Hume would call simple, and when it occupies only a *minimum perceptible* of time, it would seem that it is to be taken as absolutely indivisible, and so as a simple substance.

the qualification that it is not always the case that two sets of parts have definite positions in the series with reference to each other. There will be sets such that neither of them can be reached from the other by further division. This is the case, for example, with the two sets of parts of the United Kingdom, one of which consists of England, Scotland, Wales and Ireland, and the other consists of Great Britain, Ulster, Munster, Leinster and Connaught. Two sets only hold definite places in the series in reference to each other, if no part in the second set falls within more than one part of the first, while at least one part of the first set contains more than one part of the second. (It is not necessary that *each* part of the first should do so. If $B$ and $C$ formed the first set, the second set might be $D$, $E$ and $C$, where $D$ and $E$ were a set of parts of $B$.) In t' is case we may conveniently speak of the second set as Sequent to the first, and of the first as Precedent to the second.

It is to be noticed, however, that, even when neither of two sets is sequent to the other, there is always to be found a set which is sequent to both, because, in any whole which has no simple parts, there is always some set of parts which can be reached by division from each of any two sets of parts. Thus the set of counties of the United Kingdom would be sequent to both the sets given above.

It is no objection to our theory that it involves an infinite series, for not all infinite series are vicious. But some infinite series are vicious. In the next chapter we shall consider whether such a series as this would in any case be vicious.

The result of this chapter is to leave us, so far, with the want of order, discussed in the last chapter, in an aggravated form. If there had been simple substances, they might have ranked together with the universe as the most fundamental unities of the existent. They might, indeed, have more claim to such a position than the universe itself. This chance, then, of finding some fixed points in the unending complexity of wholes and parts, is lost. But when we consider further all that is implied in the fact that every substance is divisible, we may succeed in finding a principle of order which will be sufficiently far-reaching.

# CHAPTER XXIII

## THE CONTRADICTION OF INFINITE DIVISIBILITY

**182**. We have come to the conclusion, then, that no simple substances can exist, and that every substance that does exist is divided into parts, which again have other parts, and so on to infinity. We must now enquire whether this infinite series of sets of parts involves any contradiction. If we did arrive at the conclusion that it did involve a contradiction, we should no doubt be bound to scrutinize with additional care our conclusion that no simple substance could exist. For, if we found ourselves compelled to adhere to that conclusion, we should be confronted with a hopeless difficulty. We have seen that some substances do exist. And we have just decided that all substances must consist of parts of parts to infinity. If we were compelled to add to this the further conclusion that no substance can, without contradiction, be divided into parts of parts to infinity, we could not escape from contradiction in any way. If, on the other hand, we should find that such an infinite series of parts of parts would involve a contradiction unless the substance had a certain nature, we should be certain that all substances had that nature, since under no other conditions could they have the infinite series of sets of parts which they do have.

I believe that this is the case—that the infinite series in question does involve a contradiction unless the substance is of a certain nature, and that we may conclude, therefore, that it is of that nature. The discussion of this question will occupy the present chapter, and the first of the next Book.

The mere fact that a series is infinite is, as we have seen, no reason for condemning it as vicious. The infinity of some series renders them vicious, but other infinite series are perfectly legitimate. Nor can we argue that infinite divisibility would be vicious, in the case of substances, because it would admittedly be vicious in the case of characteristics[1]. But it seems to me

[1] Cp. Section 175.

that, unless certain conditions are complied with, it is vicious for another reason.

**183.** This reason depends on the occurrence, between a substance and its parts, of a relation which I propose to call Presupposition. I should define Presupposition as follows. When the occurrence of the quality $X$ determines intrinsically the occurrence of either the quality $Y$ or the quality $Z$ (whether as belonging to the same subject as $X$, or to some other), but does not intrinsically determine whether it shall be $Y$ or $Z$ which does occur, then $X$ is said to presuppose $Y$ or $Z$. In this statement, however, though it seems the natural way to express the relation, the phrase " $Y$ or $Z$ " is used ambiguously. For we have said both that $X$ intrinsically determines $Y$ or $Z$, and that it presupposes them, whereas nothing can both determine intrinsically and presuppose the same thing. A more accurate expression is that $X$ determines intrinsically $Y$-or-$Z$, but that it either presupposes $Y$ or presupposes $Z$, according as $Y$ or $Z$ does actually occur[1]. (In this statement $Y$ and $Z$ are to be taken as standing for any number of terms not less than two.)

Thus the possession by any substance of the quality of being human intrinsically determines that the same substance shall be male-or-female, and presupposes either that it is male or that it is female, according to which it is. Again, the possession by any substance of the quality of being a human parent intrinsically determines that some other substance shall be son-or-daughter, and presupposes either that it is a son, or that it is a daughter.

It may be the case that whatever is either $Y$ or $Z$ is also $W$. Then $X$ will intrinsically determine that something is $W$, but will not intrinsically determine what sort of $W$ it is. In this case we shall say that $X$ intrinsically determines $W$, but presupposes some particular $W$. Thus, in our first case the quality of humanity intrinsically determines the quality of sexual

---

[1] I have taken in the text the case in which $X$ determines the occurrence of either $Y$ or $Z$, but excludes the occurrence of both together. If we take a case in which $X$ renders the occurrence of either $Y$ or $Z$ necessary, while the occurrence of both is possible, we may put it that $X$ intrinsically determines $Y$-alone-or-$Z$-alone-or-$YZ$, but that it either presupposes $Y$ alone, or presupposes $Z$ alone, or presupposes $YZ$, where " $Y$ alone" means " $Y$ without $Z$."

differentiation but presupposes some particular kind of sexual differentiation. And in our second case the quality of being a human parent intrinsically determines (this time in another substance) the quality of being sexually differentiated, while it presupposes some particular sexual differentiation.

**184.** The nature of presupposition may be expressed not unfairly by saying that $X$ presupposes whatever it requires but does not supply. $X$ requires $Y$-or-$Z$, for if it occurs, something must occur which is $Y$ or $Z$. But it does not presuppose $Y$-or-$Z$, for it supplies it, since it intrinsically determines it, and so, if we know that $X$ occurs, we know that $Y$-or-$Z$ occurs. But in addition to this, it either requires $Y$ or requires $Z$, and this it does not supply. For the fact that $X$ occurs does not determine whether it is $Y$ or $Z$ which occurs.

It is possible that presupposition should be reciprocal, even when the amount given about each of the terms is equal. If it were the case that the series of events in time had no first or last terms or limits, then the fact that there were events in a given hour, $M$, would intrinsically determine that there were events in any subsequent hour, $N$, and would presuppose their nature. For they must have some nature, and it would be impossible to infer what nature they had from the fact that there had been some events, whose nature was not specified, in a previous hour. But, again, the fact that there were some events in the hour $N$ would imply that there were events in the preceding hour, $M$, and would presuppose their nature.

Presupposition is a transitive relation. If $X$ presupposes either $Y$ or $Z$, and $Y$ presupposes either $T$ or $S$, and $Z$ presupposes either $U$ or $V$, then $X$ presupposes either $T$ or $S$ or $U$ or $V$. Also it is clear that, if $X$ intrinsically determines $Y$, and $Y$ presupposes either $U$ or $V$, then $X$ presupposes either $U$ or $V$—unless indeed it happens that $X$ either directly or indirectly determines one of the two, and consequently excludes the other. For $X$ clearly requires whatever is required by what $X$ requires, and therefore it must presuppose it unless it supplies it—that is, unless it determines it intrinsically.

**185.** When $X$ intrinsically determines $W$, and presupposes some particular $W$, it may happen that $X$ and $R$, taken together, would intrinsically determine some particular $W$. Then, if $R$ occurs as well as $X$, the fact that they do both occur will not presuppose some particular $W$, since it will intrinsically determine the existence of that particular $W$. Or again, we may know as a matter of fact that it is some particular $W$, and no other, which is the $W$ presupposed by $X$. When, in either of these ways, it is known what the particular $W$ is which is presupposed by $X$, we may say that the $W$ is Fixed.

Supposing that $X$ presupposes some particular $V$, and also some particular $W$, it may be the case that the fixing of the $V$ would involve the fixing of the $W$. For example, if anything is triangular, that fact presupposes either that it is equilateral, or that it is isosceles, or that it is scalene. It also presupposes certain definite relations in which the magnitude of its three angles stand to one another. But if the relative magnitudes of the angles are given, the presupposition in the first case is fixed. If all three angles are equal to one another, the triangle is equilateral, if two are equal, it is isosceles, and if no two are equal, it is scalene.

This relation between presuppositions may or may not be reciprocal; for if the fixing of the $V$ involves the fixing of the $W$, it may or may not be the case that the fixing of the $W$ involves the fixing of the $V$. If something is a book on the shelves of a particular library, this presupposes that it has some particular subject, and also some particular place in the library. If the books in that library are arranged according to subjects, the fact that it has such and such a subject will imply that it is in such and such a place in the library. And the fact that it is in such and such a place will imply that it has such and such a subject. Thus the relation is reciprocal. On the other hand, if we know of something that it is a species recognized by zoology, without knowing which species it is, this presupposes that it belongs to some particular genus, and also to some particular order. And here the fixing of the genus involves the fixing of the order, but the fixing of the order does not involve the fixing of the genus[1].

---

[1] It may be noticed also that in some cases $V$ and $W$ may be so related that, if $V$ is fixed to one of its possible cases, it fixes what the case of $W$ is, while it

**186**. When two presuppositions are related in this way, it might be maintained that there are not really two separate presuppositions. The fact that something is a species, it may be said, does not really require *both* the genus and the order without supplying them, since, if the genus is given, the order is supplied by that fact. But I think it more accurate to say that they are both presuppositions, but that they do not both form part of the Total Ultimate Presupposition. I should define the Total Ultimate Presupposition of $X$ as being the aggregate of all the presuppositions of $X$ after all those have been removed, the fixing of which is implied in the fixing of any of those which remain. (In cases in which the fixing of either of two presuppositions reciprocally implies the fixing of the other, it is indifferent which of the two is eliminated.)

Everything which has a presupposition at all has a total ultimate presupposition. Even if it were the case that it had only one presupposition, or if it were the case that none of its presuppositions were such that the fixing of one of them implied the fixing of any other, it would still be the case that it had a total ultimate presupposition defined as above, although in the first case that total ultimate presupposition would consist only of a single presupposition, and in neither case would there be any presupposition which did not form part of it.

**187**. Having thus discussed the nature of presupposition, we must now apply the results which we have attained to the consideration of the question whether the impossibility of simple substances would in any case produce a contradiction.

Let the substance $A$ have a set of parts $B$ and $C$. Then, if we have sufficient descriptions of $B$ and $C$, we have a sufficient description of $A$—namely, the whole which has a set of two parts which have respectively the sufficient descriptions of $B$ and of $C$. (For the sake of brevity, I shall write this in future as "the whole which is composed of $B$ and $C$.") This is a

does not do so if fixed to others of its possible cases. We have seen that the fixing of the relative magnitudes of the angles of a triangle involves the determination of whether it is equilateral, isosceles or scalene. This relation is not in all cases reciprocal, for we cannot infer the exact relative magnitudes of the angles from the fact that the triangle is isosceles or scalene. But if the triangle is equilateral, we can infer that all its angles are equal.

sufficient description of $A$, for it applies to $A$, and to nothing but $A$, since there cannot be two wholes which have the same set of parts[1]. And this is true, whatever sufficient descriptions are taken of $B$ and $C$. So long as they are sufficient descriptions, it does not matter how trivial and insignificant are the qualities which compose them.

On the other hand a sufficient description of $A$ does not necessarily involve sufficient descriptions of $B$ and $C$. It may be the case that there is always *some* sufficient description of $A$ which involves sufficient descriptions of all its parts. (We shall see later that this is actually the case.) But *all* sufficient descriptions of $A$ do not involve sufficient descriptions of all its parts. It would be quite possible, for example, to find a sufficient description of some particular college, which did not even enable us to determine how many members composed any set of its parts, and which, therefore, *à fortiori*, did not enable us to determine sufficient descriptions of each of those members.

**188.** $A$ is a substance, and this quality of being a substance implies that it is not simple, and has therefore an infinite number of sets of parts. Each member of each of these sets must, of course, have a sufficient description. The nature of $A$, then, since it contains the quality of being a substance, requires sufficient descriptions of the members of all these sets. If there is nothing in the nature of $A$ which supplies these descriptions, it will presuppose them.

If the nature of $A$ presupposes sufficient descriptions of the members of any set, $M$, of its parts, it will presuppose sufficient descriptions of the members of any set of its parts, $N$, which is sequent to $M$. For if it does not presuppose them, it must supply them, since it requires them and can only escape presupposing them by supplying them. But sufficient descriptions of the members of $N$ will imply sufficient descriptions of the members of $M$, since each member of $M$ is either itself a member

---

[1] It will be remembered that, according to our use of "whole," the same parts form the same whole, even if they are connected by two different systems of relations. If $B$ and $C$ were connected as being father and son, and also by being partners in the same business, we should not say that they formed two wholes, but that they were one whole, whose parts were connected by two systems of relations.

of $N$, or is a whole made up of members of $N$, and, as we have seen, sufficient descriptions of the parts give a sufficient description of the whole. And so, if the nature of $A$ presupposes sufficient descriptions of the members of $M$, and therefore does not supply them, it cannot supply sufficient descriptions of the members of $N$, since, by supplying the latter, it would supply what they imply—namely sufficient descriptions of the members of $M$.

Since $A$ has no simple parts, it will have an infinite number of sets of parts which are sequent to any given set. And, therefore, if its nature presupposes sufficient descriptions of the members of any set of its parts, it will have an infinite number of presuppositions.

The fact that $A$ has an infinite number of presuppositions may not involve any contradiction. But when we consider the nature of these particular presuppositions, we find that a contradiction is involved.

**189**. We have seen that a sufficient description of any substance is given, if sufficient descriptions are given of all the members of any set of its parts. Now, in the first place, if this were the *only* way in which the sufficient description of a substance could be given, there would be a contradiction. The fact that $A$ is a substance presupposes the sufficient descriptions of the members of a set, $M$, of its parts. And these sufficient descriptions of the members of $M$ could only be given, on our present hypothesis, by giving sufficient descriptions of the members of sets of their parts. These members of the sets of parts of members of $M$ will also form a set of parts of $A$—the set $N$. And, in the same way, sufficient descriptions of the members of $N$ could only be given by giving sufficient descriptions of the members of sets of their parts, which members will form another set of parts of $A$—the set $P^1$. And this process will continue to infinity.

Such an infinite series will be vicious. For the sufficient descriptions of the members of $M$ can only be made sufficient

---

[1] It will be seen that $N$ comes into this argument, not as a set of parts of $A$, but as the aggregate of the sets of parts of the members of $M$. In the same way $P$ only comes into the argument as the aggregate of the sets of parts of the members of $N$. In the argument in Section 191, on the other hand, $N$ and $P$ will enter as sets of parts of $A$.

by means of sufficient descriptions of the members of $N$, and
these by means of sufficient descriptions of the members of $P$,
and so on infinitely. Therefore the sufficient descriptions of the
members of $M$ can only be made sufficient by means of the last
stage of an unending series—that is, they cannot be made
sufficient at all. But the existence of $A$, which presupposes
sufficient descriptions of the members of $M$, implies that there
are such sufficient descriptions. And therefore the fact that there
can be no such sufficient descriptions implies a contradiction.

**190.** But, it may be replied, the hypothesis which we have
been discussing is not correct. A substance can be sufficiently
described without describing sufficiently the members of a set
of its parts. The United Kingdom, for example, might be described as a Great Power, a monarchy, a nation which possessed
two established churches, and so on, till the description
became sufficient, without introducing sufficient descriptions
of any of its parts. There is therefore, it is said, the possibility
that each part of $A$, in each of its infinite number of sets of
parts, had some quality which did not consist of the possession
of such and such parts, and which distinguished it from each
of the infinite number of other substances in the universe. (We
may say that when the sufficient descriptions of the members
of $M$ are given otherwise than by means of the sufficient
descriptions of their sets of parts, the presuppositions by $A$ of
these sufficient descriptions are Independently Fixed.) In this
case it may be said, there will be no vicious infinite series. The
existence of $A$ will presuppose the sufficient descriptions of each
of its parts in every set, but each of these presuppositions will
be independently fixed by the ultimate fact that this part has
such and such a sufficient description. It will no longer be
necessary to seek to give definiteness to each sufficient description by reaching the end of an endless series.

It seems doubtful, however, whether this is a possible alternative. Since $A$ exists, we know that there exist an infinite
number of substances, each of which is described, though not
sufficiently described, by its position in the series of such substances—that is, as being a member of a particular set of $A$'s
parts, and as being a part of some particular member of the

precedent set. The supposition is that each of these substances will also have a quality or qualities which, either by themselves or in conjunction with those mentioned in the last sentence, form a sufficient description of it. Now these additional qualities must be independent of the position of the substance in the series. They cannot be dependent on its position with regard to sequent terms in the series, for that would lead to the vicious infinite discussed in the last Section. And they cannot be dependent on its position with reference to the precedent terms of the series, for then those precedent terms would imply a sufficient description of the sequent term and would not presuppose it. And our present hypothesis is that they do presuppose it.

The concurrence then of these additional qualities with those which arise from the position of the substance in the series, must be ultimate and undetermined. And can we suppose that there are an infinite number of ultimate concurrences of this sort—that, for each of the infinite number of substances required by the absence of simple substances, there occurs a quality or qualities such as to give a sufficient description?

It seems to me that we cannot accept this supposition, in which case this attempt to avoid the contradiction involved in infinite divisibility would break down. But, even if this were not so, the existence of such sufficient descriptions of the terms, independent of their place in the series, would fail to remove the contradiction.

**191.** If each part had such a sufficient description, it would, no doubt, be sufficiently described without reference to the parts of which it consisted. But this would not affect the fact that it would also be sufficiently described by means of sufficient descriptions of all the members of any set of its parts—this, as we have seen, is true of any whole.

Now how would this affect the total ultimate presupposition of $A$? The presupposition of sufficient descriptions of the members of the set $M$ (which we may call the presupposition $\mu$) will not be part of the total ultimate presupposition presupposed by $A$. For when the presupposition $\nu$—the presupposition of the sufficient descriptions of the members of the set $N$—is fixed, it fixes the presupposition $\mu$. And thus, by the definition of total ultimate presupposition, one of the two presuppositions does not form part of it, while, since the fixing of $\mu$ would not involve the fixing of $\nu$, it is not indifferent which of the two is left out. It must be $\mu$ which is omitted.

But if we take any set of parts $P$, which is sequent to $N$, we shall reach a fresh presupposition by $A$—the presupposition, $\pi$, of sufficient descriptions of the members of the set $P$. And the fixing of $\pi$ will fix $\nu$, so that $\nu$ also must be eliminated from the total ultimate presupposition. And the same fate will befall $\pi$, and so on without end. No presupposition of this series could remain in the total ultimate presupposition unless the set of parts to which it referred had no set sequent to it. Accordingly the total ultimate presupposition presupposed by $A$ will contain neither $\mu$, nor any presupposition whose fixing implies the fixing of $\mu$.

This, however, is impossible. For the total ultimate presupposition was defined as the aggregate of all the presuppositions, after those had been removed, the fixing of which was implied by the fixing of any of those which remained. It is therefore impossible that the total ultimate presupposition presupposed by $A$ should contain neither $\mu$, nor any presupposition whose fixing implies the fixing of $\mu$.

Let us state this consideration in other words. We saw in Section 189 that, if no presupposition in the series is independently fixed, a contradiction arises. It is therefore necessary —since they must be fixed somehow—that at least one of the presuppositions must be independently fixed. But, as we have seen, it is not necessary for any of the presuppositions which are precedent to any presupposition to be independently fixed, since it will be fixed by the fixing of any sequent presupposition. And every presupposition is precedent to some presupposition. Therefore it is *not* necessary for any presupposition to be independently fixed[1]. And thus we have a contradiction.

The infinite series of presuppositions of $A$, then, will involve

I do not say that no presupposition *is* independently fixed. Apart from the difficulty raised in Section 190, which has been waived for the purpose of the present argument, I see no reason why they should not all be independently fixed. The contradiction is that every term in the series can be fixed otherwise than independently, and that therefore it is not *necessary* that any term should a contradiction, whether presuppositions can or cannot be fixed independently. As it is sometimes maintained that all infinite series involve a contradiction, it may be well to repeat that, although the contradiction would not arise unless the series were infinite, it does not arise merely from the fact that it is infinite, but from the relations in which each term stands to the term sequent to it.

**192.** The nature of any substance, then, cannot presuppose sufficient descriptions of the members of any set of its parts. And, as it certainly requires them, it must supply them. Now there are two ways in which the nature of anything can supply sufficient descriptions of other things. It can include them or imply them. Let us first consider inclusion.

It might seem at first sight as if there was no difficulty at all about this. For the nature of $A$ certainly includes sufficient descriptions of all its parts. It is part of the nature of $A$ that it has a part with a description which sufficiently describes $B$, a part with a description which sufficiently describes $C$, and so on with all the other parts in all the sets. Such a description would contain an infinite number of parts, because $A$ has an infinite number of parts, each of which must be separately described in this description of $A$. But a description is not necessarily vicious because it contains an infinite number of parts. And if this description is part of the nature of $A$, then that nature supplies, as well as requires, sufficient descriptions of all the parts of $A$.

But when we look further we shall see that such a description would involve a contradiction unless there were something in the nature of $A$ which implied sufficient descriptions of the endless series of parts, without including those descriptions. And therefore we are driven to implication—the other way in which what is required can be supplied—as the only way in which contradiction can be avoided.

**193.** For, without this, the infinite number of parts of the description would require an infinite number of ultimate concurrences between additional qualities and those which arise from the position of the part in the series. And, as was said in Section 190, it does not seem that such an infinite number of ultimate concurrences can be accepted.

**194**. And a contradiction would also arise for reasons analogous to those discussed in Section 191. The description of $A$ which includes sufficient descriptions of all its parts is adequate for a certain purpose—the purpose of providing those sufficient descriptions. Now it is clear that a description which is adequate for a given purpose may be more than adequate for that purpose —that is, it might be such that it would still have been adequate if certain parts of it had been omitted. And thus we get the conception of a Minimum Adequate Description for any purpose —a description which is sufficient for that purpose, and not more than sufficient.

It is clear that for every adequate description for any purpose, there must be at least one minimum adequate description which will differ from it by the omission of elements superfluous for the purpose, or will be identical with it, if no element in the original description is superfluous[1].

Now what would be the minimum adequate description in the case which we are considering here? It could not contain the sufficient descriptions of the parts which are members of any set of parts $M$, because sufficient descriptions of those parts are implied by sufficient descriptions of the parts which are members of any sequent set of parts $N$. It is therefore superfluous for our purpose to retain them both, and not superfluous to retain the latter. The former, therefore, must go. But, in the same way, the latter must also go in their turn, because they are implied by sufficient descriptions of any set of parts, $P$, which is sequent to them. And so on without end. Thus there will be no minimum adequate description. The only possible

---

[1] An adequate description might have more than one minimum adequate description. Let us take a case where the adequacy is for the purpose of providing a sufficient description. Then "the kindest and the best of men" has two minimum adequate descriptions, since either "the kindest of men" or "the best of men" would be a sufficient description. And again, two adequate descriptions might have the same minimum adequate description—*e.g.* "the kindest of men and a court official" and "the kindest of men and a British peer," would each have "the kindest of men" as its minimum adequate description for the purpose of providing a sufficient description.

minimum adequate description would consist of sufficient descriptions of the parts of $A$ which are members of a set of parts which had no sequent to it. And since $A$ has no simple parts, there can be no such set.

And thus there is a contradiction. There must be a minimum adequate description for the description in question, and yet there cannot be one. There is only one way in which this can be avoided. A chain of implications must run downwards from precedent sets to sequent sets, such that sufficient descriptions of the members of the precedent set imply sufficient descriptions of the members of the sequent sets. In this case the inclusion of the description of the precedent set will render inclusion of the descriptions of the sequent sets unnecessary, since they can be deduced from it. And thus the minimum description of $A$ which is adequate for providing sufficient descriptions of all its parts will be the description of the parts of the precedent set, from which the chain of implications starts.

Of the two ways in which the nature of $A$ could supply the sufficient descriptions of its parts, we have now seen that inclusion without implication would involve a contradiction. We have therefore no hope left but in implication. We must find a description of $A$ which, while it may include sufficient descriptions of the members of one or more sets of its parts, implies sufficient descriptions of the members of the infinite number of sets of parts which are sequent to the last of these.

Can we find such a description? We have seen that any sufficient description of the members of a set of parts implies a sufficient description of the whole, and therefore that any sufficient description of the members of a sequent set of parts implies a sufficient description of the members of a precedent set of parts. But the reverse is not true. Many sufficient descriptions of a whole do not imply sufficient descriptions of the members of any one set of its parts, much less of the infinite number of such sets. But if the contradiction is to be avoided, there must be some description of every substance which does imply sufficient descriptions of every part through all its infinite series of sets of parts. To discover what such a description could be will be our first task in the next Book.

# BOOK IV

## DETERMINING CORRESPONDENCE

# CHAPTER XXIV

## DETERMINING CORRESPONDENCE

**195.** In the last Chapter we saw that, from the fact that no substance can be simple, it would follow, under certain circumstances, that the nature of a substance involved a contradiction, and that, therefore, no substance could exist. This contradiction would arise, we found, if the nature of any substance, $A$, presupposed sufficient descriptions of sequent sets of its parts to infinity. This condition can be analyzed into two elements— firstly, that the fact that $A$ is a substance implies that it has parts within parts to infinity, and that those parts have sufficient descriptions, and, secondly, that no description of $A$ implies some sufficient description for each of its parts.

The first of these elements is obviously true, if no substance can be simple. For then the fact that anything is a substance implies that it has parts within parts to infinity, and each of these must have a sufficient description. If, therefore, no description of $A$ implies some sufficient description for each of its parts, then the nature of $A$ involves a contradiction.

But we have seen that substances do exist, and the nature of an existent substance cannot contain a contradiction. We can be certain, then, that there must be some description of each existent substance which does imply sufficient descriptions of all the parts of $A$[1]. We are entitled to assert this, even if we do not know of any description of $A$ which would do this. And if we come to the conclusion that only a description of a certain

---

[1] If an argument were offered to us, in which we could detect no error, to prove that there could be no such description of $A$, it would be obvious that there was some mistake somewhere, since all the conclusions combined would produce a contradiction. In that case there might be no reason for doubting the last argument rather than for doubting one of the others. But since the other propositions have been accepted as certain, and no argument has ever been offered to prove that there could be no such description of $A$, it is this last proposition which we ought to reject.

type could do this, we shall be entitled to assert that a description of this type must be true of $A$. Can we arrive at any conclusion as to the type of description in question?

We saw at the end of the last Chapter that the description may be one which includes sufficient descriptions of the members of one or more sets of its parts, so long as it implied, without including, sufficient descriptions of the members of the infinite number of sets of parts which are sequent to the last set included in the description. In what way could such implications be determined?

**196**. There are certain realities, other than substances, each of which does imply an infinite series of other realities. Would it be possible to get what we want by a law which asserted that each part of $A$ was in a certain one-to-one correspondence with each term of such an infinite series, the nature of the correspondence being such that, in the fact that a part of $A$ corresponded in this way to a reality with a given nature, there would be implied a sufficient description of that part of $A$?

What infinite series are there of this sort? We get such series with propositions. For example, " $M$ is $N$ " implies "it is true that $M$ is $N$," and again "it is true that it is true that $M$ is $N$," and so on infinitely. But a one-to-one correspondence with the terms of such a series as this would never give us the series of parts of $A$. For the infinite series in the case of the substance is an infinite series of sets of parts, and the number of members in each set increases as we pass from precedent to sequent sets. No one-to-one correspondence with such a series as this series of propositions could give the required increasing plurality in the later set of parts, and such a series, therefore, cannot help us.

Again, there are the infinite series of derivative characteristics which were discussed in Chapter IX. And here we can get an increasing plurality in the later terms. Take the case of $M$ being equal to $N$. This relationship, in the first place, involves two more relationships, since both $M$ and $N$ have relationships to the relationship of equality of which they are terms. In the next stage there are involved four more relationships. For the relationship between $M$ and its relationship of equality to $N$

has relationships both to $M$ and to the relationship of equality, and a corresponding fact is true of the relationship between $N$ and the relationship of equality. In the third stage eight fresh terms are involved, and so on infinitely.

Would it be possible to determine the parts of $A$ by a correspondence to the series of relationships generated in this way by the relation of any two terms? But in this case, like the last, there is no uniform kind of correspondence which could prevail between the terms of such a series, and the parts of $A$. For in this series the fresh terms generated in each stage are not parts of the terms in the stage above, but are intercalated between all the terms generated in all the previous stages. With the parts of $A$, on the other hand, the new terms introduced in each stage—that is, in this case, in each set of parts—are parts of the terms in the stage above, and do not occupy positions between them. No principle of one-to-one correspondence, therefore, with the terms of the first series, could determine the series of the parts of $A$.

Of course propositions, and those characteristics which are not simple, have parts, and some of them have parts of parts. But it would be impossible to get our infinite series of sets of parts of substances by any correspondence to them, because it is not the case that every part of a proposition or of a characteristic has again parts. On the contrary, every characteristic which is not itself simple is made up of simple parts, and every proposition can be analyzed into members which cannot be analyzed further.

Can we hope to obtain what we want by means of any correspondence of the series of sets of parts of $A$ with any other infinite series of substances? But, if the series to which it is to correspond is not a series of parts within parts to infinity, correspondence to it can never give us what we want. And, if it is a series of parts within parts to infinity, will not the same difficulties arise about it as arose about $A$?

**197.** I believe that there is one way out of the difficulty, and only one way.

Let $A$ have a set of parts, $B$ and $C$. (The number of parts in the set may be any number, finite or infinite.) Let it be true in the first place, that each of these parts has a set of parts corresponding to each set of parts of *A*. In the second place, let it be true that the correspondence is of the same sort throughout, that it is a one-to-one relation between the members of the sets of parts, and that it is such that a certain sufficient description of *C*, which includes the fact that it is in this relation to *some* part of *B*, will determine a sufficient description of the part of *B* in question. And, in the third place, let it be true that the correspondence is such that, when one determinant is part of another determinant, then any part determined by the first will be part of a part determined by the second.

For the sake of brevity, I shall write *B! C* for that part of *B* which corresponds to *C*, and *B! C! D* for that part of *B* which corresponds to that part of *C* which corresponds to *D*, and so on. I shall call such a correspondence a Determining Correspondence, since by it, with the help of sufficient descriptions of *B* and *C*, we can determine a sufficient description of *B! C*. I shall speak of *C* as the Determinant of *B! C*, and of *B! C* as the Determinate of *C*, or as determined by *C*. I shall say that *B! C! D* is Directly Determined by *C! D*, and Indirectly Determined by *D*, which is the determinant of its determinant. I shall call *A* a Primary Whole, and *B* a Primary Part. *B! C*, *B! C! D*, *B! C! D! E*, and so on, I shall call Secondary Parts. I shall call *B! C* a secondary part of the First Grade, *B! C! D* a secondary part of the Second Grade, and so on[1].

**198**.  If the conditions mentioned in the last paragraph but one are fulfilled, it follows that sufficient descriptions of the primary parts will determine sufficient descriptions of parts within parts of *A* through an infinite series. For in *B* we have *B! B* and *B! C*, and in *C* we have *C! B* and *C! C*. And all these four are parts of *A*, and will have parts correspondent to them both in *B* and *C*. In *B*, then, there will be *B! B! B*, *B! B! C*, *B! C! B*, and *B! C! C*. In *C* there will be *C! B! B*, *C! B! C*, *C! C! B*, and *C! C! C*. Each of these eight, again, will have

---

[1] I do not define here the terms used in this paragraph, as their meanings will turn out to be rather wider than is required to cover the cases now before us. The definitions will be given in Section 202.

parts correspondent to it both in $B$ and $C$, and so on without end.

We have thus got an infinite series of parts of parts of $A$, where the sufficient description of each set of parts implies the sufficient description of the set of parts below it. And thus the infinite series is no longer vicious. It was vicious before, as we saw in the last chapter, because a sufficient description of each stage in the series was implied by a sufficient description of a lower stage, while a sufficient description of a higher stage presupposed a sufficient description of a lower one—that is, implied that there should be such a description, while not implying what it was. And this, as we saw, rendered it impossible that the presupposition should have a total ultimate presupposition, while, on the other hand, it could not be without one.

Now, however, we have found a sufficient description of one set of parts which implies sufficient descriptions of all lower sets. Since it implies those descriptions, it does not presuppose them. And thus the difficulty about the total ultimate presupposition is removed.

And, again, the series would not be vicious because it involved an infinite number of ultimate concurrences. For both the sufficient description of each secondary part, and its place in the series, would follow from the sufficient descriptions of the primary parts.

**199.** The third condition is essential, as, if it were not inserted, it would not be necessary that determining correspondence should determine parts of *every* part of $A$, though it would determine an infinite number of parts in every *primary* part of $A$. Without the third condition, it would be possible, for example, in the case given above, that seven of the parts of the third set should fall within three of the parts of the second set, while the remaining part of the second set should be itself the eighth part of the third set, corresponding both with a part of the first set and with a part of the second. It might, for example, be true of the same part that it was *B! C* and *B! C! D*, or that it was *B! C* and *B! B! B*, or any other combination. It might also be a member of the fourth set of parts, and of every sequent set of parts. In that case determining correspondence would not determine any part of that part, while at the same time, being a substance, it must have parts within parts to infinity. And thus, in the case of that part, the vicious presupposition would not be avoided. But the insertion of the third condition removes this possibility.

**200.** The sufficient description which thus implies sufficient descriptions of each of this infinite series of parts of parts of $A$ implies sufficient descriptions of *all* parts of $A$. It is true that some parts of $A$ will not be found in the infinite series. For example, the part which consists of $B!\ C$ and $B!\ B!\ C$ will not be found there, nor, if $A$ has three primary parts $B$, $C$, and $D$, will the part consisting of $B$ and $C$ be found there. But when, *e.g.*, we had reached in the series sufficient descriptions of $B!\ C$ and $B!\ B!\ C$, these would imply a sufficient description of the part consisting of these parts. And, if we are right in our conclusion that an infinite series of sets of parts involves a contradiction unless it is determined by determining correspondence, we are certain that every substance which is not in the series of determining correspondence can be divided into substances which are in that series. For if there were any such substance which could not be so divided, then, since every substance is divided into parts of parts infinitely, there would be infinite series of sets of parts which were not determined by determining correspondence. And this would be a contradiction.

The sufficient description of members of the set of primary parts of $A$ will, of course, give us a sufficient description of $A$. For, as we saw in the last chapter, a sufficient description of the members of any set of parts of a whole gives a sufficient description of the whole.

**201.** Is it necessary, it might be asked, to take the primary parts of $A$ as an ultimate fact, in order to imply the sufficient description of all sequent sets of parts of $A$? Could not the same result be produced by means of another substance in connection with $A$. Suppose that, besides $A$, there was $G$, and that the relation between them was such that $A$ and $G$ had each a set of parts corresponding to every set of parts of the compound substance composed of $A$ and $G$. This would certainly produce the infinite series of implications required to determine all the parts of $A$. But then it would be the compound substance composed of $A$ and $G$ which would be the primary whole, and $A$ and $G$ would be its primary parts, and therefore the original formula would still be applicable.

There are three respects in which the conditions might be different from those given in Section 197, and yet the correspondence might be such as to avoid the vicious infinite series. In the first place, we have so far taken cases in which each primary part of $A$ has a set of parts corresponding to each set of parts of $A$. But this is not necessary. It is sufficient if each primary part has a Differentiating Group, consisting of two or more primary parts of $A$, and if it has a set of parts corresponding to each set of parts of that group. If $A$ has the primary parts $B$, $C$, and $D$, sufficient descriptions of an infinite series of sets of parts within parts of $A$ would be determined if $B$ had parts corresponding to $B$ and $C$ and to their parts, while $C$ had parts corresponding to $C$ and $D$ and to their parts, $D$, finally, having parts corresponding to $D$ and $B$ and to their parts. Nor is it necessary that a primary part should be a member of its own differentiating group. The differentiating group of $B$ might be $C$ and $D$, while those of $C$ and $D$ might be respectively $D$ and $B$, and $B$ and $C$.

It is not necessary, then, that every primary part should be a determinant of parts in every other primary part of $A$. And, in the second place, it is not necessary that every primary part should be a determinant at all. Let $B$ and $C$ have each $B$ and $C$ as its differentiating group. Then all parts of $B$ and $C$ have sufficient descriptions determined by the relation between $B$ and $C$. Now if the parts of $D$ were determined by $B$ and $C$, and by their parts, all parts of $D$ would have sufficient descriptions determined. And thus sufficient descriptions of all parts of $A$ would be reached, although $D$ was not a determinant of any part of $A$.

In the third place, it is possible that in the case of *some* primary parts, the place of the differentiating group may be taken by a single primary part. If, in the case just given, the parts of $D$ had no determinant except $B$ and its parts, the infinite series of sets of parts of $D$ would have their sufficient descriptions determined, since there is an infinite series of parts of parts within $B^1$.

In order that this should happen, the sufficient descriptions of the infinite series of sets of parts of $B$ must be determined. And therefore it is necessary that in each primary whole there should be at least one group of primary parts in which determining correspondence is Reciprocal. (I call determining correspondence Reciprocal in any group of primary parts when each member of the group determines, either directly or indirectly, secondary parts of each of the other members, and when no secondary part of any member is determined by any primary part outside the group.) It is only by means of such reciprocity that an infinite series of implications of sufficient descriptions can be established in the first place, though one such infinite series, when it has been established, may establish another without reciprocal determination.

**202.** We are now in a position to give definitions of the terms of whose use we gave examples in Section 197. Determining Correspondence may be defined as follows. A relation between a substance $C$ and the part of a substance $B$ is a relation of determining correspondence if a certain sufficient description of $C$, which includes the fact that it is in that relation to *some* part of $B$, (1) intrinsically determines a sufficient description of the part of $B$ in question, $B! C$, and (2) intrinsically determines sufficient descriptions of each member of a set of parts of $B! C$, and of each member of a set of parts of each of such members, and so on to infinity[2].

---

[1] In this case the highest series of sets of parts of $D$ which would be determined by determining correspondence would consist of $D! B! B$, and $D! B! C$. These are directly determined, not by primary parts, but by secondary parts of the first grade ($B! B$ and $B! C$) and will be themselves secondary parts of the second grade, so that $D$ will have no secondary parts of the first grade. In the same way, if $D$ stands in the place of a differentiating group for $E$, the highest set of parts in $E$ which are determined by determining correspondence would consist of $E! D! B! B$, and $E! D! B! C$, which are secondary parts of the third grade.

[2] The determining correspondence, which is a relation between the two substances, is, of course, not to be confounded with the relation of intrinsic determination, which is a relation between certain sufficient descriptions of the two substances.

We have seen that such an infinite series cannot be determined unless (3) the sufficient description of $C$ also includes a statement that each member of a set of $C$'s points has some substance to which it stands in a relation of determining correspondence, as the part of $B$ does to $C$ itself; unless (4) either $B$ and $C$ form a group, or part of a group, in which determination is reciprocal, or else each of them is itself determined, either directly or indirectly, by a relation of determining correspondence to substances which are in such a reciprocal relation to one another; and unless (5) when one determinant is part of another determinant, any part determined by the first will be part of a part determined by the other. These three conditions, however, do not form part of the definition, but can be deduced from it, since, as has just been said, the second clause in the definition could only be true in cases in which these three conditions were also true.

Proceeding with our definitions, a Primary Whole is a substance (1) such that it is not necessary, in order to describe sufficiently any of its parts, to introduce any determining correspondence with anything except another of its parts, and (2) such that it is not necessary to introduce determining correspondence with any of its parts to describe sufficiently any substance outside it, and (3) such that it has no part of which the previous clauses (1) and (2) are both true[1].

Primary Parts may be defined as follows. When a set of parts of a substance is such that none of its members are determined by determining correspondence, and that, from sufficient descriptions of all its members, there follow, by determining correspondence, sufficient descriptions of the members of an infinite series of sequent sets, then the members of that set are called Primary Parts.

Any member of any of these sequent sets is called a Secondary Part. If it is directly determined by determining correspondence with a primary part, it is called a secondary part of the First

[1] The difference between a primary whole and a reciprocally determining group is that, while the latter is self-contained in respect of the determination of its own secondary parts, its parts can determine secondary parts which are outside the group. In a primary whole, on the other hand, no part has either a determinant or a determinate outside the primary whole.

Grade. If it is directly determined by determining correspondence with a secondary part of the first grade, it is called a secondary part of the Second Grade, and so on.

The Differentiating Group of any primary part $B$ consists of those primary parts, to which, and to the secondary parts of which, the parts of $B$ correspond.

**203.** We have seen that every primary part in a primary whole need not have parts directly determined by all the primary parts in that whole. Is it necessary that it should have parts indirectly determined by all of these primary parts? It is clear that this is not the case. For, as we have seen, it is possible that some primary parts should not be determinants at all. And if $D$, for example, determines nothing, it cannot determine something which determines something else.

But even if every primary part in some primary whole was a direct determinant of something, it would not follow that all these primary parts determined parts of all the others, either directly or indirectly. Suppose that, of four primary parts, $B$, $C$, $D$, and $E$, the differentiating group of $B$, and also that of $C$, was $B$ and $C$, while the differentiating group of $D$, and also that of $E$, was $B$, $D$, and $E$. Thus each of the four parts would be a determinant. And they would all fall within the same primary whole, since $B$ must be within the same primary whole as $C$, and also within the same primary whole as $D$ and $E$. Yet neither the parts of $B$ nor the parts of $C$ would be determined, either directly or indirectly, by $D$ or $E$. $B$ and $C$ form a system such that their parts are determined by nothing outside that system.

But though their parts are not determined, either directly or indirectly, by $D$ or $E$, they both determine parts of $D$ and $E$, $B$ determining them directly, and $C$ indirectly through $B$. And of any two primary parts in the same primary whole it is necessary that each of them should either determine parts of the other, or itself have parts which are determined by that other, or both. For without this, the two primary parts would belong to two primary wholes, and not to the same one.

**204.** We saw in the last chapter that sufficient descriptions of the members of a sequent set will always give sufficient descriptions of the members of a precedent set, since the parts in a precedent set are wholes made up of the more numerous members of the sequent set. Determining correspondence ensures that sufficient descriptions of the members of a precedent set will give sufficient descriptions of the members of a sequent set. But there is a difference between the two cases. For *any* sufficient descriptions of the members of the sequent set will give sufficient descriptions of the members of the precedent set, while all that determining correspondence involves is that *some* sufficient descriptions of the members of the precedent set will give sufficient descriptions of the members of the sequent set. The members of the precedent set may have other sufficient descriptions which would not do this. But this result is, as we have seen, sufficient to remove the contradiction.

**205.** We have spoken of primary wholes by that name because they are self-contained as far as determining correspondence goes. But, unless the whole universe forms a single primary whole, a primary whole will also be a part. It will be a part of the universe, to begin with, and, if there are more than two primary wholes in the universe, each of them will be a member of various groups of primary wholes, each of which groups will be a separate substance. And there will also be substances which consist of one or more primary wholes, together with one or more parts of other primary wholes. We may speak of wholes of which primary wholes are parts as Super-primary Wholes.

Between such wholes and their parts there will be no relation of determining correspondence. And so, while any sufficient descriptions of the parts will imply sufficient descriptions of the wholes, there will be nothing to ensure that any sufficient descriptions of the wholes will imply sufficient descriptions of the parts. It is thus possible that the nature of a super-primary whole will presuppose sufficient descriptions of all its parts. But that will not produce a contradiction, because the series of presuppositions generated will not be infinite. A super-primary whole may, in some cases, be divided into other super-primary wholes. But a finite number of steps will analyze it into a set of parts, all of which are primary or secondary parts. These, of

I

course, will each have an infinite series of parts within parts, but these series will not be vicious, because, being within primary parts, the terms of each series will be related by determining correspondence.

**206.** To sum up the results of this chapter—the absence of simple substances does not involve a contradiction if the universe has a set of parts which answer to our definition of primary parts. (These primary parts may form one primary whole, or may be divided into any number of primary wholes.) The theory that the universe has such a set of parts I shall call the theory of the determining correspondence of substance.

Are we entitled to accept this theory as proved? We have found that there are no simple substances, and therefore the nature of the existent must be such as to prevent the absence of simple substances from involving a contradiction. For this, as we have seen, it is necessary that sufficient descriptions of the unending series of parts should be implied in sufficient descriptions of their wholes. And we have seen that this will be the case if the theory of the determining correspondence of substances is true.

But would it be possible to imply the sufficient descriptions of the parts by sufficient descriptions of their wholes in any other way besides this? If so, we cannot be sure that the theory of determining correspondence is true. But what has to be done is to imply an infinite series of stages, each stage with more members in it than the stage before it, and, as we have seen, to imply it in something which does not itself contain such an infinite series. And how could this possibly be done except—to use a metaphor which is not inappropriate—by that reflection of a plurality on itself which does imply an infinite number of stages, each containing more members than the one before it? And when we try to specify the sort of reflection which must take place, we can see that, to give sufficient descriptions, this reflection must take the form which we have called determining correspondence.

I submit, therefore, as the legitimate conclusion from this chapter and the two which precede it, that we are entitled to adopt the theory of determining correspondence as proved.

# CHAPTER XXV

## DETERMINING CORRESPONDENCE AS CAUSAL

**207.** We have now established that a relation of determining correspondence holds between various substances. And it may be well at this point to enquire whether this relation is to be called a relation of causality. The question is, in a sense, only verbal. We shall not here endeavour to discover any fresh characteristics of the relation of determining correspondence, but to decide whether the characteristics which it is already known to possess are such as to make the name of causality appropriate to it. But the question, though in this sense verbal, is not therefore trivial. Causality is a term which has occupied a prominent place in almost every philosophical system—in those which deny the validity of causation no less than in those which assert it. And it is therefore not unimportant to discover the relation of our system to these others in this respect. If determining correspondence is a case of causality, then causality does hold between some existents, since determining correspondence has been shown to hold between some existents.

What, then, is meant by causality? There would be general agreement that, unless causality is to be rejected altogether, the beheading of Charles I must be held to have caused his death, while it did not cause his birth, or the death of Henry VIII. And, again, the uxoriousness of Charles I caused him to be contemptible, while it did not cause him to be King of England or President of the United States. What is the relation which is thus considered to hold between the beheading of Charles I and his death?

**208.** There are three things which would be universally admitted to be necessary to this relation. The first is that it is a relation of determination, and of what we have called intrinsic determination. The occurrence of the beheading of Charles I determines the occurrence of his death. And the determination is clearly intrinsic, and not merely the extrinsic determination which, as we have seen, holds between each fact in the universe and every other fact. For causality is a relation which may hold between $A$ and $B$, and not between $A$ and $C$. There may be no causal relation between the execution of Charles I and the last eruption of Vesuvius. And the proposition "Charles I was beheaded" implies the proposition "Charles I is dead." This shows that the determination is intrinsic.

In the second place, the relation of causality only holds between existents. We should not say that the definitions and axioms of Euclid were the cause that two sides of a triangle are longer than the third side, though they do determine that they are longer. And we should not say that the law of the tides was partly caused by the law of gravitation, though we should say that the height of the sea at a particular time and place had the attraction of the moon as part of its cause.

Again, the beheading of an English king in the eighteenth century intrinsically determines the death of that king. But we should not say that it caused it, because, in point of fact, no English king was beheaded in the eighteenth century, and so the relation of determination is not between existents. All that we can say is that, if a king of England had been beheaded in the eighteenth century, it *would* have caused his death—that is, that, if the terms had been existent, the relation of causality would have held between them.

In the third place, the relation of causality is always a relation between qualities (including relational qualities). Our ordinary language, indeed, conceals this. We speak of Luther as a part-cause of the Reformation, and of the beheading of Charles I as the cause of his death. And both Luther and the three events are not qualities, but substances, each of which has many qualities. Indeed, instead of saying that the beheading caused the death, we might describe the substances by other qualities, and say that an action by a masked man caused an event deplored by the White Rose League.

But when we look more closely into the matter we see that the relation is really between two qualities. It is only one quality in the earlier event which is held to determine one quality in the later. That the earlier was the beheading of Charles I determines that the later was the death of Charles I. But that the earlier was an action by a masked man does not determine that the later was an event deplored by the White Rose League. The intrinsic determination, and therefore the causality, is a relation which connects only one quality in each substance, and does not connect the others.

And, again, when the uxoriousness of Charles I is said to be the cause that he is contemptible, it is clear that the relation must be between qualities. For in this case both the qualities belong to the same substance. And nothing can be the cause of itself.

**209.** These three points about the nature of causality are, I think, beyond dispute. In the fourth place, it is commonly held that the two terms of the relation can be distinguished from each other as respectively cause and effect, and that the cause cannot be subsequent to the effect, so that the prior term is the cause, except in cases where the two terms are either timeless or simultaneous in time.

If this were all, the point would merely concern nomenclature. The earlier term would be called the cause, and the later the effect. There would, however, be no difference between cause and effect in cases where the two terms are timeless or simultaneous. And the possibility of timeless or simultaneous causation is often, though not always, admitted.

But now we come to three features which are sometimes held to distinguish all causes from effects. And the assertion of these distinctions is combined with the assertion that a cause cannot be subsequent to its effect. By means of these features, if we accepted them, we should be able to distinguish between cause and effect even in cases of timeless and simultaneous causation. And now the distinction between cause and effect has become more than a question of nomenclature. For it is a question of fact whether, in all cases of intrinsic determinations between existent qualities, one of the two terms has any of these features, while the other has not, and whether, if this is so, and if the two terms occur at different times, it is always the earlier term which has them.

The first of these features which is sometimes held to distinguish the cause from the effect is that the cause determines the effect in some way in which the effect does not determine the cause. It is often held, for example, that our choice between resisting a temptation and yielding to it would not be determined if it were not caused, even if it were itself the inevitable cause of certain effects.

In the second place, it is sometimes held that the cause explains the effect in some way in which the effect does not explain the cause.

In the third place, it is sometimes held that the cause exercises a certain activity on the effect. Even if the occurrence of $A$ intrinsically determines the occurrence of $B$, this is not, it is said, sufficient to constitute causation unless an activity is also present.

Now it seems to me that all these features, which have been held by different thinkers to differentiate the cause from the effect, must be rejected—the first on the ground that such non-reciprocal determination of one term by the other is not limited to the determination of the earlier by the later, and the second and third on the ground that no such explanation, and no such activity, are to be found in causal relations at all.

**210.** Let us first consider the non-reciprocal determination. It is, of course, often the case that the determination of two qualities which are causally connected is not reciprocal. Beheading is the cause of death. And, while beheading determines death, death does not determine beheading, since there are many other ways in which death can occur. Here then, the earlier does determine the later, in a way in which the later does not determine the earlier. But in other cases non-reciprocal determination goes the other way. Drinking alcohol must precede intoxication. And here it is the later which determines the earlier. For I cannot get drunk without drinking alcohol, but I can drink alcohol without getting drunk.

And we find that the determination may run non-reciprocally from earlier to later, or from later to earlier, according as the qualities taken are taken in a more or less precise form. In so far as it is taken in a less precise form, it is more probable that it will be determined without determining. We have seen that drinking alcohol is determined by getting drunk, and does not determine it. But any event which is a drinking of alcohol is also a drinking of a definite amount under definite conditions. And if we take this more definite quality we find that the drinking now determines the drunkenness, and not *vice versa*. For it would be impossible to drink that amount under those conditions without getting drunk, while it would be possible to get drunk without drinking that amount under those conditions—much less drink, for example, might be sufficient for a man with a different constitution.

Thus, if the cause is to be taken, as it always is taken, as something which cannot be subsequent to the effect, we cannot say that the cause determines the effect in a way in which the effect does not determine the cause.

**211.** Then, secondly, it is asserted that the cause explains the effect in some way in which the effect does not explain the cause. Now if explanation here merely means that the events are taken as an instance of a general law, then, of course, causality does give an explanation. If I ask why the event $B$ has, among other qualities, that of being the death of a human body, I may be told that it was immediately preceded by the event $A$, which was the beheading of the same body, and that there is a general law that the beheading of a body is immediately followed by its death. But this does not explain the quality of $B$ in any way in which it does not explain the quality of $A$. They are both included in the general law.

But it is more than this which is meant when the cause is said to explain the effect. It is supposed that a causal law shows in some way *why* the occurrence of $X$, the quality in the cause, implies the occurrence of $Z$, the quality in the effect, and that, as a consequence of this, a particular case of $Z$ is explained by its relation to $X$ in some deeper and more thorough manner than by being shown to be an instance of a general law, while the occurrence of $X$ is not explained in the same way by its relation to $Z$.

This, however, is a mistake. Either the causal law in question is ultimate, or it can be deduced from some more general law which is ultimate[1]. And, it must be remembered, an ultimate law need not be self-evident. It may be one which we can only reach by induction. In that case the implication by the occurrence of $X$ of the occurrence of $Y$ presents itself to us as a mere fact. We see that it is so, but that is all about it. There is no question of any "why," and there is no explanation, except in the sense that the case has been brought under a general law.

But even if the ultimate causal law should be self-evident, we should not have reached the sort of explanation which is asserted here. It might possibly be said that the self-evidence of the relation was in a sense the explanation of it. But it would be no more the explanation of the later by the earlier than it would be the explanation of the earlier by the later.

**212.** There remains the view that the cause exerts an activity on the effect. This, also, seems to me to be quite unfounded. If we ask for the proof of the existence of such an activity, we are usually referred to introspection. When I will to move my hand, and my hand is moved, I am directly aware, it is said, of an activity which I am exerting in my volition.

Even if there were such an activity in such cases, it would give us no reason to believe that there was any such activity when the cause was not a volition, nor any indication of what the cause would in that case be like. And therefore some of the more consistent supporters of this view are driven to maintain that nothing but a volition is ever a cause—all events which are not the effects of human volitions being the direct effects of divine volitions, and having no other causes. It would, however, be a very strained and inconvenient use of the word cause, which compelled us to say that the *only* cause of the destruction of Lisbon was a divine volition, and that the earthquake had no effect at all.

---

[1] I believe that the astonishing view, held by some philosophers, that cause and effect are identical, may be due to their unwillingness to admit that all cases of causality bring us finally to ultimate laws which cannot be deduced from others. If cause and effect are identical, it is thought, the only law required to connect them will be the law that a thing is itself. But whatever the relation of identity may be and do, it is not the same relation as that which is called causality. Nor is a thing explained in any way by the fact that it is identical with itself.

But I do not believe there is any such activity to be perceived, even when our volitions are causes. In my own case I can perceive no such activity. And I *can* perceive something which could be mistaken for such an activity. I am conscious of willing. And then I am sometimes conscious of a feeling of tension or strain within myself. But this is all. Now this feeling is not the volition, nor an element in the volition. It is an effect of the volition, and is subsequent—though only slightly subsequent—to it. But I think that it is wrongly supposed to be the volition, or an element in it, and that its quality of being a tension is mistaken for the quality of being an activity. In this way, I think, the belief arises that a volition is a cause which exerts an activity. Thus I submit that we must reject the view that we are directly aware of an activity in the cases where the causes are our volitions. And no other reasons, except this asserted direct awareness, have ever been given why we should believe such an activity to exist.

**213**. A cause, then, cannot be distinguished from an effect, in respect of its determining or explaining the effect, or of exercising activity on it. It can only be distinguished as the term of the relation which is prior to the other in time, if either is prior to the other. In cases in which the terms are timeless or simultaneous, neither of them can be called the cause[1].

What is the reason of the belief that it is the earlier term which exerts activity, or which determines or explains the later? Professor Taylor gives two reasons to which this may be due. "(*a*) Even granting that an event may be determined by subsequent events, yet, as *we* do not know what these events are until after their occurrence, we should have no means of inferring by *what* particular events yet to come any present event was conditioned, and thus should be thrown back on mere unprincipled guess-work if we attempted to assign its, as yet future, conditions. (*b*) A more important consideration is that our search for causes is ultimately derived from the search for *means* to the practical realization of results in which we are

---

[1] We might, however, reasonably call one term the cause if it *appeared* as being in time, and as being prior to the other, though in reality both terms were timeless.

interested. We desire to know the conditions of occurrences primarily in order to produce those occurrences for ourselves by setting up their conditions. It is therefore essential for our practical purposes to seek the conditions of an occurrence exclusively among its antecedents[1]."

Two other reasons might also, I think, be given. Our ordinary unreflective notion of causality has been largely moulded by persons who accepted the doctrine of undetermined free will. Now, according to that doctrine, if such a free will existed, a free volition would determine what succeeded it. But it would not determine what preceded it, since its occurrence is independent of conditions. There would thus be a class of important events which determined what succeeded them, but not what preceded them. And from this it would be an easy step to the belief that events could only be determined by their antecedents and not by their consequents.

In the second place, as we shall see in Book VII, the direction of the time series from earlier to later is more fundamental to the series than the direction from later to earlier. And this might produce the view that activity, or explanation, or determination, proceeded from earlier to later.

**214.** It may be remarked in passing that the view that each causal series must have a first cause, while it need not have a last effect, seems to be due, to a considerable extent, to the belief that the cause determines or explains the effect in a way in which the effect does not determine the cause. Determining and explaining are transitive relations. If $Z$ is determined by $Y$, and $Y$ by $X$, then $Z$ is determined by $X$. And the same is the case with explanation. If determination and explanation were always of the effect by the cause, then nothing is causally determined or explained except by the earliest term in the whole series—the first cause. If there is no first cause, nothing in the series is causally determined or explained at all. And if it is held that everything which is causal must be completely determined or completely explained, then there must be a first cause, while there is no corresponding necessity for a last effect.

We have seen, however, that an effect can determine the

---

[1] *Elements of Metaphysics*, I, 5, Section 5.

cause in just the same way in which the cause can determine the effect. Nor is there any sense in which the cause can explain the effect, and in which the effect cannot explain the cause. It follows, therefore, that an infinite causal regress would not be vicious on this ground, and that, so far as we can yet see, it might exist[1].

**215.** Our conclusion, then, is that causality is a relation of intrinsic determination between the occurrence of existing qualities, and that, when one quality occurs before the other, it is convenient to speak of the earlier quality as the cause, but that the cause is not distinguished from the effect in any other way, and that, where the relation is timeless or simultaneous, neither of the two terms can be called the cause.

This result differs from the ordinary view of causality in one respect only. The ordinary view holds that there is some additional difference between the cause and the effect besides their relative positions in time, and that this additional distinction could be found in cases which were not temporally separated. And, therefore, it would not allow that there were any causal relations in which one term was not the cause, and the other the effect.

This is doubtless an important difference. But it is not sufficient to make the name of causality inapplicable to the relation as defined by us. For in any case in which the two terms of the relation are, or appear as being, at different moments of time, we shall be using terms in just the same way as that in which they are used on the ordinary view. And it is this class of cases with which mankind is mostly concerned. Even in cases of timeless or simultaneous causation, we shall agree with the ordinary view in holding that they are cases of intrinsic determination between the occurrence of existing

---

[1] I do not say that this is the only ground which has led to the assertion that there must be a first cause, while there need not be a last effect. Another ground, I think, is the belief that an infinite past is impossible, since it would be a completed infinite, while an infinite future would not be completed. I cannot see, however, in what sense an infinite past is more completed than an infinite future. Each is bounded in one direction by the present. Each is unbounded in one direction. The fact that the infinite past is unbounded in one direction, and the infinite future in the other, does not seem to me to make the first less probable than the last. This, however, is a digression.

qualities. And this is, after all, the most essential point on any view of causation. When a man says that the beheading of Charles I was the cause of his death, the essence of the assertion is that the beheading involved the death, so that from the fact that he was beheaded it could be inferred that he died, and, if he had not died, it could be inferred that he had not been beheaded. For some people the assertion may mean more, but this is always the most important part of the meaning.

**216.** Since we have defined causality in this way, we must answer the question with which this chapter began in the affirmative. Determining correspondence is a causal relation. A certain quality in each secondary part of the first grade is intrinsically determined by a certain quality in some primary part. A certain quality in each secondary part of the second grade is intrinsically determined by a certain quality in each secondary part of the first grade, and so on infinitely.

Thus, if we are right in holding that we have demonstrated the theory of determining correspondence, we have demonstrated that causality does occur. And not only have we demonstrated that causality does occur, but we have demonstrated the validity of a particular causal law. For we have shown that the specific relation which exists between the determining quality and the determined quality is a relation of that particular sort which we have called determining correspondence.

And not only have we demonstrated the occurrence of a particular causal relation, and therefore the validity of a particular causal law, but we have demonstrated that this relation occurs in every part of the universe, however small. For every part of the universe is either a determinant of determining correspondence, or determined by it (or both), or else can be divided into parts determined by determining correspondence.

**217.** This is a result of great importance, but we must note that it does not involve what would be normally called the universal validity of causation. We see that every part of the universe, however small, consists of substances, some of the qualities of which are terms in causal relations. But it has not been shown that all the qualities of every substance are terms in causal relations.

It would, I think, be generally considered that, in order that causality should hold universally, it would be necessary that the occurrence of any quality of any substance should be intrinsically determined by the occurrence of some other quality. The statement that this is the case is what is usually called the Law of the Uniformity of Nature. But there does not seem any reason to say that this would make causality hold universally more than it would be made to hold universally if the occurrence of any quality of any substance intrinsically determined the existence of some other quality. It does not seem more important that each quality should be determined, than that each quality should itself determine[1]. Let us consider both cases.

In order that each quality should be determined, it would be necessary that the following statement should be true. Let $G$ be any quality which occurs. Then, in each case in which $G$ occurs, a quality $H$ can be found, which occurs in a relation $M$ to the occurrence of $G$, and which is such that, in each case in which $H$ occurs, it will stand in the relation $M$ to some occurrence of $G$.

In order that each quality should determine, it would be necessary that, in each case in which $G$ occurs, a quality $K$ can be found which occurs in a relation $P$ to the occurrence of $G$ and which is such that, in each case in which $G$ occurs, it will have an occurrence of $K$ standing in the relation $P$ to it.

Thus $G$ might be death in a human body. The $H$ which would be found in connection with a particular case of $G$ might be beheading of a human body. The relation $M$ would then be that they were qualities of the same body, and that death immediately followed beheading. The law, therefore, would be that whenever a human body was beheaded, the death of that body immediately followed.

Again, with $G$ as the death of a human body, $K$ might be isolation from beings still living on this planet, and $P$ might be that the isolation befell the self which had previously been

---

[1] The common belief that the first is more important is, I think, connected with the belief that an event is explained by its cause but not by its effect.

living in that body. The law would then be that, whenever a body died, the self previously living in it would be isolated from beings still living on this planet.

The universal validity of causality would involve that such laws as these were true of whatever quality was taken as $G$. I do not say that causal laws invariably take such a form as this. They do take it in some cases, but in others (especially, though not exclusively, in the sciences of inorganic matter) the laws of most importance take a quantitative form. For example, a change in the temperature of water determines a change in the space it occupies, and the amount of the one change is connected with the amount of the other according to some definite formula. But, if such a formula is to be true, then many laws of the type which we have given above must be true. If the changes of temperature and size are connected in this way, then, whenever the change takes place from one particular temperature to another, there must be a change from some particular size to another. And these changes will be the $H$ and $G$, of which one is always found in a certain relation to the other. And thus the universal validity of causality would involve that laws of this type should be true of every quality.

**218.** Our results have given us no reason to believe that causality is universal. If we had reached any reason for such a belief it could only have been by the establishment of determining correspondence. Now we have not shown that all qualities of all substances are related to others by determining correspondence, either directly or indirectly. All that is proved is that there must be such relations of determining correspondence as will afford sufficient descriptions of every secondary part. And this leaves it possible that there may be qualities, both of primary and of secondary parts, which neither determine a determining correspondence nor are determined by one. (It will be shown in the next chapter that the undetermined character of such qualities would not involve a contradiction.) It remains, therefore, possible that there are qualities of various substances which are neither causally determinant nor causally determined.

This, of course, still leaves it possible that causality *may* be universal. But, as far as I know, no satisfactory proof of this has yet been given, and it seems clear that the proposition that causality is universal is not self-evident.

Nevertheless, the conclusions which we have reached are of great importance. For we have shown that causal determination does occur, and that it occurs in every part of the universe, however small. And, although causal determination has not been shown to extend to all qualities of every substance, it has been shown to extend, in the case of every secondary part of the universe, to such qualities as will constitute a sufficient description of that substance. And, if we have demonstrated that causal determination extends as far as this, we have demonstrated a great deal.

**219**. There are three further points about causality as to which it may be well to say something. In the first place, it must be noticed that our statement of what would be meant by the universality of causation does not imply reciprocal determination. The $H$ which can be found for any occurrence of $G$ is to be such that every occurrence of $H$ stands in the relation $M$ to an occurrence of $G$, but it has not been said that every occurrence of $G$ will have an occurrence of $H$ standing in the relation $M$ to it. It may well be the case that different occurrences of $G$ may be related respectively to occurrences of $H$, $J$, and $L$, by the relations $M$, $N$, and $O$, and therefore, while every occurrence of $H$ stands in the relation $M$ to an occurrence of $G$, not every occurrence of $G$ has an occurrence of $H$ standing in the relation $M$ to it. Thus, in our previous example, beheading of a body determines its death, but death does not determine beheading. Death may be caused by hanging or poisoning[1].

---

[1] Of course, if $G$ does not reciprocally determine $H$, it will be necessary, if the law of the uniformity of nature should be true, that $H$ whenever it occurs should be determined by some other quality. Since, for example, death of a body does not imply previous beheading of that body, there must, if the law of the uniformity of nature be true, be some other quality or qualities, the occurrence of which or of one of which on any occasion implies beheading of a body. This quality need not, of course, be a quality of the body beheaded. There might, for example, be a law that whenever a Queen Consort of England has the quality of misleading her husband in a particular way, her husband's body will have the quality of being beheaded.

In the same way, while the $K$ which is to be found for each occurrence of $G$ is to be such that, in each case in which $G$ occurs, it will have an occurrence of $K$ standing in the relation $P$ to it, it has not been said that every occurrence of $K$ will stand in the relation $P$ to an occurrence of $G$. Thus death of the body, in our previous example, determines cessation of intercourse, but cessation of intercourse does not determine death. A man may be isolated from intercourse with other persons or this planet by the paralysis of his body, as well as by its death.

The universality of causality, then, does not involve the universality of reciprocal causality. The latter, however, has also been asserted to exist. Let us consider what is meant by this.

It is clear, in the first place, that any law which asserted that all causal determination was reciprocal would be false. We know that drunkenness determines the drinking of alcohol, and we know that the drinking of alcohol does not determine drunkenness, since there have been cases in which men have drunk alcohol without getting drunk. Here, then, is at least one case of causal determination which is not reciprocal.

If, then, universal reciprocal determination is taken to mean that every determination of one quality by another is reciprocal, it is clear that reciprocal determination does not hold universally. And when it is said that all causal determination is reciprocal, something else, less far-reaching than this, has, I think, been meant. It has been meant, not that every determination of a quality is reciprocal, but that every quality has at least one determination which is reciprocal. It would be admitted that beheading determined death without death determining beheading, but it would be asserted that all deaths by beheading have some peculiar quality which is found in no other sort of death, and that this peculiar quality and the quality of being beheaded reciprocally determine one another. Again, it would be asserted that there is some other quality which occurred whenever the quality of death occurred, and only then, so that it stands in reciprocal determination with death.

If such reciprocal determination were universal, the law asserting it might be expressed as follows. Let $G$ be any quality which occurs. Then, in each case in which $G$ occurs, a quality $H$ can be found, which occurs in a relation $M$ to that occurrence of $G$, and which is such that, in each case in which $H$ occurs, it will stand in the relation $M$ to an occurrence of $G$, and that, in each case in which $G$ occurs, an occurrence of $H$ will stand in a relation $M$ to it.

**220.** It is possible that such reciprocal determination as this should be universal. It involves no contradiction, and it is impossible to prove empirically that it is not the case. There may be many qualities, even among those for which we can find determinants, for which we cannot find any reciprocal determination with another quality. Yet for each of these there may be a determinant, unknown to us, where the determination is reciprocal. But, on the other hand, it seems impossible to prove the universality of reciprocal determination. It could not be proved from the universality of causal determination, even if the latter were itself established. For it is obvious that there is no contradiction in a determination which is not reciprocal, since, as we have seen, many determinations—such as the determination of death by beheading—are not reciprocal.

**221.** In the second place, it has sometimes been said that, if every quality was causally determined, it would follow that complete knowledge of any substance would imply complete knowledge of every other substance in the universe, and that this result would not necessarily follow if there were qualities which were not causally determined. But this seems to me to be erroneous. In one sense of the phrase "complete knowledge of any substance," the result would follow, even if all qualities were not causally determined. In another sense of the phrase it would not follow, even if they were all causally determined.

Every substance in the universe is related to every other substance in the universe. And complete knowledge of all that was true about any substance, $A$, would include knowledge of all its relations to all other substances. This, of course, includes knowledge of sufficient descriptions of all those substances, since I do not know $A$ completely unless I can identify the substance $B$ to which it stands in the relation $P$. But further, in addition to a sufficient description of $B$, every other fact which is true of $B$ adds to my knowledge of $A$, since it tells me that $A$ is in the relation $P$ to a substance of which this fact is true. A complete description of $A$, therefore, would, since it would include all facts true of $A$, include complete descriptions of all other substances. It would therefore be true that, if we had complete knowledge of $A$, we should have complete knowledge of $B$, and of every other substance, whether all qualities were causally determined or not.

But this inclusion of knowledge of all other substances in the knowledge of $A$ is not what is meant by the theory which we are discussing. What is meant is that, from a knowledge of $A$ which does not include complete knowledge of $B$, complete knowledge of $B$ might be inferred by anyone who had sufficient knowledge of the laws by which one quality causally determined another, and sufficient power of reasoning to carry out the arguments required. And there seems to be no reason to believe that the truth of this would be involved by the causal determination of all qualities.

There is nothing in the causal determination of all qualities which would exclude the possibility that there should be two substances in the universe such that no quality of either should be causally determined by any quality of the other, either directly or indirectly. Nor is there, as far as I can see, anything else which excludes the possibility[1]. It is perfectly possible that two substances should exist in the universe which are completely unrelated to each other in respect of causality. It is, of course, impossible that there should be two substances in the universe which are not related in some way, but it does not follow from this that there cannot be two substances which are not related causally.

And, even if it were the case that every substance in the universe should be causally related to every other substance in

---

[1] The only sort of causal determination which we have proved to exist is determination by determining correspondence. And we have seen that it is possible for the universe to be divided into two or more primary wholes, no part of any one of which is connected by determining correspondence with any part of the other. It would, of course, be possible that parts of two primary wholes should be connected by some other sort of causal determination; but this remains merely a possibility.

the universe, the theory which we are considering would not be proved. For it might still be the case that, though some qualities of $B$ were causally determined by qualities of $A$, there were other qualities of $B$ which were not causally determined, either directly or indirectly, by qualities of $A$. And in this case no knowledge of $A$ would enable us to infer all the qualities of $B$.

**222.** Why has it been supposed that, if every quality was causally determined, such an inference could be made from the nature of any one substance to that of any other? I am inclined to think that it is partly due to a confusion between what we have distinguished as extrinsic and intrinsic determination. It was perceived, more or less clearly, that we have no right to believe that, if anything were different from what it is, anything else would be the same as what it is. And then this negative and general extrinsic determination was confused with positive and particular intrinsic determination. We have no right to believe that, if any flower in a crannied wall had been different from what it was, Shakespeare would have written *Hamlet*. But it does not follow, as Tennyson seems to suggest, that the most complete knowledge of the flower would render it possible to infer that Shakespeare did write *Hamlet*.

Thus, even if every quality was causally determined, we should not be entitled to hold that complete knowledge of every substance could be inferred from complete knowledge of any one substance. And, even if it were, the possibility of making such inferences would be of no practical importance. The number of substances in the universe is infinite, and their relations are infinitely complicated, and there would therefore be no guarantee that the nature of any particular $B$ could be inferred from the nature of $A$, except by a thinker with a power of carrying out an argument of infinite length and complexity. It is obvious that this is of no importance with regard to the knowledge of beings whose powers, like our own, are only finite. And even if there should exist in the universe a being whose powers of inference were infinite and who was capable of acquiring complete knowledge of some one substance, the possibility of making such inferences would be of no importance to him if he were also directly omniscient, as in that case he would have complete direct knowledge of all substances, and would have no need to reach it by inference.

**223**. In the third place it remains to consider whether the possibility that all qualities are not causally determined will give any satisfaction to indeterminists, in the ordinary sense of the word—that is to say, to those who assert that, at any rate in some cases, human volitions are not completely determined. Whether it will give them any satisfaction depends upon what they maintain, or desire, to be true, and what that is does not seem very clear.

It sometimes seems that what indeterminists demand is that volitions should be contingent, both intrinsically and extrinsically, in relation to the events which precede them, though not in relation to the events which follow them. What appears to be required is that we should be able to say that, if a volition had been different from what it has been, this would give us no reason to doubt that the preceding events would have been what they have been. The protests against a "block universe," which are sometimes put forward by indeterminists, appear to signify this. It does not seem that they could be appeased by the absence of complete intrinsic determination.

If this is what is wanted, no result which we have reached will do anything to justify such a want. For its justification would require that there should be absent from the universe, not only complete intrinsic determination, but also complete extrinsic determination. And, as we have seen, the extrinsic determination of the universe is complete.

Again it sometimes seems as if what was wanted by indeterminists was that volitions should be less determined than other things. If I will to pull a trigger, and the trigger is pulled, and a man is shot, it would seem as if the indeterminist would not be contented with establishing that the volition was not completely determined intrinsically, unless it was also established that the pulling of the trigger, and the death of the man, were completely determined intrinsically. Apparently it is held to be necessary, in order that we may be responsible for our actions, not only that they should be partially undetermined, but that nothing else should be. Our results will do nothing to justify this demand. For the possibility that all qualities are not intrinsically determined, which we have seen to be still open, is not limited to qualities of those substances which are volitions.

It may be, however, that indeterminists, or at any rate some indeterminists, would be satisfied if our volitions were not completely determined intrinsically. And we have seen that the possibility of this has not been excluded. It is possible that our volitions are not completely determined in respect of all their qualities, and that among the undetermined qualities may be those, or some of those, which have ethical significance. Whether, in this case, they would gain or lose in ethical significance, is a question for ethics.

# CHAPTER XXVI

## DETERMINING CORRESPONDENCE (*continued*)

**224**. We must now proceed to consider certain further questions about determining correspondence. We have seen that from a sufficient description of $B$, which includes the fact that $C$ is in the relation $X$ to some part of $B$, there follows a sufficient description of $B! C$. But can we go further, and say that there is implied in this sufficient description of $B$, not only a sufficient description of $B! C$, but the whole nature of $B! C$? Or, on the other hand, is it possible that $B! C$ should have qualities which were not in any way implied in this sufficient description of $B$?

If any quality of $B! C$ is not implied by this sufficient description of it, then the quality is presupposed by this description. For, by the Law of Excluded Middle, $B! C$ must be either $S$ or not-$S$, where $S$ is any quality. That it should be $B! C$, therefore, implies that it is $S$-or-not-$S$, and, if it does not further imply that it is one and not the other, it will presuppose, either that it is $S$, or that it is not-$S$—whichever it actually is.

We saw, in Section 184, that any term $N$ presupposes whatever is presupposed by what $N$ implies. And a certain sufficient description of $B$ implies sufficient descriptions of all the parts of $B$ through an infinite series. If, therefore, each of these sufficient descriptions of a part of $B$ presupposed some other qualities of that part, then the sufficient description of $B$ would have an infinite series of presuppositions. Would this involve a contradiction?

**225**. We cannot decide that it would do so for those reasons which led us to conclude, in Section 191, that a contradiction would arise from the infinite series of presuppositions which was then considered. For the fixing of the presuppositions in the sequent terms of the series need not imply the fixing of the presuppositions in the precedent terms. If, for example, in the secondary parts of the second grade which make up $B! C$, we fixed the other qualities of those parts, which are presupposed by their sufficient descriptions, this would not necessarily fix, in $B$! $C$ itself, the qualities which are presupposed by its sufficient description. And, in that case, when we come to consider the total ultimate presupposition of $B$, none of these presuppositions would disappear from it because of their implication in lower terms of the same series, and therefore no contradiction will ensue.

On the other hand, the objection raised in Section 190 would apply in this case also. For there would have to be an infinite series of concurrences, in order that each of the infinite series of substances, determined by determining correspondence, should have its presupposition fixed in respect of each quality not implied by the determining correspondence. And we came to the conclusion in Section 190 that we could not accept such an infinite series as this.

If we are correct in this, it will follow that it will be impossible for all the parts of $B$ to infinity to have any qualities other than those determined by determining correspondence. But this result only follows from the infinity of the series. It would be possible that all or any of the parts for any finite number of grades might have qualities not determined by determining correspondence. And among such parts would, of course, be included all substance which could even be observed by any observer whose powers of observation were not infinite—that is, of all substances which are of any practical interest to us at present.

**226**. The question now naturally arises whether we are able to discover what relation of determining correspondence actually does occur in the universe. If we could show *à priori* that there was only one relation which was a relation of determining correspondence, or only one whose occurrence was compatible with the other results which we have reached as to the nature of the existent, we should know that that relation does occur in the universe, and that it is the only relation of determining correspondence which does occur. But I do not think that it is possible to show this *à priori*. When, in Book V, we introduce considerations of an empirical nature, it will, I think, be possible to give good reasons for believing that there is a certain relation of determining correspondence which occurs in the universe, and which is the only one which does occur. But, till then, the point must remain undetermined.

**227.** Nor are we able, as far as I can see, to lay down at present any further conditions which must be satisfied by any relation of determining correspondence which actually does occur. There are, in particular, two important possibilities which we cannot exclude. In the first place, I cannot see that it can be shown to be necessary that the same sort of determining correspondence should occur everywhere. It seems to me quite possible that, if there is more than one primary whole, the relation might be a different one in each of them. And even within one primary whole, there seems no reason to deny that *B* might have a different sort of determining correspondence with the parts of *C* from that which *D* has with the parts of *E*, or even from that which *B* itself has with the parts of *F*, or, again, from that which *G* has with the parts of *B*.

But no fresh sort of determining correspondence could be introduced into any stage after the first in the determination of the infinite series of sequent sets of parts. For in the first stage the sufficient descriptions of all the members of these sequent sets of parts must be implied. And this would not be the case if a fresh sort of correspondence, not stated in the first stage, came into force in any sequent stage. It is possible, of course, that *A* should have a set of parts which determine a sequent set by a relation which has every characteristic of determining correspondence, except that of generating an infinite series of further sequent sets. And the set so determined might determine another set by another relation which had again every characteristic of determining correspondence except that of generating such a series. This might continue for any finite number of sets. But it would not be determining correspondence, since none of the relations would possess the characteristic of generating the infinite series of sets. Eventually, if the original contradiction is to be avoided, we must reach a relation of determining correspondence, which will generate such an infinite series. And then, for the reason given above, no fresh sort of determining correspondence can be introduced after the first stage in such a series.

**228**. In the second place, we cannot at present exclude the possibility that there might be more than one species of determining correspondence extending over the whole universe, or over a part of it. It might, for anything we can see yet, be possible that the universe should have two sets of parts, which were such that none of the members of either were directly determined by determining correspondence, and also such that from sufficient descriptions of all the members of either set there followed, by determining correspondence, sufficient descriptions of the members of all sequent sets[1]. In that case the universe would have two sets of parts, each of which was by our definition a set of primary parts, and each of which would start a system of determining correspondence extending over the whole universe. And the number of such sets of parts need not be confined to two.

When, in Book V, we introduce empirical considerations, we shall, I think, see good reason for rejecting both these possibilities. We shall, as was said above, find grounds for concluding that there is only one relation of determining correspondence which does occur in the universe, and we shall also find grounds for believing that there is only one set of primary parts. But at present we can go no further on this point.

**229**. Meanwhile it may be useful to consider certain forms of correspondence, of which our experience tells us, and to enquire how far they do, and how far they do not, comply with the conditions required for determining correspondence. Such a discussion may enable us to realize more clearly the nature of determining correspondence.

Let us begin by enumerating certain characteristics which we have found to belong to determining correspondence. (1) A relation between a substance $C$ and part of a substance $B$ is a

---

[1] It will be remembered that a whole can be divided into two sets of parts, neither of which is sequent to the other. The group of Cambridge graduates, for example, has one set of parts which consists of the group of Doctors, the group of Masters, and the group of Bachelors. It has another which consists of the group of graduates in Divinity, the group of graduates in Law, and so on. Neither of these sets is sequent to the other.

relation of determining correspondence, if it is such that a
certain sufficient description of $C$, which includes the fact that
it is in that relation to *some* part of $B$, intrinsically determines
a sufficient description of the part of $B$ in question, $B!\ C$. (2) A
relation of determining correspondence is a relation such that
one determinant term can determine more than one determinate
term. (3) It is a relation such that $B!\ C$ is determined by only
one determinant, $C$; while $C$, though it may be the direct
determinant of many parts of $A$, is the direct determinant of
only one of the parts of $A$ which fall within $B$. (4) It is, in some
cases at least, reciprocal. (5) It is such that it is possible to have
a whole divided into a set of parts, and each of these into a set
of parts, and so on infinitely, in such a way that sufficient
descriptions of all these parts are determined, by means of
determining correspondence, by a sufficient description of the
whole.

**230.** To begin with, let us consider the case of a pattern
which is drawn on a transparent surface, and the shadow of
which is thrown on sheets which stand at different angles to
that surface, no two sheets standing at the same angle. The
relation between the pattern and the shadows does conform to
some of the conditions required by a determining correspondence. It conforms to the first. For if we know the shape of the
pattern, and the angle at which each of the sheets stands to the
transparent surface, we shall have data which imply the shape
of the shadow on each of the sheets. It will conform to the
second condition, since one pattern may have many shadows
on different sheets. And it will conform to the third condition,
since each shadow can (on a sheet set at that angle to the pattern)
be the shadow of only one pattern, while the pattern can only
have one shadow on each sheet.

But it will not conform to the fourth condition. There is no
possibility of reciprocal determination, since the parts of the
pattern cannot be shadows of the shadows of the pattern. And
therefore it cannot conform to the fifth condition. If the shadows
had parts within parts infinitely, it could only be because the
pattern had, as a fact independent of the relation between it
and the shadows, parts within parts infinitely. And thus the

pattern would have had an infinite series of sets of parts, each of which would have presupposed those which were sequent to it, while it would itself be implied by them. And thus a contradiction would arise in the manner explained in Chapter XXIII.

**231.** Or, again, suppose that a collection of volumes of poetry were catalogued on some system which excluded cross-entries, and that there were several copies of the catalogue, each copy being on paper of a different colour. Then, again, the first three conditions would be satisfied. The sufficient description of $C$ would be any sufficient description of one of the volumes, which included the fact that the volume was entered in $B$, which would be sufficiently described as the copy of the catalogue which was on red paper. And this gives us a sufficient description, $B! C$, of the entry of the book in that copy of the catalogue. Thus the first condition is satisfied. The second condition is satisfied, since one book can be entered in many copies of the catalogue. And each entry will only refer to one book, while each book will have only one entry in each catalogue, so that the third condition is satisfied.

But the fourth condition is not satisfied. For the parts of the books catalogued cannot consist in catalogue entries which catalogue the catalogues. This is impossible, because books consisting of such entries would not be volumes of poetry. And therefore the fifth condition fails also. On the one hand, if only books, and not their parts, are catalogued, the catalogue entries cannot have parts within parts to infinity which correspond to anything in that which is catalogued. If, on the other hand, the parts of books are catalogued, there could only be such an infinite series in the entries, if the book catalogued had, as an independent fact, such an infinite series of parts. And this would lead, as in the last case, to a contradiction.

**232.** Suppose, however, we alter our case, and take a certain number of catalogues, each of which catalogues itself, the others, and the entries in itself and in the others. The first three conditions would be satisfied as before. And so would the fourth, since an entry of the red book would be part of the blue book, and an entry of the blue book would be part of the red book. Also sufficient descriptions would be implied of an infinite series of entries. If there were two catalogues, the red and the blue, then the red would contain entries of itself and of the blue. It would also contain entries of the entries in itself of itself and of the blue, and also of the entries of both of them in the blue. And so on infinitely.

But still the fifth condition would not be satisfied. An entry of the blue book is, as we have just said, part of the red book. And the further entries, which record the entries in the blue book of the blue book and the red book, are also parts of the red book. But they are not parts of the entry of the blue book in the red book. The entry "blue book" cannot, it is clear, have as its parts "the blue book's entry of the red book," and "the blue book's entry of the blue book." And therefore the infinite series of entries will not be a series of parts divided into parts infinitely, and we shall not have satisfied the fifth condition.

**233.** Let us now suppose that $B$ is positive, and $C$ is negative, and that they determine parts, of themselves and of each other, to resemble them in this respect, so that $B! C$ is the negative part of the positive part of $A$. In this case the first condition will be satisfied, since $B! C$ will be sufficiently described in this way. The second condition will be satisfied, since $C$ will determine $C! C$ as well as $B! C$. So also will the third condition, since $B! C$ will correspond to nothing but $C$, and $C$ is the direct determinant of only one of those parts of $A$ which fall within $B$. The fourth condition will be satisfied, since $B$ will determine a part of $C$, and $C$ will determine a part of $B$. Finally, the fifth condition will be satisfied. There will be four secondary parts of the first grade—the positive part of the positive part, the negative part of the positive part, the positive part of the negative part, and the negative part of the negative part. Each of these will again have positive and negative parts, and so on infinitely. Thus all the conditions are satisfied.

The same result might happen with other qualities besides positive and negative. And the number of qualities which were thus combined might be more than two, so that the primary whole might contain more than two primary parts. Also it would not be necessary that every primary part should deter-

mine every other, provided that some of them formed a reciprocally determining group.

But for such a determining correspondence as this, it is
necessary that the qualities should have certain characteristics.
Firstly, they must be incompatible with one another. If this
were not the case, sufficient descriptions of the parts of $B$
would not be given by saying of one of them that it was positive
and of the other that it was negative, as both descriptions
might belong to the same part. Secondly, they must be such
that a whole and its part can have the same quality. For the
infinite series will not arise unless a positive part can have a
positive part, and a negative part a negative part. Thirdly, they
must be such that a whole and its part can have different
qualities. For it is also necessary to have the positive part of a
negative part, and the negative part of a positive part. And
these characteristics must be true at any stage in the infinite
process, whether the wholes in question are primary parts,
secondary parts of the first grade, or secondary parts of any
other grade.

Whether there is any set of qualities which have these
characteristics is a question which does not concern us now.
I do not assert that there is such a set, nor, if there is, that
positive and negative are such a set.

**234.** Can we find an example of determining correspondence
in the world of spirit? Could knowledge be a term in such a
correspondence? Let us take first that knowledge which consists
in judgments. Only true judgments are parts of knowledge[1].
A true judgment is one which corresponds to a fact, and since
a judgment, which is a state of the mind of a knowing being, is
a substance, and that which is known is sometimes a substance,
there are cases of knowledge which are correspondences between
substances.

$B$ knows that a substance exists which has the sufficient
description $XYZ$. Will a sufficient description of this substance,

---

[1] I do not mean to assert that all true judgments are parts of knowledge.
It is a true judgment that the Visitor of Peterhouse in 1919 was a Bishop, but
it is at any rate doubtful whether a man could be properly said to know this,
if he made that judgment because he believed the Visitor to be the Bishop of
Gibraltar.

$C$, which includes the sufficient description $XYZ$, and also the fact that $B$ has this knowledge of $C$, give us a sufficient description of $B$'s knowledge of $C$?

In the first place, it will fail to do so, because it is possible for a man to know the same fact at two different times. There would then be two states of his mind, of each of which the description "$B$'s knowledge that a substance exists which has the sufficient description $XYZ$" would be true. And therefore this description would not be a sufficient description of either state, since it is true of both. In consequence of this, the first and third conditions laid down above would not be satisfied.

They would, however, be satisfied if the assumption were made that each of the knowing beings had only one act of knowledge of any substance which it knew at all. A substance would then be sufficiently described, if it is described as the knowledge of $B$, that is, of a substance sufficiently described as $RST$, that there exists another substance which is sufficiently described as $XYZ$.

But when this preliminary difficulty is removed, we should find others. Firstly, in many cases the fourth condition could not be satisfied, even if we grant, what I believe to be true, that every act of knowledge is a part of the knower. In that case a part of $B$ would be determined by $C$. But if $C$ is not itself a knowing being, this determination cannot be reciprocal. If I know the Great Pyramid, a part of my mind is determined by being knowledge of the Great Pyramid. But no part of the Great Pyramid can be determined by being knowledge of my mind. And, since the fourth condition fails, the fifth must fail also.

Secondly, the fifth condition would fail, even in cases when $B$ and $C$ can know one another. For it is not part of the supposition that either of them knows more than one substance. Nor would even this give us the fifth condition, unless we also supposed that the knowledge was reciprocal, and unless we supposed also that each knowing being knew the parts of everything which he knew.

Thirdly, it is not part of the supposition that the acts of knowledge of any knowing being form a complete set of parts of that being, so that there is nothing to insure that determining correspondence would be provided for all parts of $B$.

**235**. Could we avoid those difficulties by specifying still further the sort of knowledge which we are considering? Let each of the primary parts of a primary whole be a knowing being, each of which knows other primary parts and their parts, and, except that knowledge, has no parts whatever. Determination can now be reciprocal, since the primary parts which are known can also know and the secondary parts which are known can be acts of knowledge. Thus the fourth condition is satisfied. And thus we have an endless series of parts determined in $B$. There will be first his knowledge of himself and of $C$. Then his knowledge of his knowledge of himself and $C$, and his knowledge of $C$'s knowledge of himself and $C$. And so on through an infinite series.

But still the fifth condition has not been satisfied. Sufficient descriptions of the primary parts, indeed, intrinsically determine sufficient descriptions of an endless series of substances, each of which is part of the primary whole, and part also of one of the primary parts. But, beyond this point, the parts determined are not parts of parts previously determined. They are all judgments, and a judgment about a part cannot be part of a judgment about a whole, so that the reciprocal determination, while it produces an endless series, does not produce an endless series of parts within parts.

For example, in the case given above, $BkC$ (where $k$ stands for "knowledge of") implies $BkCkB$ and $BkCkC$, since in $C$ there are $CkB$ and $CkC$, and $B$ knows the parts of everything which it knows. But $BkCkB$ is not a part of $BkC$, though both are parts of $B$, and though $CkB$ is part of $C$. A judgment has parts (though not parts within parts to infinity), but a set of parts of a judgment are never all judgments, and therefore a set of parts of a judgment about a whole can never be judgments about the parts of the whole. If, for example, I know something about the United Kingdom, my judgment about the United Kingdom could not be divided into two judgments about Great Britain and Ireland respectively. Even if my judgment about the United Kingdom should be that it consists of two parts,

Great Britain and Ireland, the judgment would not consist of two judgments, one about Great Britain and one about Ireland.

**236**. Thus knowledge cannot give us an example of determining correspondence, if knowledge is taken as restricted to judgments. But there is something besides judgment which has a claim to be called knowledge. This is perception. And in the case of perception the difficulty which we have just been considering does not occur. For it must, I think, be admitted that the perception of a part may be part of a perception of the whole. If I perceive the surface of a panel as a whole[1], and at the same time perceive the details of the carving on the surface, the perception of each particular detail is part of the perception of the panel as a whole.

We can thus, I think, get an example of what determining correspondence would be, by taking a primary whole, each of whose primary parts is a percipient being which perceives other primary parts and their parts, and which has itself no parts except those perceptions. (We must also assume that the perception is, in some cases at least, reciprocal, and that no percipient has more than one perception of any perceptum.) The first four conditions would be satisfied, as they were in the case of knowledge by judgment. And the fifth condition would also be satisfied. For as $B$'s perception of $C$'s perception of $B$ would be part of $B$'s perception of $C$, we should have an infinite series of parts within parts.

Of such perception as this we have no experience. Our experience, I think, if properly analyzed, shows that a self can perceive itself, and that it frequently does so. But we have no experience of any self perceiving another self, nor, consequently, of the reciprocal perception of selves. And, again, we have no experience of a percipient being with no other activity but perception, and with no parts but perceptions.

Still, we know what perception is like, and it does not seem

---

[1] Strictly speaking, of course, I do not perceive the panel, or its details. I perceive sense-data, from which I am led to a belief in the panel and the details. The sense-data thus related to the details are, it seems clear, part of the sense-data thus related to the panel, and my contention is that my perception of the sense-data related to the details is part of my perception of the sense-data related to the panel. (This subject will be discussed in Book V.)

impossible to form a conception of a society of selves which in this manner perceived themselves, and each other, and their parts. It is not useless, therefore, to have come to the conclusion that in this, if it occurred, we should have a relation of determining correspondence. And here we must leave the question till we resume it in Book V.

# CHAPTER XXVII

## EXCLUSIVE COMMON QUALITIES (*continued*)

**237.** The results which we have reached in the earlier chapters of this Book naturally lead us to the reconsideration of the question discussed in Chapter XVII, the occurrence in groups of exclusive common qualities. Are there, that is, any qualities which belong to more than one substance, without belonging to all? For if there is such a quality, the substances which possess it will form a group in which the quality in question is an exclusive common quality—that is, will belong to every substance which is a member of the group, and to no other substance[1].

In our previous consideration of the subject we found, not only that there were such qualities, but that every group possessed them. But the only exclusive common qualities which we could be certain that all groups possessed, were qualities which were mere restatements of the denotation of the group. If the group consists of the members *A*, *B*, and *C*, and if *D*, *E*, and *F* are taken as a complete list of the substances which are not members of the group[2], then we saw that there will be two exclusive common qualities in that group. One is the quality of being a member of the group which consists of *A*, *B*, and *C*, and the other is the quality "dissimilar to *D*, to *E*, and to *F*." But the first of the qualities is little more than a tautology, and the second could only be known to us if we knew all the infinite number of substances which are not members of the group, and also knew that we knew all of them[3].

---

[1] Such a quality cannot also be a quality *of* the group, since no group is one of its own members.

[2] We now know that existent substances are infinite in number, and that the substances outside any group with a finite denotation will likewise be infinite in number. But this will not affect the validity of the argument.

[3] Cp. Section 132.

It is also possible, as was pointed out before[1], for the members of a group to have some exclusive common quality which is not a mere restatement of the denotation of the group, and which therefore is not tautological, and can be known without infinite knowledge. And we know empirically that this sometimes happens. The Colleges of Magdalene and Trinity in Cambridge form a group the members of which have the exclusive common quality "to be a Cambridge College in which, in the year 1919, the Headship was not in the gift of the Fellows." At the point, however, at which we then left the subject, we know nothing about the frequency of such groups, nor had we any *à priori* knowledge as to the nature of any of the exclusive common qualities.

**238**. But now the position is different. We shall find ourselves able to show that there are qualities of certain sorts which are exclusive common qualities in groups, and which are not restatements of the denotations of the groups[2]. And although we shall not be able to show that each group has in it such an exclusive common quality, we shall be able to show that every substance does belong to at least one group which has in it such an exclusive common quality. The qualities whose occurrence can thus be demonstrated will, in every case, turn out to be relational qualities.

Let us take first those substances which are primary wholes, primary parts, or secondary parts in the system of determining correspondence. (We will call this system, for a reason which will appear in the next chapter, the Fundamental System, and will speak of these substances as being within the fundamental system.) We shall find several sorts of qualities such that each of these substances will be a member of one or more groups which have a quality of one of these sorts as an exclusive common quality.

In the first place, substances within this system are either primary wholes, primary parts, or secondary parts. And we

---

[1] Section 133.

[2] For the sake of brevity I shall, in the rest of this chapter, use "exclusive common quality" so as *not* to include those which are restatements of the denotations of the groups.

have thus three groups, each of which has an exclusive common quality—the compound quality which is the definition of a primary whole, a primary part, or a secondary part. And secondary parts, again, form an infinite number of groups—the group of secondary parts of the first grade, the group of secondary parts of the second grade, and so on. And each of these has an exclusive common quality in the definition of secondary parts of that grade.

**239**. In the second place, the primary parts are divisible into a set of groups, by taking all those primary parts which fall within the same primary whole as a separate group. In the same way the secondary parts of the first grade can be divided into groups according to the primary part in which they fall. The secondary parts of the second grade can be divided according to the secondary parts of the first grade in which they fall, and so on to infinity.

Each of these groups will have an exclusive common quality which is not a restatement of the denotation. In the group of primary parts which fall within the primary whole $A$, the exclusive common quality will be to be a primary part which falls within the primary whole $A$. In the group of secondary parts of the first grade which fall within the primary part $B$, the exclusive common quality will be to be a secondary part of the first grade which falls within the primary part $B$, and so on.

When we include in the exclusive common quality "falling within the primary part $B$," or "falling within $B! C$, a secondary part of the first grade," and so on to sequent terms, we do not bring in any element which is a mere restatement of the denotation of the group. It is true that $B$ has, among other qualities, the quality of being a group of which its secondary parts of the first grade are members. But the position of $B$ in the system of determining correspondence involves that it must have a sufficient description independent of any qualities determined by its own parts. We are thus asserting that its parts have the common quality of being parts of something which has this independent sufficient description. And this is not a mere restatement of the denotation of the group of parts. The same is true of $B! C$, or any sequent part.

The case of primary wholes is rather different, since it is possible that a primary whole may not have any sufficient description which is independent of qualities determined by its primary parts. But even if this should be so, we should not bring in any element which is a mere restatement of the denotation of the group. For we should not be saying merely that $B$ was a primary part falling within the group constituted of $B$ and $C$. We should be saying that $B$ was a primary part falling within the *primary whole* constituted by the primary parts $B$ and $C$. And the fact that the group was a primary whole is not a mere restatement of its denotation. For every primary part belongs to many groups of primary parts which are not primary wholes—groups, *e.g.*, in which primary parts from two primary wholes are included.

**240**. This, then, is the second system of groups with exclusive common qualities which can be determined to exist in the universe. In the third place, there is the system which would be formed if, instead of grouping together only the primary parts which were parts of $A$, or the secondary parts of the first grade which were parts of $B$, we took *all* parts in the fundamental system which were parts of $A$, and all parts in the fundamental system which were parts of $B$, and so on.

**241**. Fourthly, every secondary part in the fundamental system, *i.e.*, every part except primary wholes and primary parts, has a determinant. We may give the name of Final Determinant of any part to its direct determinant, if it is a secondary part of the first grade, and, if it is of any other grade, to the last of its indirect determinants. Thus $B! C, D! E! C,$ $F! G! H! C$ have all of them $C$ as their final determinant. All secondary parts, then, can be divided into groups according to their final determinant. The exclusive common quality in each of these groups will be to be finally determined by $B$, or $C$, or some other primary part. Those secondary parts which are not in the first grade, will, in addition to their final determinant, have a penultimate determinant, and those, therefore, which have the same final determinant can be subdivided into groups having the same penultimate determinant. Here the exclusive common quality will be, for example, to have the final deter-

minant $C$, and the penultimate determinant $D$, or, as it may also
be expressed, to have the determinant $D! C$. Those which are
not in the first two grades will be further subdivided into groups
in which the exclusive common quality is the possession of the
same last three determinants, and so on infinitely.

**242**. Passing to substances which are not parts of the
fundamental system, we find that their relation to that system
enables us to determine that certain groups of those substances
will have in them exclusive common qualities.

In the first place, as we have seen, every substance which is
not a member of the fundamental system can be divided into
substances which are members of that system. (We can, for
the sake of brevity, express this by saying that every external
substance can be divided into internal substances.) And every
external substance can be divided into internal substances,
which are all of the same grade. If, for example, we take the
substance which consists of $B$, $C! D$, and $D! C! E! F$, then, since
$D! C! E! F$ is a secondary part of the third grade, and $B$ and
$C! D$ are divisible into parts of the same grade, the whole
external substance can be divided into parts of that grade,
though not into parts of any higher grade. Other substances
could be divided into parts all of which were of a higher grade,
while others, again, could only be divided in this way when a
lower grade had been reached.

All external substances, then, could be divided into groups
according to the highest grade of internal substances to which
all the content of the external substance could be reduced. The
first group would consist of those external substances all of
whose content was given in a set of parts whose members were
primary wholes. The second group would consist of those substances where the highest grade in question was that of primary
parts, and so on infinitely. And this gives an exclusive common
quality for each group.

**243**. In the second place, some, though not all, external
substances will be such that all the parts of any of them fall
within some one primary whole, should there be more than one.
Those external substances, each of which has all its parts falling
within a primary whole, $A$, will form a group, in which there

will be an exclusive common quality—that of having all its parts falling within the primary whole $A$. In each such group, some, though not all, of its members will be such that all the parts of any one of them will fall within some one primary part. Then those of them, each of which has all its parts falling within a primary part $B$, will form a group, in which there will be an exclusive common quality of having all parts falling within a primary part $B$. And so on infinitely.

**244.** Thus the result is that every substance which is a member of the fundamental system is a member of a group with an exclusive common quality of the first type; that every such substance, except primary wholes, is a member of a group with an exclusive common quality of the second type; that every such substance, except primary wholes, is a member of at least one group with an exclusive common quality of the third type; and that every such substance, except primary wholes and primary parts, is a member of at least one group with an exclusive common quality of the fourth type. And, further, that every substance which is not a member of the fundamental system is a member of a group with an exclusive common quality of the fifth type, while some of them are members of one or more groups with an exclusive common quality of the sixth type. Every substance, then, is a member of at least one group in which there is an exclusive common quality besides those which are restatements of its denotation.

All these exclusive common qualities, however, are relational qualities. Each of them is the quality of standing in a certain relation to something. Can we say anything about the occurrences of exclusive common original qualities? I do not think that we can. We know empirically that in certain groups there are exclusive common qualities which are original. Some substances are happy, and some are not. And there is therefore a group of substances which has the exclusive common original quality of happiness. But it is, so far as I can see, impossible to determine anything *à priori* as to the occurrence of such qualities. And, in particular, I can see no reason to assert *à priori* that every substance is a member of at least one group which has an exclusive common original quality. Our *à priori* knowledge about the original qualities of substances, here as elsewhere, does not take us as far as our original knowledge about their original relations, and, consequently, about their relational qualities.

**245.** But in demonstrating the occurrence of exclusive common qualities, whether these properties are original or not, we have done what is really essential. In order that we may be able to build up a system of knowledge about anything that exists, it is not necessary that there should be found in it groups with exclusive common original qualities. Groups with some exclusive common qualities are necessary, but it is indifferent whether these are original or relational.

Without groups with exclusive common qualities, it would be impossible to make any general statement about substances, except such as applied to all existent substances. It would be logically possible to make a certain number of general propositions about existent substances, since some such propositions do apply to all existent substances. And there would be no logical impossibility in making propositions about particular existent substances, since each might be sufficiently described by means of qualities which it did not share with any other substance. And, further, it would be logically possible to reach such scientific propositions as can be known *à priori*. We can see that equilateral implies equiangular, for example, whether there does or does not exist a group of equilateral substances[1].

But no scientific propositions could be reached which depended on induction, since, as a basis for induction in any science, we require experience of several existent substances with a quality which is common to them, and which is not to be found in every substance. And scientific propositions reached *à priori* would no longer have the same relevance to the existent that we find these to have at present, since we could

---

[1] These three possibilities are only logical—that is, there is no logical impossibility in our having such knowledge under such conditions. As a matter of psychological fact, it would, I suppose, be impossible that such knowledge, or any knowledge, could arise in a being who was unable to discover, in the course of his empirical experience, qualities which belonged to some of the substances he knew, without belonging to all.

find no groups of substances in which the conditions of the propositions were realized even approximately.

We do not, indeed, need the arguments of this chapter, or any other philosophical arguments, to assure us that there are groups of substances having exclusive common qualities in them. Each of us can reach this conclusion by an argument from his own perceptions which is shorter and more certain than any such argument can be. I have perceived more than one sense-datum, which is a sense-datum of red. And I have perceived other sense-data which are not sense-data of red. It is clear, therefore, that there is more than one substance which has the quality of being a sense-datum of red, and that all existent substances have not that quality. And this alone is sufficient to prove that a group can be found in which there is an exclusive common quality.

But such an argument as this cannot prove to us that every substance belongs to such a group. And therefore it would still remain possible that there are substances to which no general propositions would apply, except those which apply to all substances. But the arguments of this chapter have shown us that every substance belongs to at least one group with an exclusive common quality, and that therefore every substance has at least one quality which belongs to it, and to some other substance, without belonging to all other substances. This result is of great interest and importance. And it is important and interesting even though all the exclusive common qualities of which we can be certain are relational and not original.

In the case of the first type of exclusive common qualities in internal substances we were able to determine à priori, not only the type of the qualities, but the qualities themselves. And the same was the case with the first type in external substances. But the other types are different. The qualities of these types are derived from relations to some particular part of the fundamental system. They can only be known if those parts are known. Now sufficient descriptions of all parts of the fundamental system follow by principles which are known à priori from sufficient descriptions of the primary parts. But there is no way by which sufficient descriptions of the primary parts can be deduced *à priori*. These must be known empirically, if they are to be known at all. The qualities of some types, therefore, can only be known empirically. And, although every substance has not been shown to be a member of a group with an exclusive common quality of those types, yet this has been shown about every *internal* substance, except primary wholes.

**246**. It does not follow that because we know a substance we shall be able to know what groups it belongs to in which there are exclusive common qualities of one of these six types. For to know this we must know the place of the substance in the fundamental system, or, if it is outside it, the place of its parts in that system. And we might know a great deal about a substance without knowing this. In particular, we might know of some group or groups with an exclusive common quality to which the substance belongs, without knowing to what groups it belongs in which the exclusive common quality comes under any of these six types. Trinity College in Cambridge, as we have seen, belongs to a group which has in it the exclusive common quality of being a Cambridge college whose Headship is not in the gift of the Fellows. But we may know this without knowing what qualities it has which come under any of the six types.

# CHAPTER XXVIII

## ORDER IN THE UNIVERSE

**247.** In Chapter XXI we came to the conclusion that we had at that point, no reason to believe that the universe was ordered. We defined an ordered universe as one which possessed at least one of three characteristics. The first was that the parts should determine one another according to general laws. This was called causal order. The second was that its parts should be connected with one another by such a relation that they should form a single series. We called this serial order.

The third we called order of classification. We said, to begin with, that the parts of a whole may be said to form a classifying system, when there is such an arrangement of parts within parts as to give each part a definite place in the whole with relation to other parts, and when each group of parts formed by the arrangement possesses some exclusive common quality other than those which are merely restatements of the denotation of the group[1]. And we said that a whole may be said to possess order of classification if its parts can be arranged in a classifying system of such a nature that the exclusive common characteristics in the groups are of fundamental importance to the parts which possess them. The greater the extent to which the system carries the classification, the more perfect will be the order.

Without considering the question whether the universe possesses serial order, we can now see that it possesses both the other characteristics. For we saw in Chapter XXV that causal determination, though it possibly did not extend to all qualities of all substances, did extend to some qualities of every substance, and to such an extent as afforded a sufficient description of every substance determined by it.

---

[1] Such a system must, of course, provide exclusive descriptions of each part in the system, as otherwise they could not be identified, and it would not be known what part was in any particular place.

And the same relation of determining correspondence which ensures this, ensures also that the universe possesses order of classification. For by means of that relation, the parts of the universe can be arranged in a classifying system based on qualities which are of fundamental importance. Such a system may be called a Fundamental System.

**248**. The system in question is one which divides the universe, in the first place, into primary wholes, then divides each of these into their primary parts, each of these into secondary parts of the first grade, each of these into secondary parts of the second grade, and so on infinitely[1].

Each of the groups thus formed will, as we saw in the last chapter, have in it an exclusive common quality which is not a mere restatement of the denotation of the group. In the group of primary wholes that exclusive common quality will be the quality of being a primary whole. In the group of primary parts which fall within the primary whole $A$, the exclusive common quality will be that of being a primary part which falls within $A$. In the group of the secondary parts of the first grade which fall within the primary part $B$, the exclusive common quality will be to be a secondary part of the first grade which falls within the primary part $B$. In the group of the secondary parts of the second grade which fall within $B! \, C$, the exclusive common quality will be to be a secondary part of the second grade which falls within $B! \, C$, which is a secondary part of the first grade. And so on with all the others.

Here we have a system which arranges all the content of the universe. It does not, indeed, contain all substances as members. It does not contain as members such substances as that which consists of $B$ and $C$, in the case in which $B$ and $C$ are not the whole of $A$. Nor does it contain as members such

---

[1] The first step in this system will of course drop out, if it should prove to be the case that the universe is a single primary whole. It might be thought that between primary wholes and primary parts there should come another stage, that of differentiating groups. But these groups may overlap. The differentiating group of $B$, for example, may be $BCD$, and the differentiating group of $E$ may be $CDF$. And thus division by these groups would not arrange the parts of the universe in one definite system, in which such part is either united to or separated from every other in the grouping at each particular stage.

substances as that which consists of *B! C* and *C! D! E*. But
though the system does not contain them as members, it does
contain their parts as members.

**249**. Why should this system be regarded as more fundamental than other systems of classification? In the first place,
this system of division of the universe is involved in the fact
that there is a universe at all. The universe is a substance.
Every substance is divided into parts of parts infinitely. And
the only way to avoid the contradiction which would otherwise
be involved in this infinite series is that the universe should
contain primary parts (arranged in one or more primary wholes)
the parts of each of which should be in determining correspondence with other primary parts, and their parts. And since this
relation of primary parts and their parts to one another gives
us the system which we are now considering, that system is
implied in the fact that there is a universe. It does not seem
possible that any other system than this is implied in that fact,
except a system which is implied in this system. And this is
sufficient to entitle us to regard the system as specially fundamental to the universe.

And, in the second place, we are not certain that any system
of classification extends over the whole universe, except this
system, and any other which is implied by this. The infinite
number of parts of the universe could, indeed, be arranged in
an infinite number of ways. Any two or more could be grouped
together, and any two or more of these groups could again be
grouped, and so on. But such an arrangement would not be a
system of classification unless each group of parts formed by it
possessed some exclusive common quality which is not a restatement of its denotation. And we do not, so far as I can see,
know that any arrangement has this quality, except the one
which we are now considering, and any which may be implied
in it. This gives us a second reason for regarding this system as
fundamental.

In the third place, the system which we have described,
while it does not include every part in the universe, does, as we
have seen, include the parts of every part, and therefore implies
the existence of every part which it does not include, and has a

definite relation to every division in every arrangement (whether systematic or not) that can be made of the parts of the universe. And this cannot be the case with any system of arrangement which does not depend on determining correspondence. For it can only be the case with a system which contains parts of every part of the universe, that is, a system which contains parts of parts to infinity. And, as we have seen, no such system can exist unless it is determined by determining correspondence.

For these three reasons we may regard such a system as a fundamental system, and as therefore producing order in the universe. And such a system has two other characteristics which render the order produced by it more perfect. The first is that, since its divisions are carried on to infinity, it never leaves any content in any of its divisions which cannot be further determined by the system. The second is that the principle which has determined any division is the same principle that determines the sub-divisions of that division to infinity— namely, the same sort of determining correspondence[1].

We saw in an earlier chapter[2] that, so far as we had yet gone, the possibility was not excluded that there should be two or more independent systems of determining correspondence, each of which extended over the whole universe. Considerations to be introduced in Book V will give us good reason to suppose that this is not actually the case. But, if it were the case, the universe would still be an ordered universe. It would have several systems of classification, independent but not incompatible, each of which would be based on qualities of fundamental importance, and each of which, therefore, might be called a fundamental system, as opposed to systems of classification which were not based on qualities of fundamental importance, and to arrangements which were not systems of classification at all.

**250.** There are, of course, an infinite number of arrangements of the infinite number of parts of the universe. Such of these arrangements as cannot be deduced from the fundamental

---

[1] As contrasted, for example, with a system which should classify mankind by races, should then classify the persons of each race by sex, and then the persons who were of the same race and sex by age.

[2] Section 228.

system, may, whether they are systems of classification or not, be considered as more or less expressing the fundamental nature of the universe in proportion as they depart less or more from the arrangement of the fundamental system.

In the first place, there are those divisions which divide groups which the fundamental system does not divide, without making any alteration in that system. For example, if the differentiating group of $B$ should be $C$, $D$, $E$, and $F$, then $B$'s secondary parts of the first grade would be $B! C$, $B! D$, $B! E$, $B! F$. These four members would in the fundamental system form one group, between which, and the four groups formed by the parts of the four members respectively, the fundamental system would give no intermediate groups. But if it should happen, for example, that $B! C$ and $B! D$ possessed an exclusive common quality which was not shared by $B! E$ and $B! F$, then there would be two intermediate groups, one of $B! C$ and $B! D$, and one of $B! E$ and $B! F$, which would give a supplementary systematic arrangement. And, even if there were no exclusive common quality, this would still be a supplementary arrangement of the parts in question, although it would not be systematic.

In such a case as this the arrangement, while it supplements the fundamental system, cannot be said to depart from it. But, in the second place, there are arrangements which do depart from the fundamental system. Such, for example, would be an arrangement which brought together $B! C! D! E$ and $C! F! G! D$, as the only members of a set of parts of some higher part. For then these two parts would be brought as close to one another as any two parts could be, and would have a common whole which they shared with nothing else, while in the fundamental system they would have no common whole short of the primary whole, and each of them would have substances much nearer to itself than the other was.

Such an arrangement, then, will depart from the fundamental system. And it will depart from it more or less according to the number of cases in which parts are grouped differently in the two systems, and according as the difference in their relative positions in the two systems is large or small.

**251.** We have thus, theoretically, a test of the degree to which any arrangement, other than the fundamental system, expresses the fundamental nature of the universe, since it will do so more or less in proportion as it departs less or more from the fundamental system. But this would only be of practical importance if we were able to determine the places in the fundamental system of the substances included in the arrangement to be judged.

And even if we were able to determine the places in the fundamental system of those substances which we know empirically, it would not follow that the fundamental system would give us much aid in those classifications and divisions which we find it necessary to make in order to deal with the subject-matter of our empirical knowledge. It is clear that it might not help us if we were seeking for a classification which is to serve some special need of our own, because, if our need has no simple and definite relation to the fundamental qualities of the things dealt with, the classification which suits our needs may be one which, from the point of view of those qualities, may be trivial and fantastic. It would, for example, be trivial and fantastic, from any general standpoint, to classify a collection of pictures by the state of the gilding on their frames. But if a curator had to decide how a grant for regilding the frames should be expended, such a classification would be the one which he would require.

Even, however, when we have no such special need to consider, but are only desirous of arranging what we empirically know in such a way as to understand it best, it does not follow that the fundamental system would give us much aid towards that classification. Let us suppose, for example, that the universe was a single primary whole, and that its primary parts were material atoms. In that case we should know of no existence outside our primary whole, since nothing else existed. And we should know nothing of the particular natures of any primary part, or of any secondary part, since we have no empirical acquaintance with any atom, or with any part of any atom. Everything which we know empirically would be a group of primary parts within one all-embracing primary whole, and consequently the only arrangements in the universe which could help us to arrange what we know empirically would be arrangements of primary parts within their primary whole. And such arrangements could not be found in the fundamental system, since that system goes in one step from a primary whole to the set of its primary parts.

It is not, indeed, probable that the primary parts are in any case material atoms—this question will be discussed in Book V. But it is quite possible that, in some part of the field which each of us knows empirically, each primary part would occupy so small a portion of that field that it could not be known separately, in which case the same consequences would follow.

It is, of course, a further question whether the arrangement which was best for the purpose of understanding what we know empirically could ever be one which did not merely supplement the fundamental system but positively departed from it. But I can see no ground for denying the possibility of this.

**252.** We now pass to another point, which, while not bearing on the order of the universe, as we have used that term, is sufficiently akin to it to be treated conveniently in the same chapter. We saw in Chapter XXI that, besides the absence of any reason, at that point, to believe the universe to be ordered, there was another respect in which we failed, at that point, to detect what we ventured to call any grain in the universe. This was that we had no reason to hold of any substance that it would be more appropriately called a unity of manifestation, or organic unity, than a unity of composition, or, again, more appropriately called a unity of composition than a unity of manifestation. We saw that our empirical knowledge of certain wholes was such that it seemed far more natural to speak of the wholes as compounded of the parts than to speak of the parts as the manifestation of the whole. In other cases, again, to speak of manifestation seemed at least as natural as to speak of composition. But we saw that this apparent difference between the two classes of cases might be deceptive, and we had nothing else by which to decide. We did know that both expressions were true of every substance. We had no reason to hold that, when the whole nature of the substance was taken into account, one expression was more appropriate to that nature than the other.

**253**. But we are now in a different position. We are able to see that primary and secondary parts—that is, all members of the fundamental system except primary wholes—are more appropriately called unities of manifestation than unities of composition. For we find that, if we take a certain sufficient description of any one of them, it will imply sufficient descriptions of a set of its parts, that a sufficient description of any one of these parts will again imply sufficient descriptions of a set of its parts, and so on infinitely. And this chain of implications from whole to part renders it more appropriate to say that each whole is manifested in its parts, than to say that it is composed of them.

It is true, no doubt, that sufficient descriptions of each member of a set of parts will also determine a sufficient description of the whole. It might be thought that this fact would balance the other, so that the expressions of unity of manifestation and unity of composition would be equally appropriate. But it must be remembered that the series of implications from part to whole is not a series which is valid by itself, as apart from the series of implications from whole to part. For such a series would be infinite, since there are no parts which are not also wholes. And, as we saw in Chapter XXIII, such an endless series would be vicious, unless there were also the series of implications from whole to parts. There is no corresponding limitation with regard to the series from whole to parts, which, even when taken by itself, involves no contradiction. This latter series of implications must, therefore, be taken as the more characteristic of the two, and it is therefore more appropriate to speak of the parts in the fundamental system as unities of composition.

**254**. When we consider substances which are not members of the fundamental system, the position is different. If we limit ourselves to what we know about their natures *à priori*, it is more appropriate to speak of them as compounded of their parts than as manifested in them. For we have no reason to believe that any sufficient description of the whole would imply, without including, sufficient description of its parts, while we do know that, with them as with every other substance, sufficient descriptions of their parts do imply a sufficient description of the whole. This does not mean that an infinite series could exist of parts within parts of such substances, sufficient descriptions of each of which were implied by sufficient descriptions of its parts, without any implication of sufficient descriptions of the parts by sufficient descriptions of the wholes. That, as we have seen, would be a contradiction. But it would be avoided by the fact that, as we have seen, any substance $H$, which is not a member of the fundamental system, is divided into parts which are members of the fundamental system. Then a sufficient description of $H$ will be implied by sufficient descriptions of those parts of $H$, while, to find sufficient descriptions of the latter, we shall not have to pursue the series of implications from parts to wholes. For, since these parts of $H$ are members of the fundamental system, sufficient descriptions of them will be implied in the sufficient descriptions of precedent members of the fundamental system. Thus we may say, in general, of substances which are not members of the fundamental system, that each of them is more appropriately called a unity of composition, but that each of them consists, in the long run, of parts which are more appropriately called unities of manifestation.

But, in the case of some such substances, we know empirically that there is a sufficient description of the whole which implies, without including, sufficient descriptions of a set of its parts. A substance, for example, might have a sufficient description which contained as an element that it was a company of actors in a pantomime of the type normal in 1870. Such a description would imply sufficient descriptions of a set of its parts. For it would imply that the company contained four actors, and no more, and that they were respectively clown, pantaloon, harlequin, and columbine. And it would be a sufficient description of an actor to say that he was, for example, clown in such a company. For the company was already sufficiently described, and such a company would only contain one clown. Thus the sufficient description of the whole would imply sufficient descriptions of a set of its parts, by virtue of the law, known to us empirically, that a company of such a type contained a clown, a pantaloon, a harlequin, and a columbine, and that it contained only these. We know then that sufficient descriptions of some substances which are not members of the fundamental system[1] do imply sufficient descriptions of their parts, and it is very possible that this happens in the case of many other substances, though we have no reason to suppose that it happens with all.

When a sufficient description of such a substance does imply sufficient descriptions of its parts in this way, it is as appropriate to call it a unity of manifestation as a unity of composition. But it does not seem to me to be *more* appropriate to call such substances unities of manifestation, as it is with substances which are members of the fundamental system. The reason that it was more appropriate in the case of the latter was, as we saw, that an infinite chain of implications from whole to part ran through the fundamental system, which was intrinsically valid without depending on a series in the reverse direction. But in the case we are now considering the implication from whole to parts is not carried to infinity—the sufficient description of the pantomime company implies a sufficient description of the clown, but the latter does not imply sufficient descriptions of sets of his parts to infinity. This can only be done by determining correspondence—only, that is, in the case of members of the fundamental system. There seems, therefore, no reason to consider either expression more appropriate. It is equally suitable to say that the company is compounded of the clown and the others, as to say that it is manifested in them.

**255.** Thus, with a substance which is not a member of the fundamental system, it is possible that the two forms of expression may be equally appropriate, or that unity of composition should be preferable, while of primary and secondary parts, which are all members of the fundamental system, it is certain

---

[1] If two substances partially overlap one another, we are certain they are not both members of the fundamental system, since no members of it can overlap one another. Now some substances whose sufficient descriptions imply sufficient descriptions of their parts do partially overlap each other. Two pantomime companies can, for example, have the same clown, while their other members are different.

that in every case unity of manifestation is the more appropriate expression. But the fundamental system, besides primary and secondary parts, contains primary wholes. Is either form of expression the more appropriate for those latter?

At first sight it might appear that a primary whole was more appropriately called a unity of manifestation. For that sufficient description of a primary part, $B$, in which sufficient descriptions of all its parts are implied, must be one which gives sufficient descriptions of all the other primary parts which directly differentiate $B$. It is only because we start by knowing that $B$ is differentiated by $C$, for example, that we know that it has the part $B! C$. And these sufficient descriptions of the determinants of $B$ must include sufficient descriptions of *their* determinants. Unless we know that $C$ is differentiated by $D$, we shall not know that $B$ has the parts $B! C! D$. Thus the sufficient description of $B$ which we require must include sufficient descriptions of all the substances which differentiate it, directly or indirectly. All of these substances are to be found in the same primary whole as $B$, and a sufficient description of that primary whole could be found which contained sufficient descriptions of them. Thus it might be said that a sufficient description of the whole stands to sufficient descriptions of its primary parts in the relation in which sufficient descriptions of primary parts stand to sufficient descriptions of their parts—namely, that the whole infinite series of sufficient descriptions of the parts depends upon it. And if primary parts are more appropriately called unities of manifestation, the same, it might seem, would be the case with primary wholes.

But this is erroneous. Doubtless that sufficient description of $B$ in which sufficient descriptions of all its parts are implied, does involve sufficient descriptions of other primary parts of $A$, which could be included in a sufficient description of $A$. But this sufficient description of $A$ would contain as parts sufficient descriptions of the primary parts. It would state that $A$ was a primary whole, containing such and such primary parts, and that each of these primary parts had such and such primary parts as its differentiating group. It would therefore include the sufficient descriptions of the primary parts. But the sufficient descriptions of the primary parts imply those of their parts without including them. And thus the primary wholes do not stand to their parts in the same relation as the primary parts do to theirs.

On the other hand, any sufficient descriptions of the primary parts will imply a sufficient description of their primary whole. The process, therefore, which best expresses the nature of their mutual relations is from primary parts to primary wholes, and not *vice versa*, and primary wholes will be more appropriately called unities of composition than unities of manifestation.

The same will be the case with the universe itself. The universe is either one primary whole, or consists of more than one primary whole. If it is a primary whole, we have seen already that it is more appropriately called a unity of composition. If it consists of several such wholes, it is clear that those wholes cannot be determined by determining correspondence with the universe, because, by the definition of a primary whole, nothing in it is in determining correspondence with anything outside it. The universe, then, would be more appropriately spoken of as a unity compounded of the primary wholes, for the same reason that a primary whole is more appropriately called a unity compounded of its primary parts.

Of course it is possible that the sufficient description of a primary whole should imply sufficient descriptions of its primary parts, or that the sufficient description of the universe should imply sufficient descriptions of the primary wholes, in the same way that a sufficient description of the pantomime company implied sufficient descriptions of its members—that is, in some other way than by determining correspondence. But we have no reason to believe that this is the case, and, if it were, it could only, as with the pantomime company, make the two expressions equally appropriate, without making unity of manifestation the more appropriate of the two.

**256.** The result of all this seems to be that, although the universe and the primary wholes are very real unities, yet the primary parts occupy a position of unique significance in the fundamental system, and so in existence. It is from them that the infinite series of implications begins, by which every substance of lower grades in the fundamental system, and indirectly every other substance, is determined. For although, as we have seen, the parts of any primary part *B* can only be implied by bringing in something besides *B*, all that has to be brought in are the other primary parts which differentiate *B* directly or indirectly.

It is sometimes asked whether the true account of the universe is a pluralism or a monism. The answer must be that it is both, since the universe is unquestionably a unity, and unquestionably has parts. But if it is asked which aspect is the more fundamental, the answer must be that pluralism is the more fundamental, because, as we have just seen, the primary parts, which are a plurality, have this position of unique significance. It expresses the relations of the universe and the primary parts more appropriately—so far as we can determine those relations *à priori*—to say that the universe is composed of the primary parts than to say that it is manifested in them. And this leaves the balance on the side of pluralism.

It must not be inferred from this, however, that the unity of the universe and the individuality of the primary parts are so related that a high degree of the one is incompatible with a high degree of the other. On the contrary, we shall find reason in Book V to believe that the closeness of the unity of the universe is due to the fact that its primary parts are connected by a relation which is only possible between terms which are highly developed individuals.

Before closing our discussion of this subject, it may be well to remind ourselves that, in the case of those groups which have no sufficient descriptions which imply, without including, sufficient descriptions of their parts, we are not always driven to use that sufficient description of each group which is implied in sufficient descriptions of its parts. It may well have other sufficient descriptions, and one of them may be more convenient to use. It is highly probable that no sufficient description of the group of Cambridge graduates could be found which implied without including sufficient descriptions of its members. But it does not follow that we cannot sufficiently describe it except by saying that it is the group consisting of a member sufficiently described as $XYZ$, another sufficiently described as $UVW$, and so on through all people who have been or will be graduates of Cambridge. It is possible to describe the group sufficiently by defining graduation and sufficiently describing the University of Cambridge.

**257.** We saw that, while a substance was manifested in and compounded of the substances which are its parts, the *nature* of a substance, which is a compound quality, is manifested in and compounded of the simple qualities of which it is made up. It seems to me that it is always more appropriate to say that it is compounded of them than that it is manifested in them, since the simple qualities themselves are logically prior to the compound quality which consists of them.

# CHAPTER XXIX

## LAWS IN THE UNIVERSE

**258**. For the validity of such a fabric of knowledge as we accept in everyday life, it is essential that there should occur in the universe exclusive common qualities which are not mere restatements of the denotations of groups. Without this it would be impossible to classify in any manner the parts of the universe. But, though this is essential, it is not sufficient. For such a fabric of knowledge to be valid, it is also essential that there should be general laws in the universe, according to which one such exclusive quality of the universe should intrinsically determine another in such a way that the determination occurs more than once in the universe[1]. And it is essential that we should be able to know such laws.

There are other laws which do not answer to this description. Any statement that any quality intrinsically determines any other quality is a law. And, in the first place, there are the laws in which the determinant quality does not occur in the universe at all, and in which therefore the relation of determination also does not occur in the universe. The quality of being a phoenix determines the possession by the same substance of the quality of occupying space. This is a law, but the relation of determination does not occur in the universe, because no existent substance is a phoenix.

In the second place, there are the laws where the relation of determination occurs only once in the universe. Such is the law that the quality of being a universe determines the possession by the same substance of the quality of infinite divisibility. And, again, if a monotheistic theory of the universe were correct, a law that the quality of deity determines some other quality in the same substance would fall in this class.

[1] Such laws are often expressed in the form that a combination of the qualities $X$ and $Y$ determine the quality $Z$. But the qualities $X$ and $Y$ make together a single compound quality, so that this form can be reduced to the one given above.

In the third place, there are the laws where the qualities connected are not exclusive qualities, but belong to every substance. Such is the law that the quality of being a substance determines the possession by that substance of the quality of infinite divisibility.

The laws which we are here considering may be distinguished from the first and second of those classes by calling them Laws in the Universe. The first class do not apply to the universe at all. Each of the second has only a single example in the universe, and therefore, though they might be said to be laws *of* the universe, could not appropriately be said to be laws *in* it. The distinction from the third class may be met by calling the laws which we are considering Exclusive Laws in the Universe, since the qualities with which they deal are exclusive qualities.

**259**. Is it possible to know such laws *à priori*? It is not possible to know them completely *à priori*, because we do not know *à priori* that anything exists at all, and therefore cannot know *à priori* that any law applies to what does exist. But it is possible to know *à priori* that some such laws are valid if anything does exist. If anything exists, we know *à priori* that the system of determining correspondence applies to it. And we know *à priori* that if two substances, G and H, have each the quality of being determined by determining correspondence, and also the quality of being parts of the same substance, K, which is also determined by determining correspondence[1], then G and H will each have the quality of being determined by the same relation of determining correspondence. For, as we saw in Section 227, no fresh sort of determining correspondence can be introduced in any stage after the first in the determination of the infinite series of sequent sets of parts. And, therefore, G and H must both be determined by that relation of determining correspondence by which K is determined. Now this is a law in the universe. For there is more than one substance in the

---

[1] In most cases the highest grade of substances which are determined by determining correspondence are secondary parts of the first grade, so that G and H could be parts of the second, or of any lower grade. But in some cases, as was pointed out in Section 201, the highest grade of substances determined by determining correspondence may be secondary parts of some grade lower than the first.

universe which is determined by determining correspondence, and every one of them will have parts which are determined by determining correspondence. And it is an exclusive law in the universe. For it is not every substance which is in the position of *G* and *H*. Primary wholes, for example, primary parts, and secondary parts of the first grade, can never be in that position.

**260**. But in order to justify our *primâ facie* system of everyday knowledge, we shall want more than this. For that system involves the validity of laws in which the intrinsic determination of one quality by another, which is asserted by them, cannot, so far as we can see at present, ever be known *à priori*. All the laws of inductive science are of this nature. We have, or claim to have, good reason for thinking them to be true, but they cannot be known *à priori*. Our only ground for believing them is that we have verified them (or the more ultimate laws from which they are deduced) in so many cases that we are justified in believing that they are valid in all cases.

On the validity of such laws as these depends the whole of science, except pure mathematics. And it is on the validity of such laws that the whole conduct of our life is based. If they are not valid we should have no reason to put bread in our mouths rather than stones, to put our hands in water rather than in fire, or to approach a cat more readily than a tiger.

*Primâ facie*, then, there are exclusive laws in the universe which we do not know *à priori*. But have we any philosophical justification for asserting that this is true? Is it possible, that is, to show *à priori* that, since there is a universe, there are exclusive laws in it whose nature is not known *à priori*?

**261**. We have seen that, since there is a universe, the parts of that universe must be connected by determining correspondence. Now determining correspondence connects, in each case, one particular part of the universe with some other particular part, and we cannot tell *à priori* which particular part is connected with any other. Further, in each case there must be some particular relation of determining correspondence which connects the two parts. And we saw above (Section 226) that we could not tell *à priori* what this particular relation was, or even if it was the same relation in every case.

And this justifies us in asserting that there are laws in the universe which are not known *à priori*. For it follows from the results in Section 259, that, if we take any substance $K$ which is determined by determining correspondence to a substance $C$, so that it may be described as $B!$ $C$, and if the particular relation of determining correspondence in this case is $X$, there will be a law connecting the quality of being a part of $K$ with the quality of standing in the relation $X$ to a part of $C$.

Let us suppose, for example, that the relation of determining correspondence by which $C$ determines $K$ is the perception of the determinant by the determinate. Then we shall get the law that whatever has the quality of being a part of $K$ has also the quality of being a perception of a part of $C$. Or if the relation of determining correspondence is one of resemblance in respect of positivity or negativity, we shall get the law that whatever has the quality of being a part of $K$ has also the quality of resembling a part of $C$ in respect of positivity or negativity.

Such laws as these are exclusive laws in the universe. To be a part of $K$ is a quality of the existent, and so is the quality which it involves. They are both exclusive qualities, since neither of them is possessed by all substances. And the determination of one of them by the other occurs more than once in the universe, since $K$ has more than one part—has indeed, an infinite number of parts.

And, while we know *à priori* that, given the existence of a universe, such a law as this must be true, we cannot tell *à priori* what the law will be. For we cannot know *à priori* what particular determinant part will determine any particular determinate part, nor can we know *à priori* what particular relation of determining correspondence will hold between them.

In a similar way we may be certain that, if $H$ is a part of $K$ which is determined by correspondence with that part of $C$ which is determined by correspondence with $D$—if, that is, $H$ can be described as $B!$ $C!$ $D$—and if the relation of determining correspondence between $B!$ $C!$ $D$ and $C!$ $D$ is perception, then every part of $H$ will be a perception of a part of $C!$ $D$. And so also of all parts of $K$ of whatever grade.

**262**. We must not say however, that every part of $H$ will be a perception of a part of $C$'s perception of $D$. It is possible, as we have seen, that the relation of determining correspondence which holds between $C$ and $B!$ $C$ is different from that which holds between $C$ and $C!$ $D$, and that the first might be perception while the second was some other relation. In that case we cannot be certain that the perception of a part of $C!$ $D$ would be a perception of a part of $C$'s perception of $B$.

But if it is the case, as we shall find reason to believe in Book V, that there is only one sort of determining correspondence which occurs in the universe, and that this relation is perception, this objection would no longer hold, and we could conclude that every part of $H$ would be a perception of a part of $C$'s perception of $D$, and that this part of $C$'s perception of $D$ would be a perception of a part of $D$.

And again, on the supposition that there is only one sort of determining correspondence in the universe, we can extend our conclusions to the parts of primary parts. If, for example, the relation of determining correspondence is perception, there would be a law that the parts of any primary part $B$, which had a determining group consisting of $C$ and $D$, would be perceptions of $C$ and $D$, and of the parts of $C$ and $D$. And it could not be known *à priori* that any particular law of this type would be a law in the universe, for we could not know *à priori* what the sort of determining correspondence in the universe would be, nor could we know *à priori* what the differentiating group of any particular primary part would be.

**263**. But even without the supposition that there is only one sort of determining correspondence in the universe, we have found that the range of law in the universe is very extensive. We have not, indeed, reached the conclusion that every quality of every existent substance is determined by an exclusive law in the universe. But we have found that some quality is determined by such a law in every substance which forms part of a substance determined by determining correspondence. And such substances include the whole substantial contents of the universe an infinite number of times.

And the extent to which determination by these laws is carried in the case of each of these substances is very great.

For although we do not know that it determines every quality of each of them, we do know that it determines each of them enough to give an exclusive description of it—a description which, by the aid of the sufficient descriptions of the primary parts to which it refers, becomes a sufficient description. And thus the laws determine enough about the qualities of each of these substances to distinguish it from all other substances.

And these laws, as we have seen, cannot be known *à priori*. It is proved that each of them can be deduced from the system of determining correspondence together with certain facts—that there is a universe, that it contains, for example, a substance $K$, which is determined by determining correspondence with $C$, and that the relation of determining correspondence in this case is perception. Now the system of determining correspondence, as we have seen, is a law which can be known *à priori*, and, while the facts in question cannot be known *à priori*, they are not laws. But the combination of the two elements gives something which is a law and which cannot be known *à priori*.

As was said at the beginning of this chapter, it is necessary for the validity of the fabric of knowledge which we accept in everyday life that there should be exclusive laws in the universe, and that we should be able to know such laws, and also that we should be able to know such laws in cases where we do not know them *à priori*. We have now seen that there are exclusive laws in the universe of a type such that we cannot know them *à priori*. How does this result affect the credibility of our belief that we do, in point of fact, know some such laws without knowing them *à priori*?

**264**. A law which is not reached *à priori* can only be reached by induction, or by deduction from some other result which has been reached by induction. Now every induction can be put in the form that, since $X_1$, $X_2$, $X_3$, etc., have been found in the relation $Y$ to $Z_1$, $Z_2$, $Z_3$, etc. (where $X$ and $Z$ are qualities, and $X_1$, $Z_1$, etc., are different occurrences of those qualities), therefore any occurrence of $X$ stands in the relation $Y$ to an occurrence of $Z$, though it has not yet been observed to stand in it.

In the case of such a law as "drinking prussic acid determines death," it is clear that this is the case. $X$ is the quality of drinking prussic acid, $Z$ is the quality of being dead, and $Y$ is the relation that $Z$ immediately follows $X$ as a quality of the same body.

Or, again, take the law that the weight of gold is proportionate to its bulk. Here $X$ is the quality of being gold. $Z$ is the complex quality of possessing a bulk and weight which are in a certain definite proportion to each other—so many pounds to so many cubic inches. $Y$ is the relation of belonging to the same substance at the same time. When, in various pieces of gold, $X_1$, $X_2$, and so on, we always find that $Z$ is a quality at the same time of the same substance, we conclude that $Z$ is always found in that relation to $X$. That is to say, we conclude that the weight is in a certain definite proportion to the bulk—from which, of course, follows the wider proposition that it is in *some* definite proportion to the bulk.

Take, again, the law that a change in the temperature of water determines a change in its bulk, the magnitude of the change in the temperature determining the magnitude of the change in its bulk. Here $X$ is the quality of being water which is changing its temperature. Since such a change of temperature is quantitative, every such change must have a definite magnitude, though changes of all magnitudes are equally examples of $X$. $Y$ is the relation of being qualities of the same substance at the same time. $Z$ is the quality of being water which is changing its bulk in such a way that the magnitude of that change stands in a certain definite proportion to the magnitude of the change in that case of $X$ to which it is related by $Y$. When in various cases in which the quality $X$ occurs, we find that the quality $Z$ stands in this relation to it, we conclude that, whenever $X$ is found, $Z$ will stand in this relation to it— that is, that every change in the temperature of water determines a change in its bulk, the magnitude of the latter change being determined by the magnitude of the former.

In cases such as the two last, the conformity of the induction to the type we have laid down is not so obvious as in cases like that of the prussic acid, which involved no quantitative element. It has therefore been sometimes thought that laws which involved quantity did not conform to that type. But this is erroneous, for, as we have just seen, quantitative laws can be reduced to this type. Thus we are entitled to assert that all induction concludes that every occurrence of $X$ stands in the relation $Y$ to an occurrence of $Z$, on the ground that, in certain cases, the occurrence of $X$ has been found by observation to stand in the relation $Y$ to the occurrence of $Z$. (It will also, of course, be an essential condition of the inference that no occurrence of $X$ has been observed in which the absence of $Z$ was observed.)

**265**. Under what conditions will it be justifiable to reach such a conclusion on such grounds? It is clear, to begin with, that we are not entitled to hold that every occurrence of $X$ will be accompanied by the occurrence of $Z$, unless we are entitled to hold that $Z$ is intrinsically determined by $X$. For no number of cases in which $X$ is accompanied by $Z$ could be held to justify us in asserting that $X$ is accompanied by $Z$ in other cases, if, on the ground of some wider induction, we have good reason to believe that $X$ does not intrinsically determine $Z$. Supposing that it were the case that on the day of the admission of each Warden of the Cinque Ports there had been a magnetic storm of exceptional intensity, no sensible man would expect that such a storm was likely to happen at the admission of the next Warden, because very wide experience has convinced us that such characteristics as these are not related to each other by intrinsic determination.

Now can induction, by itself, and without aid from any results reached *à priori*, give us good reason to believe that any one quality does intrinsically determine any other? I do not see that it can. Suppose that we know a hundred cases of the occurrence of $X$, and that we know by observation that each of them is accompanied by $Z$. Will this by itself exclude the supposition that $X$ does not intrinsically determine $Z$?

If $X$ does not intrinsically determine $Z$, the connection of $X$ with $Z$ in each of the observed cases may be called merely contingent. By saying that in any particular case the connection of $X$ with $Z$ is contingent, I do not mean that there is no reason why, in this particular case, $X$ should be accompanied by $Z$, but that there is no reason why $X$ as such, and wherever it occurs, should be accompanied by $Z$. There may be circumstances which intrinsically determine that Charles I, who was a King of England, should be beheaded, and that Charles II, who was also a King of England, should not be beheaded. But the fact that Charles II was not beheaded shows that the connection between being King of England and being beheaded is contingent in any case in which it does occur.

If then, the connection between $X$ and $Z$ is contingent, the presence of $X$ in each of the hundred cases leaves it possible that $Z$ should or should not occur in that case. This gives a great number of possible combinations—the number is $2^{100}$. Now of these combinations, the one in which each of the hundred cases of $X$ is accompanied by $Z$ is no less probable than any one other—though, of course, enormously less probable than all the others taken together. If, then, there is no intrinsic determination of one of the qualities by the other, one of these combinations must occur, and be contingent. And, since, if this hypothesis is true, the combination in which $Z$ is found in every case is no more unlikely to occur than any other, how can its occurrence render it improbable that the hypothesis is true?

Can we argue that this particular combination, though it could exist contingently, would also exist if $X$ did intrinsically determine $Z$, and that it is more probable that $X$ should intrinsically determine $Z$ than that, of all the great number of possible contingent combinations, just that one should occur which would produce the same result as would be produced by intrinsic determination? But such an argument would not be valid unless we previously knew something about the occurrence of intrinsic determinations in the universe. For, unless we knew this, we should have no means of judging as to the relative probability of an intrinsic determination and of a contingent connection. There might, for anything we knew, be no intrinsic determinations at all. And, if we were ignorant whether there were any such determinations, it would be impossible to estimate the relative probability, in any particular case, of an intrinsic determination and of a contingent connection.

**266**. Thus it appears that we must know something as to the occurrence of intrinsic determinations in the universe before we can accept any induction as valid. This result will not be affected by the number of instances in which the connection of any two qualities has been observed. Nor will it make any difference if the induction, instead of being based on simple enumeration were fortified by any of the methods which, if induction is valid at all, make an induction more certain. There would still remain the possibility of the result arising contingently, and the impossibility of judging the relative probability of this and intrinsic determination.

Nor should we be entitled to trust induction because we find that it works in practice. If we did this we should believe in an induction, in cases in which it had not been verified by observation, because, in other cases, inductions which had been made had been verified by observation. To argue in this way from the correctness of some inductions to the correctness of others would itself.be a process of induction, and, if it were used as a defence of induction in general, would involve a vicious circle.

We must therefore be able to know, without induction, that in some cases an exclusive quality of the existent does intrinsically determine another in such a way that the determination occurs more than once in the universe. Without this, we shall have no basis for induction. Whether we have, even with this, a basis for induction, will be considered later.

**267.** It is true that, in a certain class of cases, we have not to wait for the theory of determining correspondence in order to be certain, without induction, that such intrinsic determination does take place. We know *à priori* that the quality of being or appearing green intrinsically determines the quality of being or appearing spatial. This requires no experience, but is evident as soon as the meaning of the terms is known. And I know, not by induction, but by observation, that the quality of being or appearing green does occur more than once in the universe. The same is the case with the quality of being a feeling of pain and the quality of having a certain intensity, and so with many others.

But such cases as these will not help us. For with them we only know *à priori* that there are intrinsic determinations because we know *à priori* what the intrinsic determinations are.

Now when we attempt to prove an intrinsic determination by induction, we do not know *à priori* that there is such an intrinsic determination—if we did, it would be superfluous to try to prove it by induction. Intrinsic determinations, therefore, which are known *à priori* can never be such as are required in order to justify our inductions.

Nor can we argue that, because some intrinsic determinations—those which are known *à priori*—occur, it is probable that others—which are not known *à priori*—occur likewise. For this would be itself an induction, and, if we based the validity of all inductions upon it, there would be a vicious circle.

And, even if there were not a vicious circle, the argument from intrinsic determinations known *à priori* to others which are not known *à priori* would be very precarious on account of the great difference between the two classes of cases. In the first, the determination is evident from the meaning of the two qualities. In the second, not only is our knowledge of the law itself dependent on experience, but apart from experience we can lay down no probabilities as to what the law—if there is a law—will be. Apart from experience I have no reason to suppose that cutting off Charles I's head would kill him. And I have no reason to suppose that it would not kill Oliver Cromwell or George Washington. Apart from experience I have no reason to suppose that my will to move my hand will move my hand, and will not move my foot, or destroy Pekin. To argue from the occurrence of the one sort of intrinsic determination to another, so different from it in such important features, would give very little ground for belief.

**268**. It is therefore necessary, for the validity of induction, that we should be able to know, without the aid of induction, that in some cases an exclusive quality of the existent does intrinsically determine another in such a way that the determination occurs more than once in the universe, and that the nature of the determination is such that we cannot know it *à priori*. And this we are entitled to assert in consequence of the results which we reached in the earlier part of this chapter. For we found that exclusive qualities of the existent did intrinsically determine other exclusive qualities in cases in which the determination in question could not be known *à priori*. And we found that this intrinsic determination was very widely spread throughout the universe. We found that some quality was so determined in every substance which is a part of a substance determined by determining correspondence, so that the substances in which such qualities occurred included the whole substantial content of the universe an infinite number of times over, and that every substance whatever had parts which were determined in this way. Further, we found that the qualities thus intrinsically determined are in each case sufficient to give a sufficient description of the substance which has them.

We are therefore entitled, without resting our conclusion on induction, to conclude that there do occur in the universe a large number—indeed an infinite number—of such intrinsic determinations as induction claims to discover. And thus we have removed the objection to the validity of inductions mentioned in Section 265. For we have eliminated the possibility, on which that objection rested, that there might be no intrinsic determination of one quality by another, except in those cases in which the intrinsic determination itself was evident *à priori*.

**269.** But there are two other objections to the validity of induction, rather similar in nature to the one which we have just discussed, and our theory of determining correspondence, as at present developed, will not help us with either of them. Granted, in the first place, that there is intrinsic determination throughout the universe, and that inductions assert intrinsic determination, what reason have we to hold that the intrinsic determinations which are asserted to be reached by induction either are, or follow from, any of those intrinsic determinations by determining correspondence which have been proved to exist? And, if they do not, then the results reached by induction can derive no advantage from the establishment of determining correspondence, but are in the same position as before.

It might seem at first sight, indeed, that the conclusions commonly reached by induction, which we are seeking to justify, could not possibly be determined by determining correspondence. For those relations between qualities which are asserted by induction, either in science or in everyday life, are not relations of determining correspondence. Nor are the qualities which they are held to connect such as we shall see reason later to believe can be connected by determining correspondence.

It might, however, be possible, when we introduce empirical considerations in Books V and VI, to show that the qualities, and the relations between them, which are dealt with in science and in everyday life, might be an appearance of which the reality was the qualities, and the relations between them, which form the system of determining correspondence. And it might be possible to show that the relation between the appearance and the reality was such that the validity of laws in the reality would involve the validity of laws in the appearance.

But if this went no further than a demonstration that such a solution was possible, it would not be sufficient. For then it would be also possible that the qualities and their relations which are dealt with in the inductions were not the appearance of the qualities and their relations which form the system of determining correspondence. And in that case the establishment of determining correspondence would not help us.

It might be said that when $X$ had been found with $Z$ a hundred times, so that the chance of its happening contingently was only one in $2^{100}$, it would be much more probable that it did not happen contingently, but was due to one of the intrinsic determinations which we now know to exist. But I do not see how it is possible to estimate the chance that it should be due to one of these intrinsic determinations, so as to compare it definitely with the chance—doubtless extraordinarily small—that it is due to contingency. The question whether the former is more probable than the latter is certainly more definite than the question in Section 265, when we did not know whether there were any such intrinsic determinations at all. And the affirmative answer is now to an undefined degree more probable, since we have eliminated one alternative which would involve a negative answer—the alternative that there are no intrinsic determinations at all, except those which are evident *à priori*. But I cannot see how the chance that it should be due to an intrinsic determination by determining correspondence could be made so definite as to be definitely pronounced greater than some other chance, however small the latter may be.

**270**. And, if this objection were got over, there would still be a third. Supposing that to the fact that in all our hundred cases $X$ had been found with $Z$, we could add the certainty that $X$ was a quality which was intrinsically determinant of something, and that $Z$ was a quality which was intrinsically determined by something—should we then have any basis for the conclusion that $X$ intrinsically determined $Z$, or was any part of a compound quality which intrinsically determined $Z$? I do not see that we should. It would remain possible that $X$ intrinsically determined $W$, which we had not observed, and that $Z$ was intrinsically determined by $Y$, which we had not observed, and that the connection between $X$ and $Y$ in the hundred cases we had observed was purely contingent. The chance of this last, indeed, is only 1 in $2^{100}$. But on the other hand there is the possibility that the real determinate and determinant are for some reason inaccessible to our observation. And 1 do not see that the chance that this possibility is not actual could be made so definite as to be definitely pronounced greater than some other chance, however small the latter might be.

**271**. Thus it would seem that a philosophical basis for induction has not yet been found. Of the three objections which we have considered, the first, as we have seen, is removed by the establishment of determining correspondence. The second might possibly be removed by a development of the theory of determining correspondence. But the third could not be removed by determining correspondence at all.

Nor does there seem much reason to hope that it can be removed in any other way. For it is difficult to see how philosophy could ever go further in aid of induction than to show that every quality intrinsically determined another, and was intrinsically determined by another. And we have seen that even if philosophy could do this—and it has not yet done so—it could not provide a philosophical basis for induction.

But, however fully we accept this conclusion, we shall all of us continue to accept the validity of induction. We cannot demonstrate that the chance that the other alternative hypotheses are false is more than one to $2^{100}$. But we cannot help regarding it as much greater than this. And therefore when we have to chose between accepting one of those hypotheses or believing that the concomitance of $X$ and $Z$ in our hundred cases cannot be contingent, we invariably accept the latter. We do not, of course, assert that $X$ by itself intrinsically determines $Z$—the concurrence of some other quality, $V$, may be necessary. But we do conclude without hesitation that $X$ either intrinsically determines $Z$ by itself, or is a member of a group of qualities which intrinsically determines $Z$. We should do this if the qualities had been found together a hundred times, as in our example. And of course we often have cases in which they have been found together for many more than a hundred times, as in the case of the concomitance of the quality of being leaden with the quality of sinking in water, and of the quality of being beheaded with the quality of being dead. To suppose that the qualities only come together in the same way in which, in a particular year, the qualities of being Lady Day and being rainy may come together is a conclusion which we feel it impossible not to reject.

Is this due to a blind and unreasonable psychological impulse, resembling the impulse which tends to make each of us regard himself and his own interests as more important in the universe than they really are, or that other impulse which tends to make us believe everything good of our friends and everything bad of our enemies? Or is it the case that the probabilities really are as we tend to judge them to be, and that we really see them to be so, though we can assign no mathematical proportions? It might be rash to deny that the latter was possible. But it would be much more rash to assert that it was actually the case, and, since this is so, we must adhere to our conclusion that a philosophical justification of induction has not yet been found.

# CHAPTER XXX

## THE DIFFERENTIATION OF PRIMARY PARTS

**272.** In this Book we have so far considered in what way the secondary parts in the system of determining correspondence could be sufficiently described by their correspondence with primary parts, and what consequences would follow from their possession of a nature which permits this. We have now to consider in what way the primary parts themselves can be discriminated from one another. In some way or another they must be discriminated, because, as we have seen, every substance must be discriminated from every other, by means of a sufficient description which applies to that substance alone. Moreover, secondary parts could not be sufficiently described by their determining correspondence with primary parts, unless those primary parts are themselves discriminated.

**273.** In the first place, two primary parts could be distinguished from each other by the fact that their differentiating groups were different, and that, in consequence, their secondary parts corresponded to different primary parts. $B$ and $C$, for example, could be distinguished from one another, if the differentiating group of $B$ was $E$ and $F$, so that its secondary parts of the first grade were $B! E$ and $B! F$, and the differentiating group of $C$ was $G$ and $H$, so that its secondary parts of the first grade were $C! G$ and $C! H$. For the possession of any set of its parts is a quality of any whole, and this quality would be different in $B$ and $C$[1].

We have no reason to hold that no two primary parts have the same differentiating group—indeed, we have not excluded the possibility that all primary parts have the same differenti-

---

[1] It would not be necessary that the groups should have no members in common. It would be sufficient if no two groups had *all* their members in common.

ating group. But, on the other hand, it is possible that no two primary parts have the same differentiating group.

It is possible that some primary parts should only be discriminated from one another in this way. But it is impossible that all primary parts should be discriminated only by differences in their differentiating groups. For this would lead either to a vicious circle or to a vicious infinite series.

If $B$ and $C$ are to be discriminated by the fact that one of them has determining correspondence with $E$ and $F$, and the other with $G$ and $H$, this presupposes the discrimination of $E$, $F$, $G$, and $H$. For unless $E$ and $F$ were discriminated from $G$ and $H$, it would be impossible to discriminate $B$ and $C$ by their respective correspondence with them.

Now, if there is no other way to discriminate primary parts, $E$, $F$, $G$, and $H$ could only be discriminated by the differences in their differentiating groups of primary parts, and the members of those groups, again, by the difference in their own differentiating groups, and so on. And this would always involve either a vicious circle or a vicious infinite series. If the series returns upon itself, so that $B$ could only be discriminated from $C$ by its relation to a term which could only be discriminated by its relation to $B$, there is clearly a vicious circle. For then $B$ can only be discriminated by a process which can only take place if the discrimination of $B$ is previously given. If, on the other hand, the series never returns upon itself, then it is a vicious infinite series. For the discrimination of $B$ would depend on the discrimination of $E$, that on the discrimination of $K$, and so on. That is, $B$ could not be discriminated without the last term of this series. And, as the series has no last term, it could not be discriminated at all.

Thus this cannot be the only way of discriminating all primary parts. But, as was said above, it remains possible that it should be the only way of discriminating *some* primary parts. If $B$ and $C$ were discriminated by their differentiating groups, and then $E$, $F$, $G$, and $H$ were discriminated by the possession of qualities, or combinations of qualities, such as were possessed by no other substance in the universe, there would be no vicious circle or infinite series. For then $B$ and $C$ would have sufficient descriptions. If the sufficient descriptions of $E$ and $F$ are represented by $X$ and $Y$ respectively, $B$ can be described as the only primary part whose differentiating group consists of a substance with the sufficient description $X$ and a substance with the sufficient description $Y$. And this will not only be an exclusive description of $B$, but also a sufficient description of it.

**274.** There must, then, be some other way in which primary parts can be discriminated from one another. And there are several others. A second way in which they could be discriminated would be by the relations in which they stood to other substances, other than the relation, which we have just discussed, of having these substances as members of their differentiating groups. $B$ might be the only substance which stood in the relation $Y$ to $E$, and the relation $Z$ to $F$.

The substances, by their relations to which primary parts were thus discriminated, might be primary parts, or secondary parts, or substances which were not members of the fundamental system at all[1]. It would, of course, be impossible for all primary parts to be discriminated only by relations of this sort to other *primary* parts, as this would again involve a vicious circle or a vicious infinite series. But some of them might be discriminated only in this way. And it would be possible that all primary parts should be discriminated by their relations to substances which were not primary parts. In that case, however, it would be necessary that the substances in question should be discriminated in some way which did not depend on the primary parts to which they were in relation.

**275.** The third possibility is that all or some of the primary parts should be sufficiently described by means of their original qualities. In such a case the primary part would be discriminated by the fact that it possessed some original quality which was not possessed by anything else. It is possible that the unique quality possessed by the primary part should be a simple quality. For example, if a certain primary part were the only conscious substance in the universe, then "conscious substance" would be a sufficient description of it. But it is also possible, and it

---

[1] Those which were not members of the fundamental system would, as we have seen, consist of parts which were members of the fundamental system.

would appear to be more probable, that any such unique original quality of a substance would be a compound or complex quality[1].

**276**. In the fourth place, the primary parts might be discriminated by qualities which were not original but derivative —qualities of standing in a certain relation to something. We have already discussed the possibility of discrimination by means of the relations in which the primary parts stand to other substances which are independently discriminated. But it is possible in certain cases to discriminate a substance by means of a relation in which it stands to another substance which is not independently discriminated. For the relation itself may be unique, or may present certain unique features. The fact that $A$ loves $B$ might afford a sufficient description of $A$ without requiring a sufficient description of $B$, if no one else in the universe, except $A$, loved anybody, or if $A$'s love of $B$ had some quality which no other love ever had, or had a degree of intensity which differed from that of any other love.

**277**. We see then that there is no difficulty involved in the fact that each primary part must have a sufficient description, and, therefore, a nature different from that of every other primary part. There are, as we have seen, several possible ways in which this could happen. And, again, it is certain that there are qualities common to all primary parts. For there are some qualities which belong to all substances, and others which belong to all substances which are primary parts. But has every primary part qualities which it shares with some other primary parts, but not with all—qualities which, among primary parts, are both common and exclusive?

If there are more than two primary parts, then every primary part will have such common and exclusive qualities of a certain sort. For then every primary part will be in at least one group which contains one or more of the others, and not all of them. And the quality of being a member of that group will be a common and exclusive quality which it will possess. But, as we

---

[1] It must be remembered that we have classed as compound qualities all collections of simple qualities, however disconnected and heterogeneous. For example, "Swedenborgian socialist diplomatist" is a compound quality.

saw earlier, such qualities are of no great importance. The more interesting question is whether every primary part has a common and exclusive quality which is not the mere restatement of the denotation of a group.

I do not see that we have any reason to suppose that this must be the case. It is of course possible—and might be said to be probable—that the uniqueness of the nature of each primary part should be due to the fact that it possessed various qualities, each of which was shared with some, though not all, of the other primary parts, while the combination was unique and belonged only to the one part. But this is not certain. It would be possible that, in some or in all cases, the nature of the primary part consisted only in the common qualities which it shared with all other primary parts, and in some quality which it shared with none of them.

If, indeed, we were certain that the universe contained more than one primary whole, we should be certain that each primary part had at least one exclusive common quality, which was not the mere restatement of the denotation of a group. For to belong to a particular primary whole is a quality, and every primary part would, on this hypothesis, have a quality of this sort, which it shared with some other primary parts, and not with all. Nor would such a quality be a mere restatement of the denotation of a group. The quality of $B$ would not be merely that it was a member of a group whose other members were $C$, $D$, and $E$. It would be part of the quality that this group, of $B$, $C$, $D$, and $E$, of which $B$ was a member, was itself a primary whole.

It is possible however that the whole universe should be a single primary whole, and then the quality of belonging to that whole would not be an exclusive quality among primary parts. And, in any case, we should have no reason to believe that there were any qualities which were common and exclusive qualities among the primary parts in a primary whole—i.e. which belonged to some of the primary parts in a primary whole, but not to all of them.

Since we are not certain that there are any such exclusive common qualities of primary parts, we cannot, à fortiori, be certain that there are general laws in the universe according to which an exclusive quality of a primary part should be intrinsically determined by an exclusive quality of anything existent, in such a way that the determination occurs more than once in the universe. For, if this did happen, the quality of the primary part would be an exclusive common quality. And thus we are not certain that there are general laws in the universe which determine qualities of primary parts. There may be such laws, but we are not entitled to assert that there are.

# CHAPTER XXXI

## THE UNITY OF THE UNIVERSE

**278.** We have now arrived at various results about various parts of the universe, and the question remains, what is the nature of the bond which unites all these parts together. In other words, what sort of unity has the universe?

Like every other substance, the universe is a unity of manifestation as well as a unity of composition. Its nature as a whole may as truly be said to manifest itself in its several qualities, as to be made up of these qualities. And, passing from the relation in which it stands to its qualities to the relation in which it stands to its parts, the universe itself may as truly be said to manifest itself in its parts as to be made up of them. It is, therefore, an organic unity.

The fact that it can be regarded as a unity of manifestation and as an organic unity is not unimportant about any substance. And, as we saw above (Section 160) this fact has a special importance in the case of the universe. But although this unity is specially important in the case of the universe, it is only the same unity which is possessed by every substance in the universe. And therefore it tells us nothing about the amount of unity in the universe. For the unity of some substances is very slight. Every group of substances in the universe, however arbitrarily selected, and however slightly connected, is, as we have seen, a substance, and therefore a unity of manifestation, and an organic unity.

I do not see that it is possible, from the results which we have reached so far, to determine anything more as to the unity possessed by the universe. But if some qualities, which we have seen to be possible, though not necessary, qualities of the universe, were actually qualities of it, much more definite and distinctive unity might be ascribed to the universe. And it is worth while to work out some of these cases, and to see what results would follow from suppositions which are at any rate possible.

**279**. Let us first consider the group of assumptions which would bring about the closest unity. It is possible that the universe should consist of several primary wholes or of one only. Let us assume that it consists of only one primary whole. It is possible either that all the primary parts in the universe should be determinants, or that some of them should be only determined and not determinant. Let us assume that they are all determinants. If they are all determinants, it is possible that every primary part should determine a part of every other primary part, but it is possible that this should not be the case. Let us assume that it is the case. Then, if this assumption is made, it is possible that every primary part directly determines a part of every other primary part, or that in some cases the determination is only indirect. Let us assume that it is in all cases direct. Finally, it is possible that the determining correspondence is of the same sort throughout the universe, or that it is of different sorts in different cases. Let us assume it is always of the same sort. We will call the view that the universe is such as it would be if these assumptions were correct, the first supposition.

**280**. On this supposition the unity of the universe is in many respects very close. To begin with, every primary part in the universe is the determinant of a part within each primary part. That is to say, the determinants of the parts within each primary part are a set of parts of the universe, and contain all its content. And this relation links the universe as a whole more closely as to each of its parts, and, through the whole, links the parts more closely to each other. And, since determining correspondence between two substances involves the intrinsic determination of the nature of the determinate by part of the nature of the determinant, there will be a relation of intrinsic determination between the natures of all the primary parts of the universe, on the one hand, and the natures of all the secondary parts in each primary part, on the other hand—a relation, that is, of causal determination.

It is not, indeed, necessarily the whole nature of the secondary part which is intrinsically determined by the whole nature of the primary part to which it corresponds. It is possible that there should be qualities in the secondary part which are not determined by anything in the primary part, and qualities in the primary part which determine nothing in the secondary part. But at any rate so much of the nature of the primary part as will distinguish it from all others stands in this relation to as much of the nature of the secondary part as will distinguish it from all other parts of the primary part to which it belongs.

It will also, of course, follow that each secondary part of the first grade throughout the universe stands in a similar relation to a secondary part of the second grade within each primary part, and so on infinitely. And this network of causal relations—much closer and more inclusive than would have been the case except on the present supposition—introduces a good deal more unity into the universe.

**281**. Another point must also be considered. In each primary part there are secondary parts which are determined by each primary part. And by our supposition the particular relation of determining correspondence is the same in every case of determining correspondence throughout the universe. From this it follows that in any primary part $B$, not only will all its secondary parts of the first grade have a one-to-one correspondence with the primary parts of the universe, but there will be a system of relations existing between those secondary parts of $B$ which may be called homologous to a system of relations existing between the primary parts of the universe. For the manner in which these secondary parts are determined by determining correspondence will depend for each of them upon three things—the fact that it *is* a secondary part of $B$, and of the first grade, the fact that the particular relation of determining correspondence is what it is, and the fact that the primary part which is its determinant has a certain nature. And the first two of the facts are, on our present assumption, the same for every secondary part of the first grade within $B$. All dissimilarities, therefore, between the determined sufficient descriptions of these secondary parts of $B$ must correspond to dissimilarities between the determinant sufficient descriptions of the primary parts, and all similarities which exist between some, but not all, of these sufficient descriptions of the secondary parts must correspond to like similarities between some, but not all, of the sufficient descriptions of the primary parts. For such dissimilarities and exclusive similarities cannot be determined by the two data which are the same for all the secondary parts in question, and must therefore be determined by the only datum which varies for the different secondary parts—that is, the various primary parts to which they correspond. Since the system of relations between $B$'s secondary parts of the first grade will correspond in this way to the system of relations between the primary parts of the universe, it may be called homologous to it. Not only will the parts of $B$ correspond to the parts of the universe, but some of the links which connect them together will correspond to some of the links which connect the primary parts together.

But what would happen, it might be asked, if the sufficient description of each primary part of the universe, to which the secondary parts of $B$ corresponded, was in each case just some simple quality, possessed by that primary part and by nothing else? Then there would be no exclusive similarities to be reproduced, and no dissimilarities, except the uniform one that each primary part had a different simple determinant quality from all the others. In this case what would be the system of relations among the primary parts which would be reproduced among the secondary parts of $B$?

But even in this case it would still be true that a system of relations of the primary parts within the universe would correspond to a system of relations of the secondary parts of the first grade within $B$. For the determinant sufficient descriptions of the primary parts would have this relation to each other— that each consisted of a different quality, and that between those qualities there were to be found no exclusive similarities or exclusive common dissimilarities. And, in the same way, that part of the determined sufficient descriptions of the parts of $B$ which distinguished them from one another would be in each case a different quality and between those qualities there would be found no exclusive similarities or exclusive common dissimilarities. And thus the system of relations of the determinates might, as in the other cases, be said to be homologous to the system of relations of the determinants. The system of relations between the parts of $B$ would indeed be one which formed only a slight unity between them, but in that respect it would correspond to the system of relations between the primary parts, which also form only a slight unity.

**282.** The extent to which the relations between the primary parts are homologous to those among the secondary parts of $B$ must not be exaggerated. We have seen that it is not necessary that every quality of each determinant primary part should enter into its determinant sufficient description, or be implied in it. The primary part may have many other qualities which are independent of this particular sufficient description, and we have no reason to suppose that there will be anything correspondent to them in the secondary parts of $B$, or that the relations which are dependent on those qualities will be homologous to any relations among the secondary parts of $B$. And, again, we have seen that it is not necessary that every quality of each secondary part should enter into its determinant sufficient description, or be implied in it. And so there may be, dependent on these qualities, many relations which are not homologous to any relations which occur between primary parts of the universe. But, after allowing for all this, it remains true that the corresponding qualities are sufficient, on the one side, to differentiate each primary part from all the others in the universe, and, on the other side, to differentiate each of the secondary parts of $B$ from all the others. And since the corresponding qualities are, at any rate, as exhaustive as this, the homologous relations cannot be insignificant.

**283.** We have established, then, that the secondary parts of $B$ of the first grade correspond to the primary parts of the universe, and that various relations between these secondary parts of $B$ correspond to relations between the primary parts of the universe. But if we take the primary parts, not in any abstract isolation, but in the relations which they really bear to each other, we have the universe as it really is. And, if we

take the secondary parts of $B$ in the same way, we have $B$ as
it really is. We are thus entitled to say that $B$, and every other
primary part of the universe, corresponds to the universe in
respect of its parts, and of relations between them.

It must be noted, with regard to this correspondence of the
primary parts with the universe, that it is only derivative. The
primary fact is the correspondence of the secondary parts of
the first grade with the primary parts, and it is from this, as we
have seen, that the correspondence of the primary parts with
the universe arises.

**284.** The universe then, on the supposition which we are
now considering, has the quality that each member of a certain
set of its parts corresponds with the universe as a whole. We
may call this quality, by a metaphor which is not inappropriate,
the quality of Self-Reflection.

Self-reflection is a form of unity. A whole which is self-
reflecting has an additional sort of unity, which is not shared
by any whole which is not self-reflecting. For a self-reflecting
whole is connected in a special way with its parts. And, through
this, the parts in question are connected in a special way with
each other, since each of them has a system of internal relations
between their own parts, all of which correspond with the same
system, and so correspond with each other.

We must distinguish between that relation of a whole to its
parts which follows from the fact that it is an organic unity,
and that other relation of a whole to its parts which follows
from the fact that it is a self-reflecting unity. In an organic
unity, as we saw in Chapter xx, the parts manifest the whole.
But the whole is only manifested in all the members, taken
together, of any one set of its parts. It is not manifested in one
member by itself. But a self-reflecting unity is reflected
separately in each member of the set of parts in which the
reflection takes place. Every substance is an organic unity, and
therefore every substance which is a self-reflecting unity possesses
two sorts of unity—organic unity and unity of self-reflection.

It may be objected that such a term as self-reflection
exaggerates the closeness of the connection between the universe
and each primary part, since there is no reason to suppose that

the primary parts resemble the universe except in the system of their internal relations. This, however, does not make the metaphor inappropriate, since a reflection is not an exact copy of the object reflected. The object may be in three dimensions, and the reflection is in two. The object may be a mountain, and the reflection may be in a hand-glass. But such differences do not prevent the one from being a reflection of the other.

**285**. If the universe is a self-reflecting unity, it is thereby distinguished from many other substances, if not from all. For the course of our argument has shown us that, if any substance is to be a unity which is self-reflecting into parts determined by determining correspondence, and self-reflecting in consequence of that correspondence, it can only be on one condition. That condition is that it should have a set of parts, each member of which has as its differentiating group all the other members of that group, and nothing but those members. That is to say, no part of it must be determined by correspondence to anything outside it. Now we saw, in Chapter XXIV, that every primary part must have some other primary part in its differentiating group, and that, therefore, some members, at least, of every set of its parts will be determined by something outside itself. And the same will consequently be the case with secondary parts, of whatever grade.

The only case, therefore, which is not excluded, is the case of a substance which is a group of primary parts, each member of which has as its differentiating group all the members of that group, and nothing but those members[1]. But if the universe is such a group, as it is on our present supposition, there can be no other substance, in the same system of determining correspondence, which is such a group. For then every primary part has all others in its differentiating group, and cannot, therefore, be a member of any self-reflecting group which excludes any primary part—that is, of any self-reflecting group except the universe.

[1] In other words, a set of parts of each member of the group would be *directly* determined by the members of the group. A reciprocally determined group is not necessarily a self-reflecting group, since a group is reciprocally determined when each member of it determines parts of each of the members of the group, either directly or indirectly.

Unless, then, there are several independent systems of determining correspondence in the universe, no other substance could share with the universe the quality of being a unity which is self-reflecting into parts determined by determining correspondence, and which is self-reflecting in consequence of that correspondence.

It is possible, no doubt, that there may be unities of self-reflection into parts otherwise determined, or in consequence of other determination. But we have no reason to suppose that this is actually the case.

It is also to be noticed that the self-reflection of the universe is not confined to reflection in each of its primary parts. Within each secondary part of the first grade there will be a set of secondary parts of the second grade, each of which will have as its final determinant one of the primary parts of the universe. And consequently it will follow, by an argument analogous to that with regard to primary parts, that each secondary part of the first grade will correspond to the universe in respect of its internal system, and may therefore be said to reflect the universe. And the same will be true of the secondary parts of all lower grades to infinity.

And this last characteristic of the self-reflection of the universe—that self-reflection in the members of one set of parts involves self-reflection in the members of the infinite series of sequent states—could not be shared by any self-reflecting unity when the self-reflection did not depend on determining correspondence. For it is only by determining correspondence that what happens in one set of parts can involve what happens in all the infinite series of sequent sets. If, therefore, the universe is self-reflecting through an infinite series of sequent sets of parts, no other substance could also have that quality, unless there was more than one system of determining correspondence.

**286**. We saw, in Sections 146 and 147, that there are two qualities which are sometimes asserted to belong to every organic unity. One is that the whole is in every part. The other is that each part expresses the nature of the whole. We saw that the fact that a substance is an organic unity did not make either of these statements literally true of that substance. But we saw also that the fact that each part of an organic whole performed an unique function in the manifestation of the whole, made the use of these expressions, though incorrect, not unnatural.

Now when an organic unity is also a self-reflecting unity, the expressions, though still not correct, are more appropriate than they would be if the unity was organic without being self-reflecting. It is less inappropriate to say that the whole is in each part if the unity is self-reflecting. For a whole, while it is manifested in its parts, is not manifested in each part separately, while in a self-reflecting unity the whole is reflected separately in each part of the set of reflecting parts. This is not equivalent to the whole being in each part, which is impossible, but it has a certain resemblance to it.

Again, it is less inappropriate to say that each part expresses the nature of the whole if a unity is self-reflecting than if it is only organic. For the nature of the whole is only very partially expressed in the fact that a particular substance is one of the parts which manifest it. But in a self-reflecting unity each of the reflecting parts has within it a system of reflection homologous to a system of relations which exists within the whole. And although this does not make each part express the whole nature of the whole, it gets nearer to it than would otherwise have been the case.

**287**. Our first supposition, then, if true, would give a unity to the universe which would be much closer than that unity which we have seen that the universe certainly does possess. But, even on this supposition, the universe will not be a whole in which the unity is more fundamental than its differentiations, or even as fundamental as its differentiations. For nothing in our present supposition lessens the force of those arguments which lead us to conclude, in Section 256, that the primary parts occupy a position of unique significance in the fundamental system, and so in existence. Sufficient descriptions of the primary parts are not necessarily implied in any sufficient description of the universe—except in one which actually contains sufficient descriptions of the primary parts as elements in it. On the other hand any sufficient descriptions of all the members of the set of primary parts of the universe implies a sufficient description of the universe[1]. And for this reason it must, I think, be said that even on the supposition which we have just been discussing, the aspect of differentiation in the universe is more fundamental than the aspect of unity.

**288**. Such are the results of our first supposition. But, as has already been said, we have no reason to believe that this supposition agrees with the facts, and we must proceed to consider what would follow from other suppositions. Let us now suppose that the first four of the assumptions which made up our first supposition are correct, but that the fifth is not. Let us assume, that is, that the universe forms a single primary whole. Let us assume that every primary part in the universe is determinant. Let us assume that every primary part determines a part in every other primary part, and that it determines it directly. Let us, however, no longer assume that the determining correspondence is of the same sort throughout the universe, but let us admit the possibility that it is of different sorts[2]. What conclusions about the unity of the universe could be deduced in the case of this second supposition?

**289**. It will still be the case, as with the first supposition, that each primary part determines, in each primary part, a secondary part of the first grade, that each secondary part of the first grade in the universe determines, in each secondary part of the first grade, a secondary part of the second grade, and so on to infinity. The network of causal relations will therefore be as close as it was on the first supposition.

But we can no longer say, as we did on the first supposition, that each primary part, and also each secondary part of every

---

[1] This follows from the general principle that any sufficient description of all the members of any set of parts of any whole implies a sufficient description of that whole (cp. Section 187). What is implied will be a sufficient description of the substance which is, in point of fact, the universe. It will not necessarily be implied that this substance has the quality of being the universe. But this does not affect the argument in the text.

[2] The sort of determining correspondence might vary with the primary part which was determinant, or with the primary part which was differentiated, or with both. But as we have seen, whatever sort of determining correspondence held between any determinant primary part $C$, and its determinate $B! \, C$, would have to hold between the parts of $C$ and the parts of $B! \, C$. (Section 227.)

grade, stands in a correspondence with the universe in respect of their internal relations, so that each of them may be said to reflect the universe. The argument by which we reached the conclusion that this did occur on the first supposition began by saying that the manner in which those secondary parts are determined by determining correspondence will depend for each of them upon three things—the fact that it *is* a secondary part of $B$, and of the first grade, the fact that the particular relation of determining correspondence is what it is, and the fact that the primary part which is its determinant has a certain nature. It then continued by pointing out that the first two of these facts were the same for every secondary part of $B$ of the first grade, and that therefore all dissimilarities and exclusive similarities in the sufficient descriptions of these secondary parts must correspond to dissimilarities and exclusive similarities in the determinant sufficient descriptions of the primary parts. But on our present supposition it is no longer the case that both the first two parts are necessarily the same for each of the secondary parts. The sort of determining correspondence which occurs between $C$ and $B!$ $C$ may possibly be quite different from the sort of determining correspondence which occurs between $D$ and $B!$ $D$. It does not, therefore, follow that all dissimilarities and exclusive similarities in the determined sufficient descriptions of the parts of $B$ will correspond to similar dissimilarities and similarities in the determinant sufficient descriptions of the primary parts. Some of them may correspond to dissimilarities and exclusive similarities in the different sorts of determining correspondence. We have no reason, therefore, to suppose that there is a system of relations which connects the parts of $B$, and which is homologous to any system of relations between the primary parts of the universe.

Now our only reason for saying that the primary parts corresponded to the universe at all was that, in the case of the first supposition, we had seen that the parts of each primary part were connected by a system of relations which was homologous with a system which connected the primary parts of the universe. And, since we are not now entitled to say this, we are not now entitled to say that the primary parts do correspond to the universe, or that the universe is reflected in them. And, on similar grounds, we shall not be entitled to say that the secondary parts of any grade correspond to the universe, or that it is reflected in them.

The second supposition, therefore, does not imply so close a unity in the universe as the first did. And the result which was reached, even on the first supposition, that the plurality in the universe was more fundamental than the unity, will be true *à fortiori* on the second supposition, as it will be also on the other suppositions which we must now proceed to consider.

**290.** Let us make our third supposition as follows. Let us still assume that the universe forms a single primary whole, that every primary part in the universe is determinant, and that every primary part determines a part in every other primary part. But let us no longer assume that this determination is in every case direct. That is, if $B$ and $C$ are two primary parts, let us admit the possibility that $B$ may have no part $B! C$, provided that it has some part of a lower grade, whose final determinant is $C$, such as $B! D! C$, $B! E! D! C$, or the like.

In this case it is clear that the connection between the universe and the primary parts is less close than in the last case. On the second supposition the primary part as a whole did not necessarily reflect the universe, but its parts had a one-to-one correspondence with the primary parts of the universe. But this will not be the case here. The secondary parts of the first grade in each primary part have no longer necessarily a one-to-one correspondence with the primary parts. If the primary parts of the universe were $B$, $C$, $D$, $E$, it would be possible for $B$'s set of secondary parts of the first grade to be, for example, $B! B$ and $B! C$, and for $C$'s set to be $C! B$, $C! D$, $C! E$. $D$, again, might have no secondary parts of the first grade at all, for it might be differentiated by correspondence with $B$ only, so that its highest set of parts would be $D! B! B$, and $D! B! C$. None of these sets is in one-to-one correspondence with the set of primary parts, and yet there would be in each primary part a part finally determined by each primary part. In the same way, the secondary parts of the second grade within each secondary part of the first grade are not necessarily in one-to-one correspondence with the primary parts of the universe.

It will, however, still be the case, as on the two earlier suppositions, that each primary part is causally related to some part of each primary part, since it does determine a part in each, either directly or indirectly. And, although the network of causal relations will not be so symmetrical as it was on the two last suppositions, it is, in this case as in those, prolonged infinitely downwards. For when a part of $B$ is once found which is determined, directly or indirectly, by $C$ (and, by the supposition, there is such a part of $B$) then all the parts of that part to infinity are determined by parts of $C$.

Does the fact that this causal relation takes place through determining correspondence unite the universe more closely than it is united by the fact that there is a causal relation? It is possible that this might be true. But this would depend upon what sort or sorts of determining correspondence did occur, and upon the nature of the characteristics of primary parts. And these are questions which must be postponed till the next Book, and, consequently, to the next volume.

The causal determination, however, is a matter of some importance. For the fact that each primary part has some part determined by every primary part does connect each primary part with all other primary parts (and so with every member of one set of parts of the universe) by intrinsic determination, and this is a closer and more vital bond than the connection by extrinsic determination which we had previously seen to connect all parts of the universe. On the other hand, since the connection here need not be direct, it is possible that in some cases the part of $B$ which is determined by $C$ may be a very small one[1]. How much this would affect the closeness of the union would again depend on those more concrete considerations which must be postponed till the next Book.

**291.** We now come to a fourth supposition. Let us continue to assume that the universe forms one primary whole, and that all primary parts are determinants. But let us drop

---

[1] It could be $B! E! F! \ldots ! C$, where the number of steps denoted by the asterisks might be any finite number.

the further assumption that every primary part determines a part in every other primary part. Let us suppose, for example, that the universe consists of six primary parts, $B$, $C$, $D$, $E$, $F$ and $G$. Let $B$ and $C$ form a reciprocally differentiating group, so that the secondary parts of the first grade which belong to $B$ are $B! B$ and $B! C$, while those of $C$ are $C! B$ and $C! C$. Let $D$ and $E$ likewise form a reciprocally differentiating group, and let the differentiating group, both for $F$ and $G$, be $BDFG$. Then it will not be possible to form, within the universe, any smaller group $K$, such that it is not necessary, in order to describe sufficiently every part of $K$, to introduce any determining correspondence with anything except a part of $K$. And therefore there are no primary wholes within the universe, which will therefore be a single primary whole. And each primary part is in at least one differentiating group, and is therefore a determinant. But each primary part does not determine a part in each primary part. For neither $D$, $E$, $F$, or $G$ determine any parts in $B$ or $C$. The parts of $B$ and $C$ are determined by the closed reciprocal group of $B$ and $C$, and have therefore no primary parts as their determinants, direct or indirect, except $B$ and $C$. In the same way, neither $B$, $C$, $F$ or $G$ determine any parts in $D$ or $E$.

What can we say about the unity of the universe on this supposition? It is no longer the case that each primary part is connected with all the others in respect of its determination of parts within them by determining correspondence. But it is still the case that each primary part is connected with each other primary part in respect of determining correspondence. For the universe is still one primary whole, and that means that no group from which any part of the universe is excluded can be self-sufficing in respect of determining correspondence. Every such group must have some part which determines, or is determined by, something outside the group. And this would join all the primary parts of the universe—and through them the secondary parts—more closely than they are joined by extrinsic determination, though less closely than they would be joined on the previous suppositions.

**292.** Fifthly, we may continue to assume that the universe forms a single primary whole, but no longer assume that all the primary parts are determinant. We may admit the possibility that some of them should be determined without themselves determining anything.

The unity of the universe which would result on this supposition would be the same as would result on the last. There will now be some primary parts which do not determine parts in *any* primary part. But this will not destroy any unity in the universe which remained on the previous supposition that there are some primary parts which do not determine parts in all primary parts.

**293**. The final supposition which we may make is that the universe forms more than one primary whole. This will diminish its unity still further. For now there are different parts of the universe which are independent of each other in respect of determining correspondence. They are not, of course, completely isolated from each other. Everything in the universe is related to everything else. And, in particular, everything in the universe is related to everything else by extrinsic determination. And it is possible that they may be related to each other causally, for there may be other causal relations besides those of determining correspondence. But we have not established the occurrence of any such other causal relations, and it is therefore possible that there may be no causal relations between the primary wholes.

It must be noticed that the assumption that only one sort of determining correspondence occurs throughout the universe may be combined, not only with the assumption that every primary part directly determines a part in every other primary part, but also with any one of the other assumptions—that it determines such a part directly or indirectly, that it is always determinant of a part in some primary part, that, at any rate, it is in the same primary whole with every other primary part, and, finally, that it is not in the same primary whole as all of them. But it will not, I think, appreciably increase the amount of unity in the universe, except in combination with the assumption that every primary part directly determines a part in every primary part.

This concludes the first part of our investigation—the endeavour to determine, as far as possible, the characteristics which belong to all that exists, or which belong to existence as a whole. There remains the consideration of what consequences of theoretical and practical interest can be drawn from the general nature of the universe, thus determined, with respect to various parts of the existent which are empirically known to us. This will find its place in a second volume which I hope to publish in a few years.

# INDEX

## OF TERMS DEFINED OR TREATED AS INDEFINABLE

*References are to Sections*